LET'S GET CODING!

Colourfully illustrated

Small coding projects for school aged children with an interest in simple FUN! computer coding in Snap!, Scratch and Python 3

2021

The author has made these twenty coding projects 'cross-platform' by using standard Scratch and Snap! 'blocks' and Python 3 code. Ideal for any small Mac/PC/Linux and raspberry pi computer. This should make it a lot easier to start and recognise basic code. All the projects use standard blocks throughout. No custom blocks or complex code. It's a FUN book of easy projects!

Let's get Coding!

20 illustrated coding projects

Published by:

www.tarquingroup.com

Printed in England

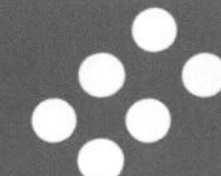

Let's Get Coding!

TWENTY Fun! projects!

Each of the following twenty projects include:	
First page:	A brief introduction to the coding project
Second page:	The block coding for Scratch (or Snap!)
Third page:	The Python code page (based on the same project)
Fourth page:	Hack your own code (with easy options)

Python 3

Snap! is based on Scratch, both are block based and are similar in many respects with some quirky ways to do the same function. Some of this is intentional as they can differ a lot - if you choose. But that has been avoided here as I have taken great care to make all the programs in this book suitable for both - as easy starter projects. You can choose your own favourite block coding program. Plus try out and hack simple Python 3 code!

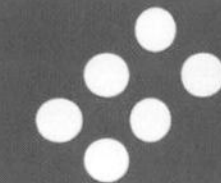

You can do this!

You can do this!

Its a huge challenge,
some coded puzzles,
that's also a game.

A little bit of coding,
is all you need to start.
You can easily make your
own games and challenges,
with a little bit of help.

You can do that!

Let's Get Started!

Where do I start?

Start with Etch-A-SKETCH. Use Scratch* block programming. You can then swop to find if Snap! is more to your liking (as the Author does). But try both and you can swop and choose either. There are 20 projects to code, and you will learn a little more bit on each project. It's a challenge to get a game working first time. Don't expect everything to work perfectly first time! It may look impossible. As I don't give up that easily, nor should you.

It can be difficult to spot a code mistake and it's usually better to ask someone you trust to check it for you. That could be a parent, School Teacher or your Computer tutor.

Be careful when typing in any 'odd' coded symbols. Start with the simplest project to get an idea of how a new program works. If you feel a bit more confident try Python. It's easy!

The Author (likes making coding books)

*See and compare Snap! and SCRATCH. See pages 8-9 and page 53

Index to projects

Index to projects

Snap! + SCRATCH blocks

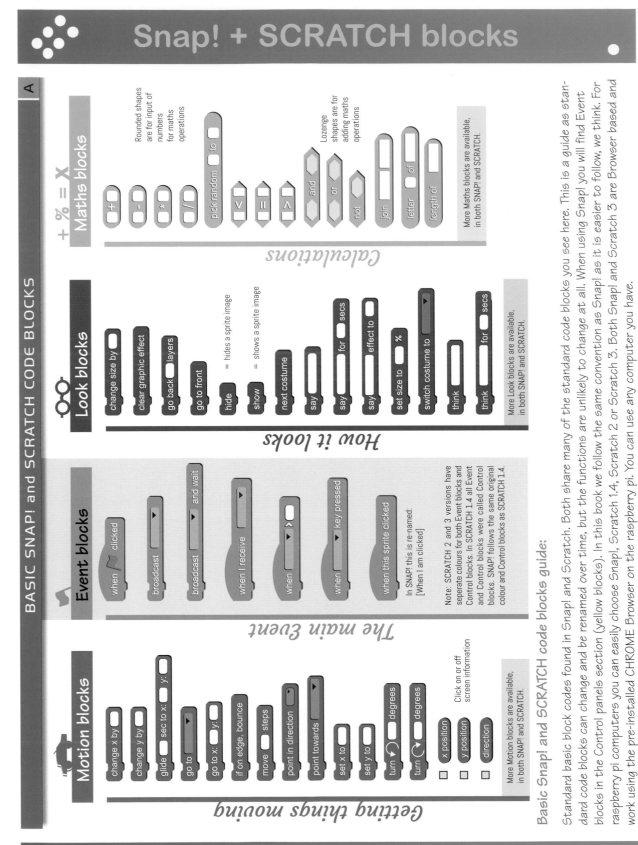

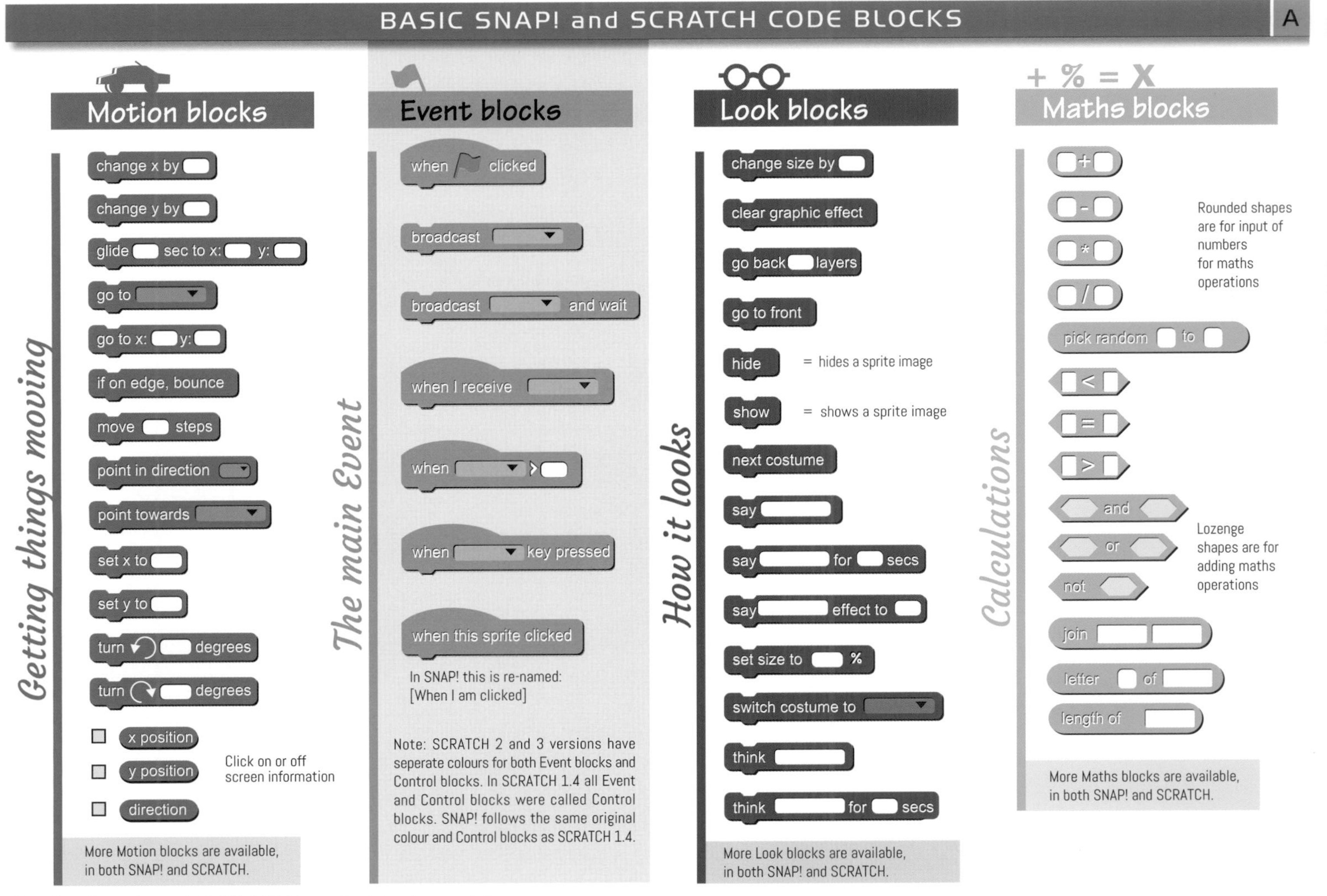

Basic Snap! and SCRATCH code blocks guide:

Standard basic block codes found in Snap! and Scratch. Both share many of the standard code blocks you see here. This is a guide as standard code blocks can change and be renamed over time, but the functions are unlikely to change at all. When using Snap! you will find Event blocks in the Control panels section (yellow blocks). In this book we follow the same convention as Snap! as it is easier to follow, we think. For raspberry pi computers you can easily choose Snap!, Scratch 1.4, Scratch 2 or Scratch 3. Both Snap! and Scratch 3 are Browser based and work using the pre-installed CHROME Browser on the raspberry pi. You can use any computer you have.

Snap! + SCRATCH blocks

BASIC SNAP! and SCRATCH CODE BLOCKS — B

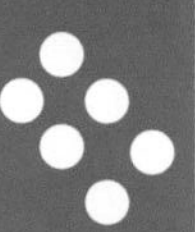
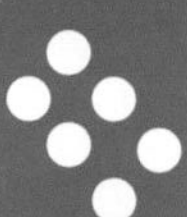

Pen blocks

Drawing with a pen

- change pen colour by
- change pen size by
- change pen shade by
- clear = clear all pen drawing
- pen down
- pen up
- set pen colour to = colour
- set pen size to 1 = 100%
- stamp = copy and duplicate

Note: Pen blocks:
SCRATCH 3 Pen blocks have been moved to 'Add extension' page. Find the 'white-on-blue' symbol at the bottom left of your screen browser. Click to reveal Pen options to import into your code project. There are more Pen blocks that you could use for your coding projects. The basics you need are shown above.

Sound blocks

Making a noise

- change volume by
- play sound
- play sound until done
- set volume to %
- stop all sounds

More sound blocks are available, in both SNAP! and SCRATCH.

Sounds blocks contain any Sound (name) that is imported from the Sound library. See how to choose a Sound below.

Note:
To import a sound into SCRATCH 3. Find the white-on-blue icon symbol at the bottom of page in your browser. Hover with your mouse over to reveal more options. Use the last of the options to 'Choose a Sound' to import into your project.

For SNAP! Sounds see Menu (where Open and Save is found) look at bottom of the Menu-list, for all 'Sounds' import.

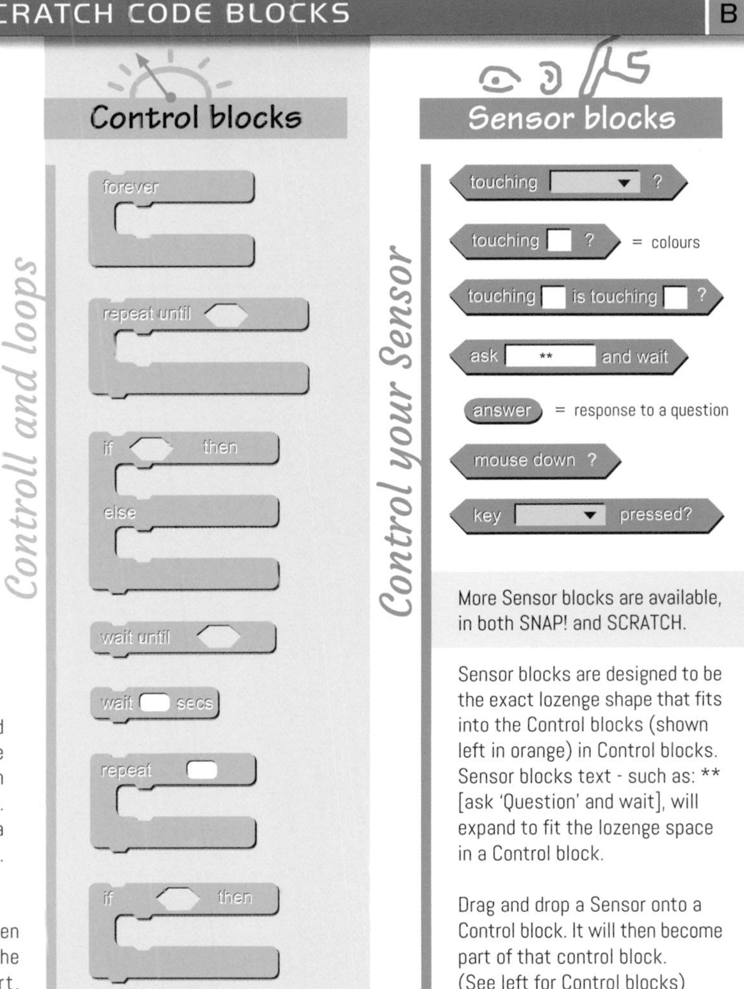

Control blocks

Controll and loops

- forever
- repeat until
- if then / else
- wait until
- wait secs
- repeat
- if then

Sensor blocks

Control your Sensor

- touching ?
- touching ? = colours
- touching is touching ?
- ask ** and wait
- answer = response to a question
- mouse down ?
- key pressed?

More Sensor blocks are available, in both SNAP! and SCRATCH.

Sensor blocks are designed to be the exact lozenge shape that fits into the Control blocks (shown left in orange) in Control blocks. Sensor blocks text - such as: ** [ask 'Question' and wait], will expand to fit the lozenge space in a Control block.

Drag and drop a Sensor onto a Control block. It will then become part of that control block. (See left for Control blocks)

EXAMPLE: how Snap! and Scratch code blocks click together...

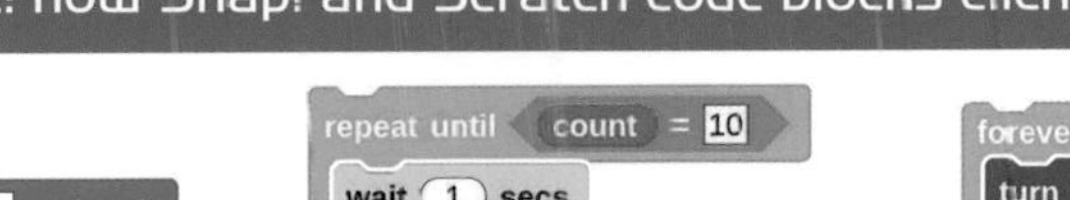
say Let's Get Coding!
say join Hello name
ask What's your name? and wait
say join Hello answer
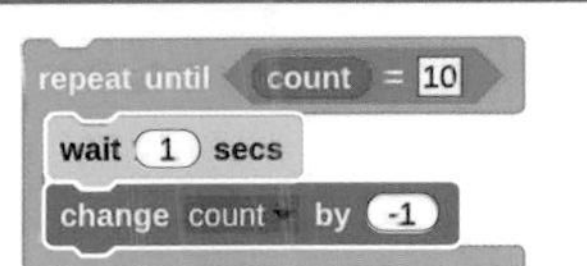
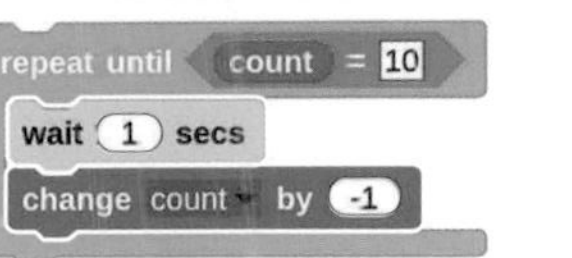
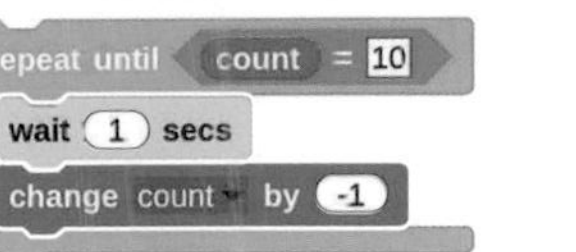
repeat until count = 10
wait 1 secs
change count by -1
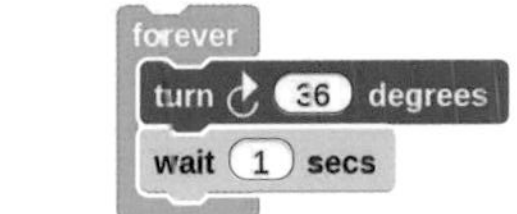
forever
turn 36 degrees
wait 1 secs
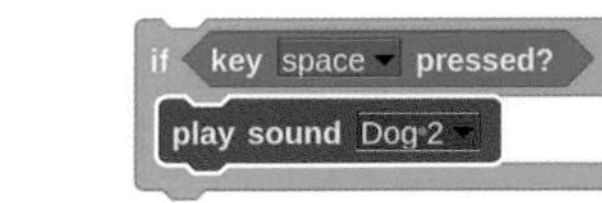
if key space pressed?
play sound Dog 2

Software

A guide for young coders:

- **YOUNGER READERS and PARENTS. All projects suitable as starter projects.**

This is NOT a book that answers all your coding questions! - It's a FUN book full of examples for making small computer games. You will need help from a parent, tutor or Teacher who already knows some code programming examples; i.e. in block and Python code programming. Both Scratch and Python are coding tools used extensively in this book. In this book you will find many easy 'block-coding' examples and a few 'hard' examples. The Author has extended that to include Python 3 *(in the most simplest form, for children)*. As such, it is based on educational projects that the Author uses for his own 'handbook' for school clubs. The book is designed to be used by a tutor or parent based on twenty fun game practical projects. How Scratch, Snap! or Python works is by 'live' demonstration of every project in the book..

Snap! Scratch and Thonny!

Scratch 1, 2 and 3 is ready installed on your raspberry pi computer. *(No install required)*

(1) Scratch: is the original block programming concept designed for children to learn code visually. Version 1.4 is still widely used in schools. Version 2 is newer web browser based (although there is an option of stand-alone version). Scratch Version 3 *(image left)* is the latest version *(raspberry pi Buster os)*. Scratch 3 is also an 'online-only' application which is 'cloud' based. The big advantage is that you can use any computer that has a modern browser. **www.scratch.mit.edu**

Snap! is a good alternative to Scratch 3 for those with a laptop Mac or PC. *(No install required)*

(2) Snap! is a recreation of the original Scratch concept and it keeps the same layout and blocks as Scratch 1.4 *(the original version)* and improved upon that idea. It has more custom code blocks and has an easy-to-use interface. It is entirely cloud based. Works on any modern browser with much the same code block operation and look as the original Scratch (v1.4). Currently the Author's favourite. **www.snap.berkeley.edu/snapsource/snap.html**

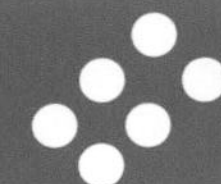

Hardware

Python 3 and THONNY is already installed on your raspberry pi computer. ***(No install required)***

(3) There are other PYTHON 'code editors' but - the one we will be using is called THONNY. This is the 'pi' standard which is easier to work with for creating the books simple games based projects. As Python is not widely taught in most primary schools, you will find THONNY is easier to use (and for installing Python modules) when learning to code for the first time. Author's favourite and used as an example throughout this book. **www.thonny.org**

Thonny

Python IDE for beginners

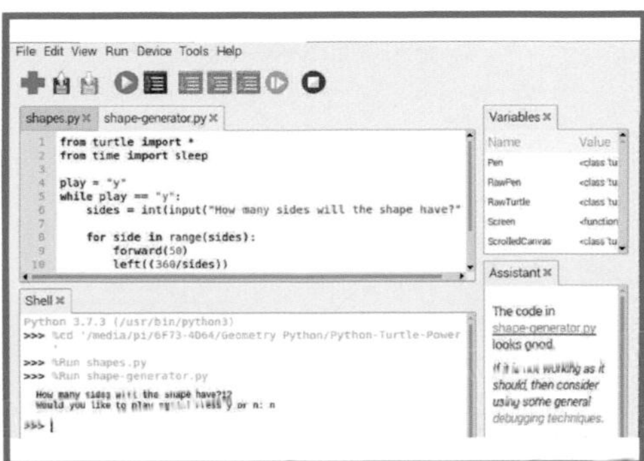

For small computers and laptops...

(left) Pi 3 Model A+ (right) Pi Zero W

The raspberry* pi is the little UK micro computer that is a low cost alternative to expensive laptops. It is user friendly to young coders as everything you need is already 'built-into' the operating system. You can program *(almost)* anything with the raspberry pi. Scratch versions 'one' and 'two' are, ready to code. Including THONNY are all pre-installed with Python 3. The Author's favourite used for this book. **www.raspberrypi.org**

**Note: raspberry pi computer does NOT have a capital 'R' in it's name!*

To extend your skills or just to meet others like yourself; try a free **CODERDOJO** that are run by volunteers around the world for you. Many are run from Schools, Colleges and Libraries near you *(see CoderDojo World Map map*)*. Get to meet other young coders with some interesting coding projects to share. I would recommend a 'CoderDojo' for those with an interest in simple computer coding. There is more to coding than you think!

www.coderdojo.com

CoderDojo's are FREE and run by raspberry pi volunteers and is an excellent way to start coding. Use any spare laptop - if you don't have a raspberry pi. You can use ANY laptop computer to start coding. The raspberry pi operating system is also available for your PC laptop, but not essential. All will work exactly the same way using the same the recommended Software programs. Otherwise you may have to download and install applications.

www.raspberrypi.org

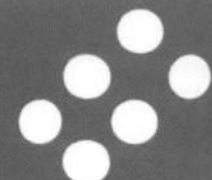

About the coding projects...

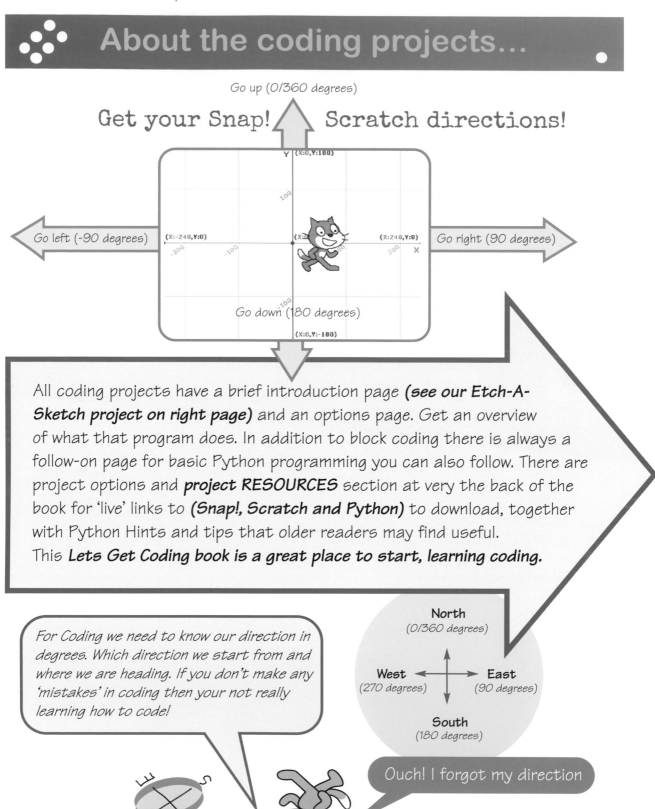

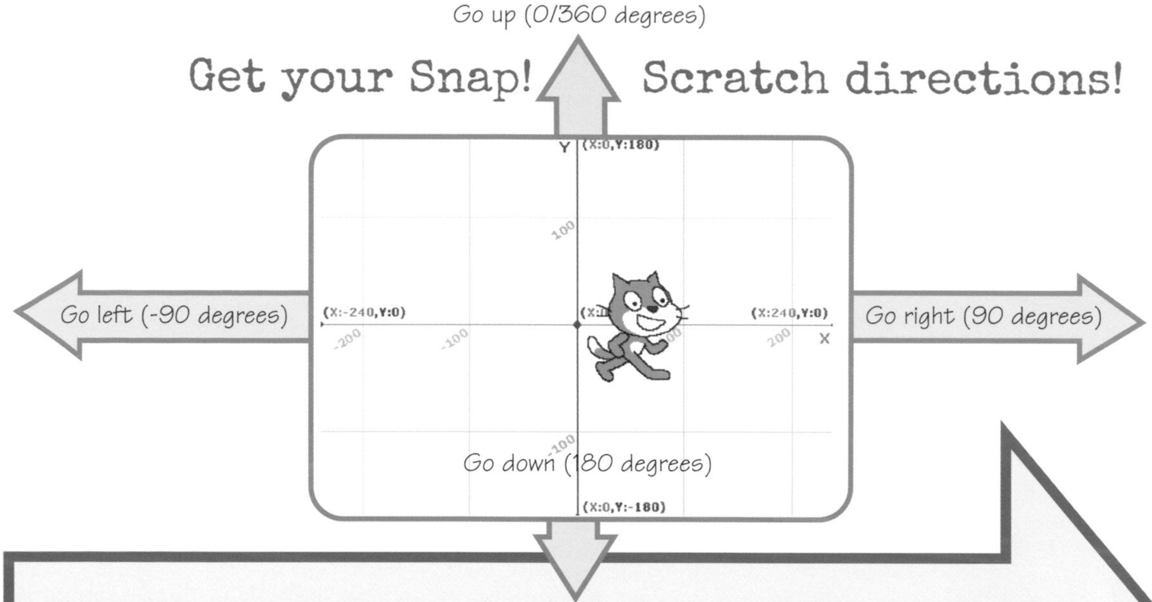

Go up (0/360 degrees)

Get your Snap! Scratch directions!

Y (X:0,Y:180)

100

Go left (-90 degrees)

(X:-240,Y:0)

-200

-100

(X:240,Y:0)

200

X

Go right (90 degrees)

-100

Go down (180 degrees)

(X:0,Y:-180)

All coding projects have a brief introduction page ***(see our Etch-A-Sketch project on right page)*** and an options page. Get an overview of what that program does. In addition to block coding there is always a follow-on page for basic Python programming you can also follow. There are project options and ***project RESOURCES*** section at very the back of the book for 'live' links to ***(Snap!, Scratch and Python)*** to download, together with Python Hints and tips that older readers may find useful.
This ***Lets Get Coding book is a great place to start, learning coding.***

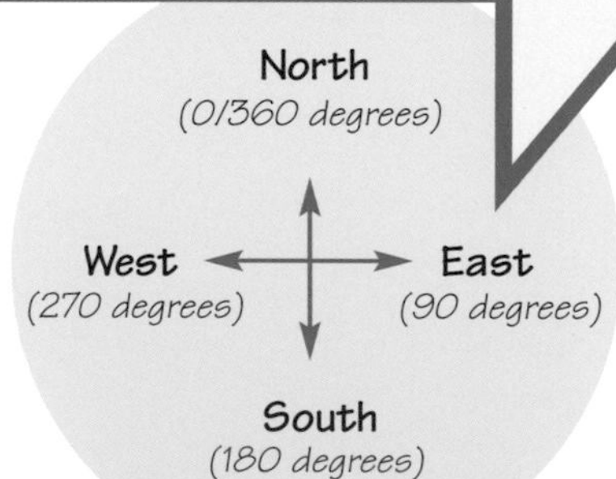

For Coding we need to know our direction in degrees. Which direction we start from and where we are heading. If you don't make any 'mistakes' in coding then your not really learning how to code!

Ouch! I forgot my direction

Drawn to 'Etch-A-Sketch'

1

Be Inspired!

Get drawn to Etch-A-Sketch!

With 'Etch-A-Sketch'. I prefer to start this project with a very short video introduction on what it means to draw in straight lines. We first play a short video introduction on the French inventor: André Cassagnes.

This video is informative and inspiring. It powers up the children's imagination who are keen to start as soon as it finishes. In class they will have learnt something in less than five minutes. That something so simple has such long lasting appeal...

This video is from the New York Times. It lasts no more than 5 mins.

A Celebration of
André Cassagnes

https://nyti.ms/2Kf6Qjj

The Author (draws on Etch-A-Sketch)

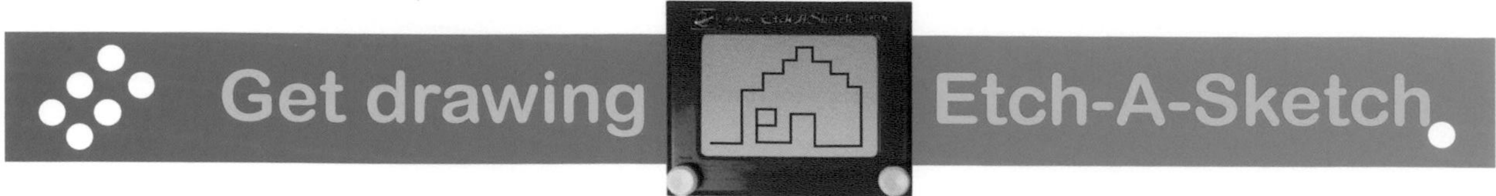

Get drawing Etch-A-Sketch

Etch-a-Sketch is something we can easily re-create in Snap! or SCRATCH code. A BIG plus is that we can now make a new colour version to play with very few code blocks to start drawing...

Let's get coding...

Sketch a Pencil. *You can draw a Pencil (if you like) or simply import one from the 'costumes' library in Snap! or Scratch. You will soon find a Pencil under 'THINGS'. But I prefer to draw my own Pencil, - as it's always much more fun to draw one!*

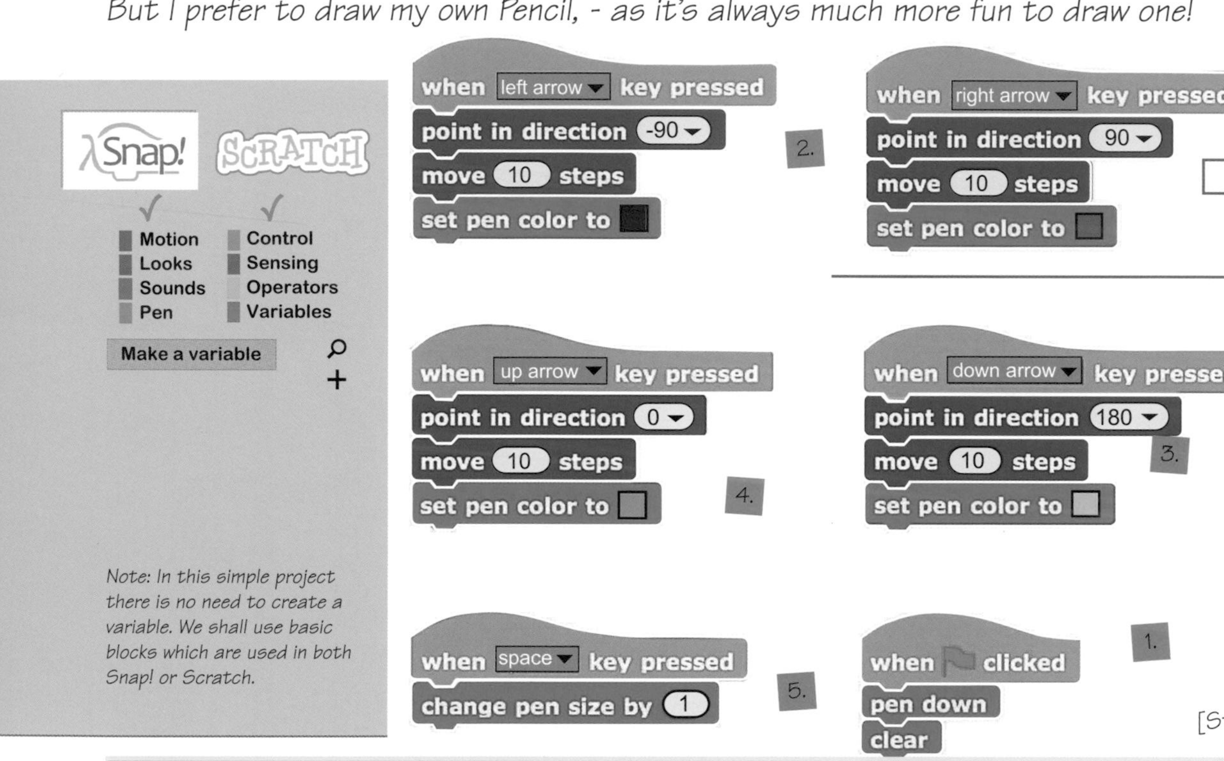

Note: In this simple project there is no need to create a variable. We shall use basic blocks which are used in both Snap! or Scratch.

[Start button]

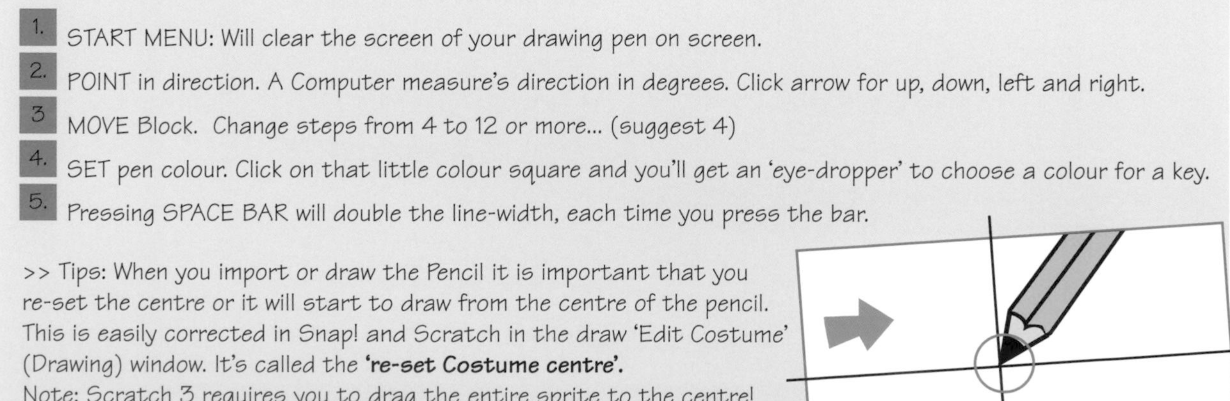

1. START MENU: Will clear the screen of your drawing pen on screen.
2. POINT in direction. A Computer measure's direction in degrees. Click arrow for up, down, left and right.
3. MOVE Block. Change steps from 4 to 12 or more... (suggest 4)
4. SET pen colour. Click on that little colour square and you'll get an 'eye-dropper' to choose a colour for a key.
5. Pressing SPACE BAR will double the line-width, each time you press the bar.

>> Tips: When you import or draw the Pencil it is important that you re-set the centre or it will start to draw from the centre of the pencil. This is easily corrected in Snap! and Scratch in the draw 'Edit Costume' (Drawing) window. It's called the **'re-set Costume centre'.**
Note: Scratch 3 requires you to drag the entire sprite to the centre!

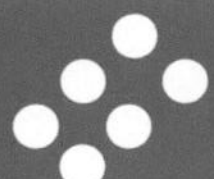

Python Coding for Turtles

It's a bit different in Python. There is a drawing package built-in and its called Turtle. We shall be using the basic import that you can use and adapt the code. Its easy and very fast!

Let's get coding...

Change THAT Pencil to Turtle! *We could import a Pencil and we will show you how to do that later. To keep things simple we are using the same basic idea, we used in Snap! (or Scratch) to make our Turtle draw. He can also draw, just like our Etch-A-Sketch block code. What is useful to know here, is that a TURTLE (turtle import*- see code below) function is always available - if you ask Python!*

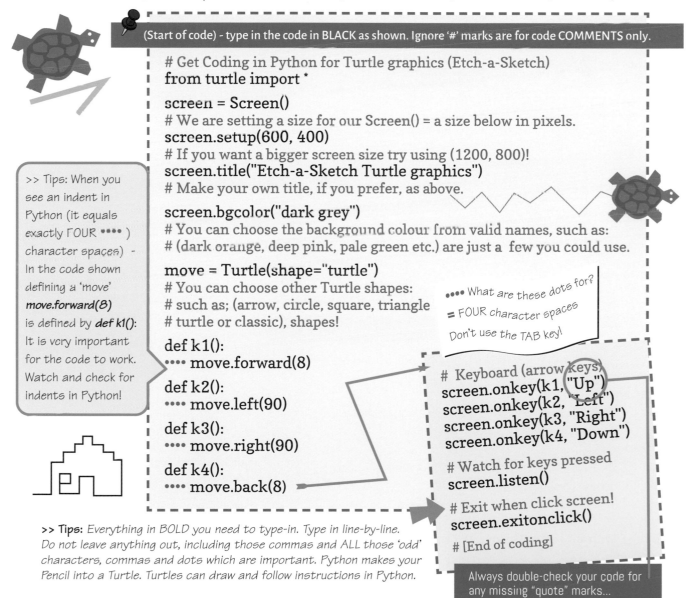

(Start of code) - type in the code in BLACK as shown. Ignore '#' marks are for code COMMENTS only.

```
# Get Coding in Python for Turtle graphics (Etch-a-Sketch)
from turtle import *

screen = Screen()
# We are setting a size for our Screen() = a size below in pixels.
screen.setup(600, 400)
# If you want a bigger screen size try using (1200, 800)!
screen.title("Etch-a-Sketch Turtle graphics")
# Make your own title, if you prefer, as above.

screen.bgcolor("dark grey")
# You can choose the background colour from valid names, such as:
# (dark orange, deep pink, pale green etc.) are just a  few you could use.

move = Turtle(shape="turtle")
# You can choose other Turtle shapes:
# such as; (arrow, circle, square, triangle
# turtle or classic), shapes!

def k1():
•••• move.forward(8)

def k2():
•••• move.left(90)

def k3():
•••• move.right(90)

def k4():
•••• move.back(8)
```

•••• What are these dots for?
= FOUR character spaces
Don't use the TAB key!

```
#  Keyboard (arrow keys)
screen.onkey(k1, "Up")
screen.onkey(k2, "Left")
screen.onkey(k3, "Right")
screen.onkey(k4, "Down")

# Watch for keys pressed
screen.listen()

# Exit when click screen!
screen.exitonclick()

# [End of coding]
```

Always double-check your code for any missing "quote" marks...

>> Tips: When you see an indent in Python (it equals exactly FOUR ••••) character spaces) - In the code shown defining a 'move' ***move.forward(8)*** is defined by ***def k1():*** It is very important for the code to work. Watch and check for indents in Python!

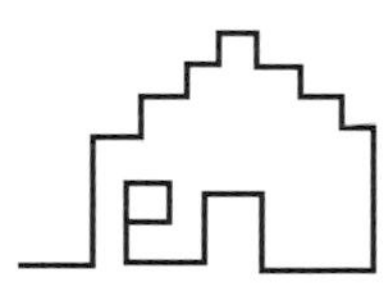

>> Tips: *Everything in BOLD you need to type-in. Type in line-by-line. Do not leave anything out, including those commas and ALL those 'odd' characters, commas and dots which are important. Python makes your Pencil into a Turtle. Turtles can draw and follow instructions in Python.*

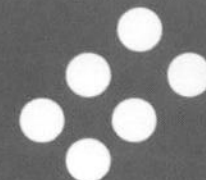

Coding options to try:

Snap! and SCRATCH option:

This is an easy option as many children get confused between the X and Y axis, so I made a little animated program (Scratch 1.4) based on what moves along an x and y axis. (see PROJECT resources below). For older children they can use the following x and y code blocks (when also understood by simple demonstration of Felix the cat *(shown on right)*. See **Project RESOURCES***

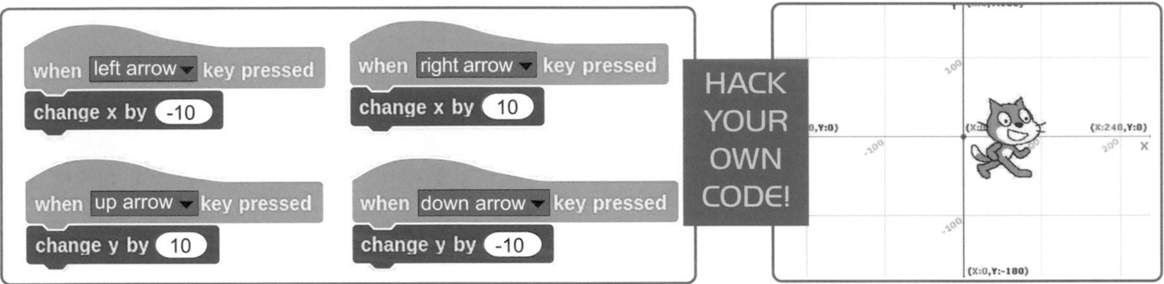

The size of screen is fixed in Scratch 1.4 (maximum 360 pixels x 480 pixels). The centre of the screen being x=0 and y=0. It is similar in both Snap! and Scratch 2. Screen sizes are based on 480 wide x 360 high (x=-240 to x=+240) and (y= -180 to +180) width, always from centre of display screen. Snap! and Scratch 3 both have a similar screen size.

PYTHON code option:

This is the simplest ETCH-A-SKETCH for Python as its very easy to (1) type-in and (2) to explain what each line of code does. I admit it may not be the 'best' Etch-A-Sketch code ever made, but it is the simplest for children to follow. I have a more advanced option for slightly more advanced coders*, i.e. those already familiar with Python 3.

Easy Python Code changes - OPTIONS - that you could make include these:

(Start of code) - type in the code in BLACK as shown

```
1. # Change the background colour of the screen:
screen.bg.color("dark green")

2. # Change the turtle shape to a circle (example)
move = Turtle(shape="circle")

3. # Change the speed of the Turtle
move.forward(12)

4. # Change size of the screen
screen.setup(1024, 768)
```

PYTHON is much faster when making changes to your coding. Simple changes such as background colour, shape, speed are all easy options to code (see page left).
The size of the screen is limited by your own screen size. Try different screen sizes to see how they look. Etch-a-sketch was a bit like a TV set. So you should set that to a 4:3 ratio which is approximately 1024x768 pixels (the smallest dots on your screen are pixels). Screen sizes can vary from one screen to another as not all computer screens are of the same size or resolution!

* See **project RESOURCES** for code and information on this and other projects.

NEXT: Your Pocket Money

2

Yikes!

What's the Compound Interest?

This program is about **Simple interest** and how it works. A simple bit of code can make all the difference in later life when the cost of money is often not well understood, even by grown-ups. Borrowing money is expensive on a credit card. But with a little bit of code you can work out what pocket money is best for 'Simple' and 'Compound interest' to work towards your pocket money savings.

Find out how a Credit card 'charges' compound interest in much the same way. Your pocket money will never be the same. Find out how rich you will be!

The Author (needs to save more)

money, money money!

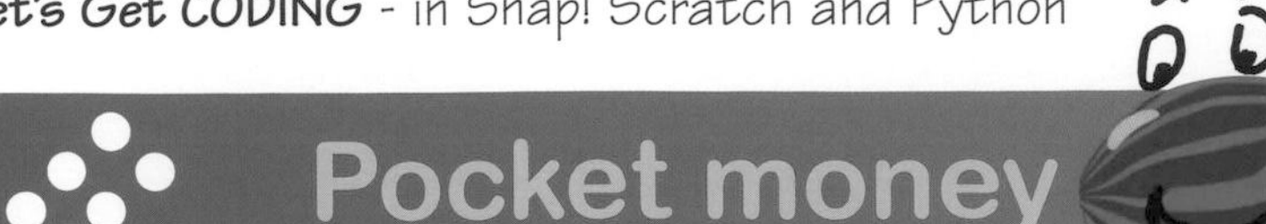

Pocket money interest!

How does your Pocket money work? Money is also 'savings' and all your money can have 'added' interest' - so called 'Simple interest', If you've never heard of it, then you will LOSE money. Savings = Pocket money. But for how long should you SAVE your own pocket money for Simple interest?

Let's get coding...

Import a Fruit costume. Import a 'costume' in SCRATCH and Snap! Place it centre in on the screen. Add four VARIABLES called [principal], [rate], [time] and [interest]. See as marked. *

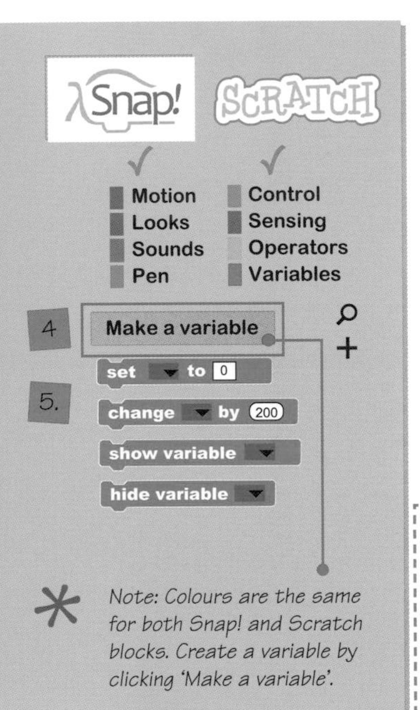

Note: Colours are the same for both Snap! and Scratch blocks. Create a variable by clicking 'Make a variable'. *

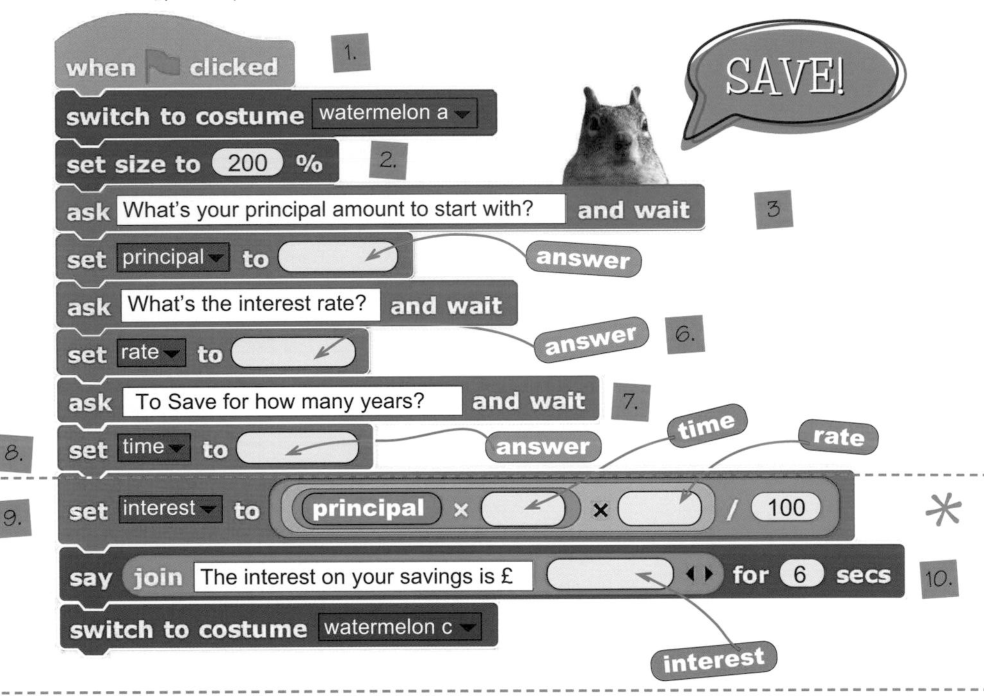

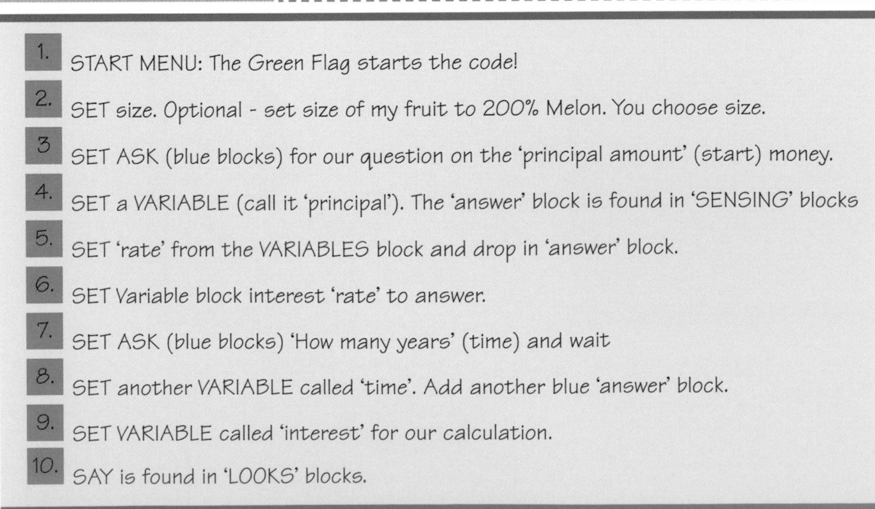

1. START MENU: The Green Flag starts the code!
2. SET size. Optional - set size of my fruit to 200% Melon. You choose size.
3. SET ASK (blue blocks) for our question on the 'principal amount' (start) money.
4. SET a VARIABLE (call it 'principal'). The 'answer' block is found in 'SENSING' blocks
5. SET 'rate' from the VARIABLES block and drop in 'answer' block.
6. SET Variable block interest 'rate' to answer.
7. SET ASK (blue blocks) 'How many years' (time) and wait
8. SET another VARIABLE called 'time'. Add another blue 'answer' block.
9. SET VARIABLE called 'interest' for our calculation.
10. SAY is found in 'LOOKS' blocks.

watermelon c

watermelon b

watermelon a

COSTUMES

(shown left)

One Sprite with three costumes - all watermellons (although you could use any other images that are provided in Snap! or SCRATCH.

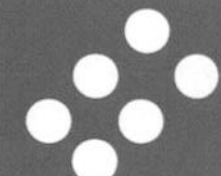

Pocket money with Python

Now let's see if it's any faster in Python! Of course it is, even without the 'Squirrel'. We can create a code that does the same calculation. But then you have to type it all in, so maybe, 'not-as-fast' is your typing code speed, which may be a bit s-l-o-w.

Let's get coding...

IMAGINE it's your money! It could be in your Bank or Building Society! We need four ***VARIABLES*** called ***[principal], [rate], [time]*** and ***[interest]*** in a way that Python understands. You can now 'Squirrel-away' some savings!

(Start of code) - type in the code in BLACK as shown. Ignore '#' marks are for code COMMENTS only.

```
# Get Coding in Python - to calculate your 'Simple  interest'.
print("This program calculates Simple interest.")
# print means on-your-screen and NOT (as some would say)
# (Not PRINT an inkjet printer), Python 'print' is to show on-screen!
principal=float(input("Enter the principal amount: £"))
# We are creating a variable float to store the amount you enter.
time=int(input("Enter the time (in years): "))
# We are creating a time as input, which is years.
rate=float(input("Enter the rate: "))
# We are creating a variable float to input the rate (as a percentage).
interest=(principal*time*rate)/100
# This simple calculation (principal x time x rate) divided by a
# 100 for a simple percentage rate calculation.
print("The simple interest is: £",interest)
# The calculation is for Simple interest ONLY for the years entered.
# [End of coding]
```

>> Tips: There are no indents in this Python code. That's easy!

But you have to be careful to add "quotation" marks where indicated and the ((double brackets)) are also important.

Do not miss out any asterisks (*) as this means to multiply in Python.

Simple interest is just a start. All banks and building societies will save your pocket money using Compound Interest. This means that your 'simple interest' is calculated monthly (or yearly) and then added to the new total. But only IF you save the same amount each year and when interest rate is the same (does not vary), you will find your pocket money grows faster each year due to 'Compound interest', that is, if you do not spend any of it!

See **'Compound Interest'** shown overleaf. It can work FOR you (or AGAINST you), so beware 'Compound Interest'.

Options to try:

How do your SAVINGS work? Banks and 'Credit cards' use a Simple AND Compound Interest calculation on how much you spend or owe them. This is exactly the opposite of how your savings work. Both savings and Credit cards are all based on 'Compound Interest' - so the more you know about that, the better off you will eventually be (with more pocket money).

SNAP!/SCRATCH - Compound Interest & Savings calculator...

Try this SAVE example (A);

if you save 10p per week for 52 weeks over a year is £52. So enter £52 as your 'principal amount'. The plan is to save for 10 years at 4% rate (typical saving rate may be less). If you save the SAME (£52) amount each year which then is re-invested added to your Compound interest you will find your total amount.

1. *Create a new VARIABLE alongside 'interest-rate' (shown right), Drag out the 'set' Variable block created.*

2. *Set a new START block (shown below) so we can reset the Compound Interest calculation back to zero each time.*

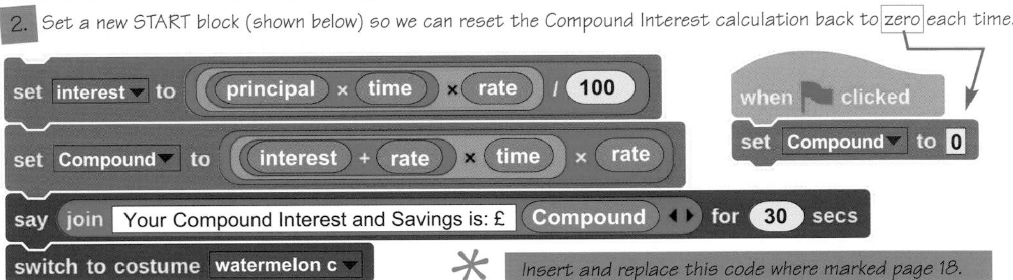

3. *Note that the Compound calculation differs slightly from the interest calculation we made earlier. The answer is then saved and inserted into next text block **'say'** for 30 seconds.*

* *Insert and replace this code where marked page 18.*

4. *Try changing the interest rate and see how fast that small amount can change the total amount over ten years. Or even longer, (say 15 years or more). It quickly adds up and you could be a **£ millionaire** - if you manage to save enough and not spend*

***APR: (Average Percentage Rate):** is often used to decribe 'Compound Interest' but excludes additional costs occurring (see example B) below.*

Python - Compound Interest & Savings calculator...

```
# Calculate your 'Compound  interest'.
principal=float(input("Enter your principal amount: £"))
time=int(input("Enter the time (in years):"))
rate=float(input("Enter the % rate:"))
simple_interest=(principal*time*rate)/100
compound_interest=(simple_interest+rate)*time*rate
print("Your Compound interest is: £",compound_interest)
# [End of coding]
```

Try this SPEND example (B);

if you spend 10p per week for 52 weeks (over a year is £52). Enter £52 as your 'principal amount'. Spend the same for 10 years at 40% rate (See Credit Cards below). If you still spend another £52 per year, you'll soon find that this includes extra bank 'COSTS'. Which get totalled up with Compound interest - so that small amount you borrowed is now much larger than ever. Beware Credit Cards!

** **Credit Cards** (using APR) work the opposite by reducing your savings and with additional charges and a high interest rate mean you lose more money than you can ever save. Beware the Compound interest (APR) of most (if not all) Credit Cards. Typically most Credit cards can charge 40% or more plus extra costs!*

NEXT: Miles-per-gallon

3

How far on a gallon of fuel?

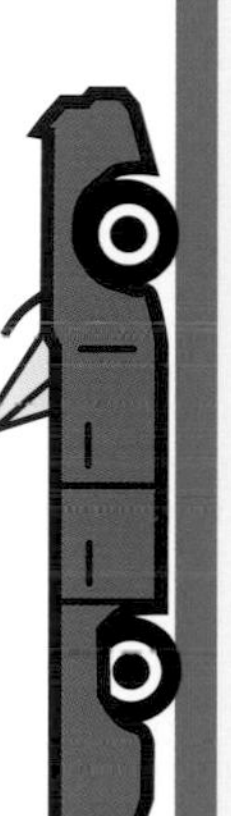

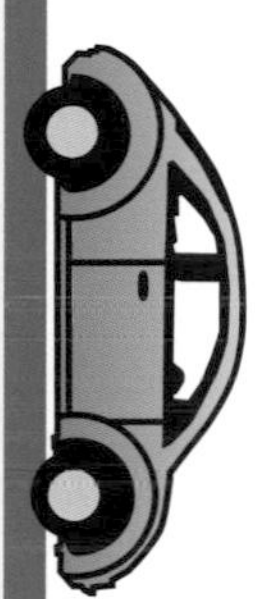

When you buy a car, it uses fuel. It may be Petrol, Diesel or Electric in which case you can work out its fuel in a similar way. Electricity is measured in Kilowatts for cars, but you can still work out how far you can go per mile. Or if you prefer per kilometre.

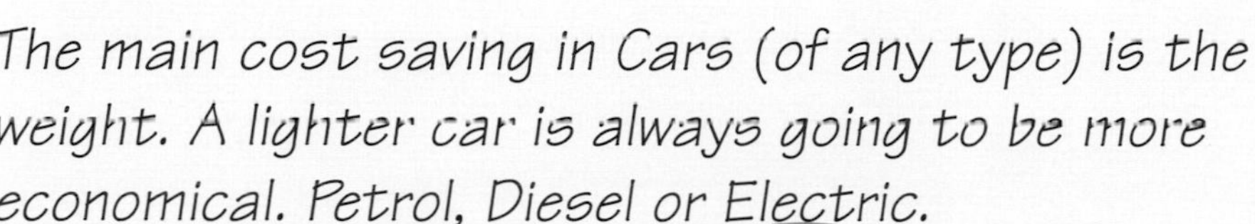

The main cost saving in Cars (of any type) is the weight. A lighter car is always going to be more economical. Petrol, Diesel or Electric.

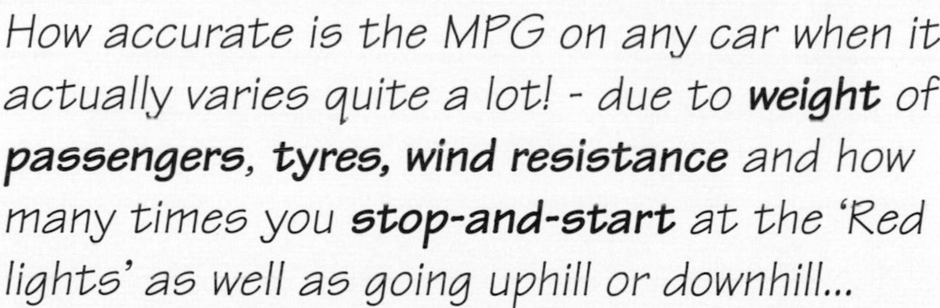

How accurate is the MPG on any car when it actually varies quite a lot! - due to **weight** of **passengers, tyres, wind resistance** and how many times you **stop-and-start** at the 'Red lights' as well as going uphill or downhill...

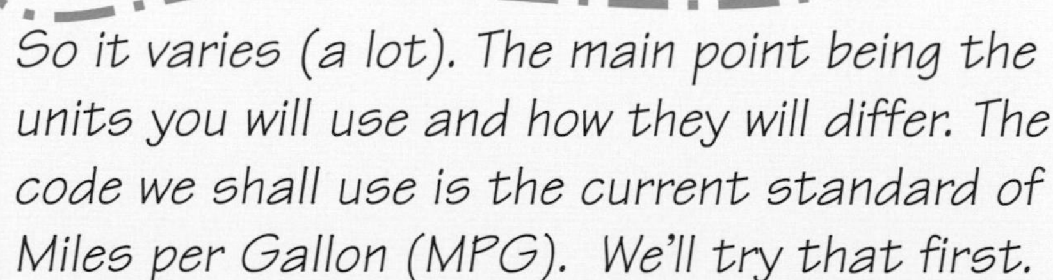

So it varies (a lot). The main point being the units you will use and how they will differ. The code we shall use is the current standard of Miles per Gallon (MPG). We'll try that first.

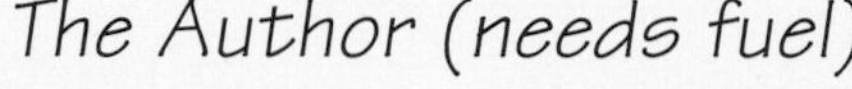

The Author (needs fuel)

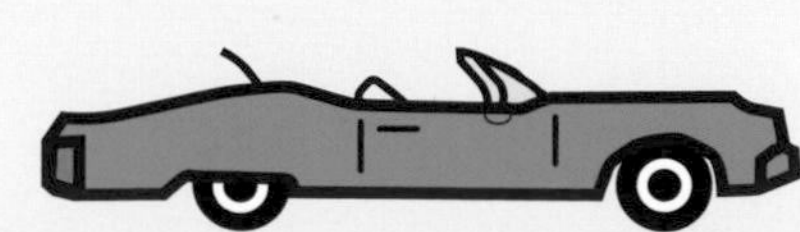

Fuel is expensive to buy! A Car's fuel uses Petrol or Diesel which is usually sold in 'Litres' (not in Gallons*). We can calculate both miles-per-gallon (MPG) and Litres with coding. We can use Snap!, Scratch or Python to do this.

Let's get coding...

IMPORT a Car. Any modern car will do. Place it centre in the preview screen. Next add three VARIABLES called **[miles]**, **[gallons]** and **[MPG]**. See sidebar ***'Make a variable'***.

Note: In Snap! import a Car by using the Costumes import function. in Scratch you need to look under 'Costumes' then import from 'Transport'. In both programs these imports are called 'Costumes'. They are pictures you can use in your coding.

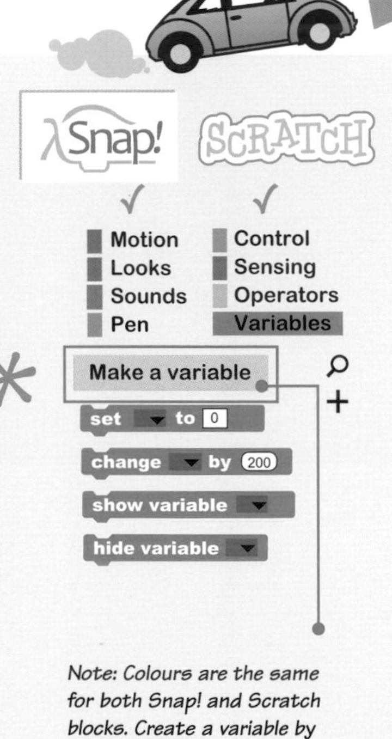

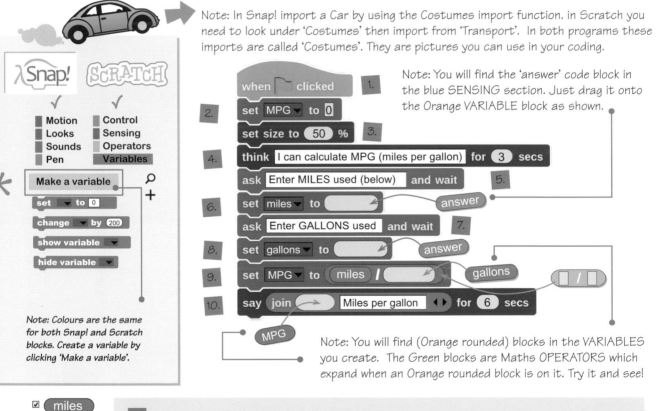

Note: Colours are the same for both Snap! and Scratch blocks. Create a variable by clicking 'Make a variable'.

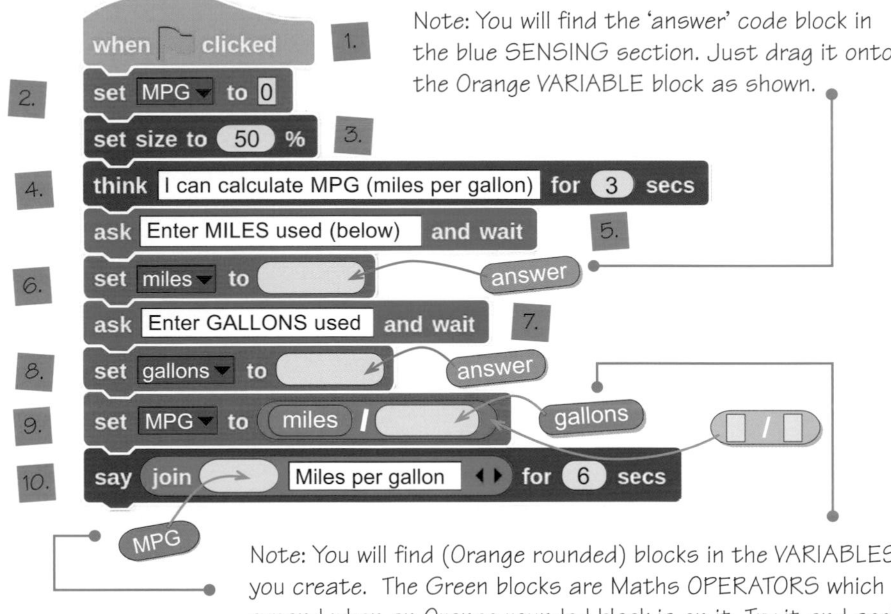

Note: You will find the 'answer' code block in the blue SENSING section. Just drag it onto the Orange VARIABLE block as shown.

Note: You will find (Orange rounded) blocks in the VARIABLES you create. The Green blocks are Maths OPERATORS which expand when an Orange rounded block is on it. Try it and see!

Using three VARIABLES as shown above.

1. START MENU: The Green Flag starts the code!
2. SET block you will have to create a VARIABLE called MPG first!
3. SET size block to a size that suits 50% for my imported Car.
4. THINK block make your question by typing in text.
5. ASK (Enter MILES) and wait for an answer.
6. SET block is created when you make a VARIABLE call it 'miles'
7. ASK block: (Enter GALLONS) and wait for an answer.
8. SET block is a VARIABLE called 'gallons". Drop in the blue block called 'answer'.
9. SET block to 'MPG. Insert a Maths operator (Green block). We are to divide miles by gallons.
10. SAY block enables us to join up a calculation (MPG) and join words together for 6 seconds.

* The author lives in England (UK). Petrol stations in the UK sell Petrol and Diesel in LITRES and (not GALLONS). Your Mum or Dad may be surprised how little miles you get per litre. Perhaps Petrol stations think its sounds cheaper if its measured in Litres.

Python for Miles-per-Gallon...

Now we could just leave it at that. But what if we code the same sequence in Python. Is it easier? Will the calculations be the same? How do we do that? Will I get 'bored' en-route?

Let's get coding...

IMAGINE a Car. It could be a Ferrari outside your house! As before, we will add three VARIABLES called **[miles_driven]**, **[gallons_used]** and **[mpg]** in a way that Python understands. Include the 'underscore' *(not a dash)* - as our example shown here. i.e. miles_driven

(Start of code) - type in the code in BLACK as shown. Ignore '#' marks are for code COMMENTS only.

```
# Coding in Python for Miles-Per-Gallon...
# Ignore all the hashtag' (#) comments.
# [START coding - use the parts in BOLD and not my comments]
print("This program calculates mpg.")
# This is statement is a BLUE block 'asking' for 'miles' user input.
miles_driven = input("Enter miles driven:")
# Convert input text to a number (called a floating number)...
# This is the 'miles' variable.
miles_driven = float(miles_driven)
# Set gallons used by the Car user... This is the 'gallons' variable.
gallons_used = input("Enter gallons used:")
# Convert gallons entered into a floating number (Maths calculation).
gallons_used = float(gallons_used)
# Calculation to divide miles by gallons used as a Maths calculation.
mpg = miles_driven / gallons_used
print("Miles per gallon:", mpg)

# [End of coding]
```

Don't type CAPITALS where there are none! **i.e. miles_driven**

Be careful to include ALL **"quotations"** when marked! **i.e. "Enter miles driven:"**

UK Cars 'gallons' convert factor:

There are 4.54608 litres in a (UK) gallon. (Approximately to six decimals). 1 Gallon UK = 4.5460899999997 Litres.

This could easily calculate the Miles-per-Litre which would be useful to know! And even if we had an Electric car, we could still find out how much 'per Kilowatt' our car does per-mile... But that's a challenge for later... (see project RESOURCES pages). Meanwhile to convert your MPG to Litres you need to find out how many Litres in a UK or US Gallon. **(litres_used = mpg /**

US Cars 'gallons' convert factor: There are 3.78541 Litres in a (US) gallon. (Approximately to six decimals). 1 Gallon US = 3.78541178 Litres.

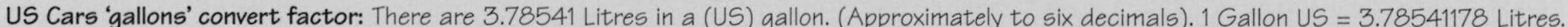

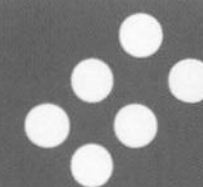

Options to try:

When buying fuel for your first Car (Diesel or Petrol) it is always sold in the UK as Litres but the Car itself is 'mileage' driven in how many 'Miles-per-Gallon' it does. Confusingly Petrol and Diesel is sold per Litre. Its easy to calculate your MPG. But how many miles do you get on a Litre? Not very far, I think!

To measure an accurate mileage of an electric car is usually averaged out, as the biggest factor by far is the overall 'weight'. Electric cars are a lot lighter but the batteries are a lot heavier. The weight of the car is the prime limiting factor extended only by a big battery. Going 'uphill' is using more power than going 'downhill' - for example. Even putting the 'heater' to 'on' is going to flatten the battery and reduce your mileage further. Most electric cars have at least 200mile range per charge. But MPG does not work here. Miles per Kw/hour is nearest, so simply changing the *(variable)* MPG to Kw/h will work and *(variable)* miles can remain the same.

Snap! or Scratch - options to consider:

When using the Snap! and Scratch block code, simply change GALLONS to (Kw/h) Kilowatt/hours. You then can find out how far per Kilowatt/hour a car travels. Most small Electric cars have 300Kw/h batteries and mileage is usually very limited to battery size. HYBRID cars can still use MPG as they still use standard fuel *(and use MPG)*, petrol engines are smaller and easily compared to a normal car for Miles Per Gallon. Typically 60 mpg for a small *(petrol/electric)* Hybrid car.

Python - Km/h to mpg and Litres to Gallons

(Start of code) - type in the code in BLACK as shown.

```
# PYTHON KMH to MPG CODE:
# This script will convert kmh to mph
kmh=int(raw_input("Enter your speed in km/h: ))
mph= 0.6214*kmh
print "Your Speed is:" kmh, "KM/H=". mph, "MPH"
# [End of coding]
```

Gallons to Litres:

To calculate 'Litres' from 'Miles-per-Gallon' just divide by 4.54608

(Litre = mpg/454608 will make that calculation for you).

More examples in project RESOURCES.

** See project RESOURCES for code and information on this and all other projects.*

NEXT: Guess the Dinosaur's age!

how old is that 'young' Dinosaur?

4

Although ancient Dinosaurs may be millions of years old, there are a few still around. Some say anyway, although you have to ask a few questions when you next see one. Better not to ask If they are a Dinosaur whilst at the table, they tend to get very hungry, depending on what age you think they are.

To avoid being eaten, you can ask the age of the baby dinosaur (Dino) in a roundabout way, too high or too low then (in five guesses) is a good game. You may even guess first time!

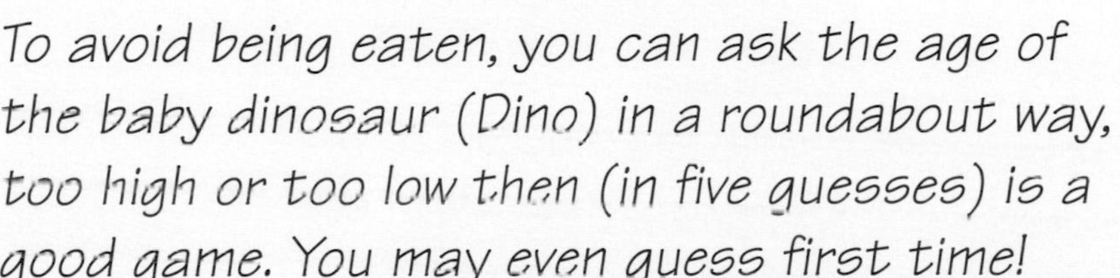

All you need to do is type-in a little bit of code to ask the age for you (much safer, I find). I found one on the next page. Be very careful typing it all in, - just in case you upset Dino!

The Author (is a bit of Dinosaur)

School aged Dinosaurs!

Dinosaurs that want to go to school is the next big thing. They can talk, add-up, go shopping and play games! So we shall now guess how old this young Dinosaur is and wonder if he is still too young to go to school?

Let's get coding...

IMPORT a Dino. Any old Dinosaur will do. Place it left-of-centre in the preview screen. Next add one VARIABLES and call it [age]. Perhaps draw a nice background by using [STAGE] if you have the time. It would be nice to have a theme-park background.

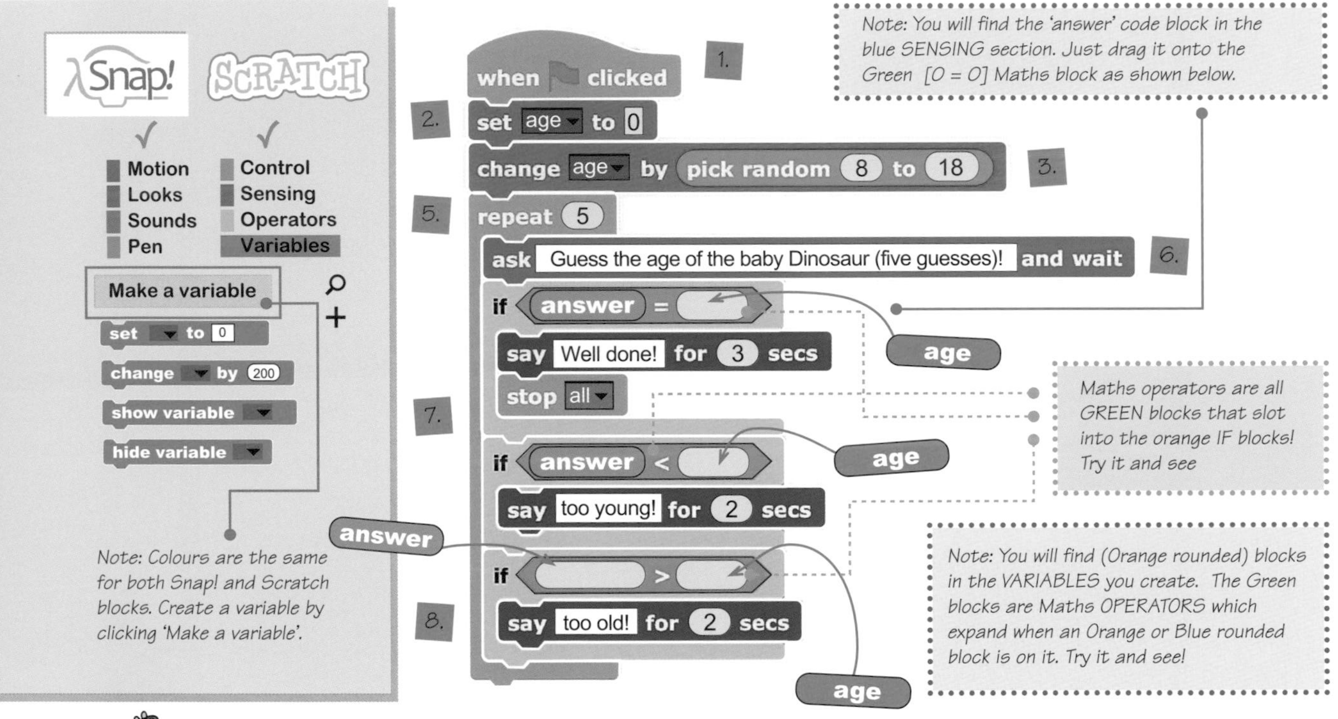

Snap!
SCRATCH
Motion
Looks
Sounds
Pen
Control
Sensing
Operators
Variables
Make a variable
set to 0
change by 200
show variable
hide variable
Note: Colours are the same for both Snap! and Scratch blocks. Create a variable by clicking 'Make a variable'.
Note: You will find the 'answer' code block in the blue SENSING section. Just drag it onto the Green [0 = 0] Maths block as shown below.
1.
when clicked
2.
set age to 0
change age by pick random 8 to 18
3.
5.
repeat 5
ask Guess the age of the baby Dinosaur (five guesses)! and wait
6.
if answer =
age
say Well done! for 3 secs
stop all
7.
if answer <
age
say too young! for 2 secs
answer
if >
8.
say too old! for 2 secs
age
Maths operators are all GREEN blocks that slot into the orange IF blocks! Try it and see
Note: You will find (Orange rounded) blocks in the VARIABLES you create. The Green blocks are Maths OPERATORS which expand when an Orange or Blue rounded block is on it. Try it and see!

Note: *To 'IMPORT a Dino' In Snap! import using the Costumes import function. in Scratch you need to look under 'Costumes' then import from 'Animals'. Snap! and Scratch have lots of 'Costumes' to choose from.*

☑ age

This is the only variable you need to create. It will ask what it is to be called. Call it age then drop it into the code we show here. Easy peasy, nice and easy!

1. START MENU: The Green Flag always starts the code running!
2. Create a new VARIABLE called [age] first. Drag block under 'When clicked'.
3. INSERT pick random numbers from maths (green blocks) (4 to 12).
4. REPEAT block sets everything inside to loop (repeat) 5 times.
5. ASK block 'asks' the question and wait for an 'answer'...
6. IF block: if 'answer' equals 'age' response then 'say' something.
7. IF block: if 'answer' is less than 'age' response then 'say' something.
8. IF block: if 'answer' is more than 'age' response then 'say' something.

School aged Python Dinosaur

Dinosaurs are quite good at Computing but a bit hopeless at coding. They just want to play games all the time. If only they could see that there is so much more to play with in Python. Maybe you can help with that?

Let's get coding...

DINOSAURS! There could be a Tyrannosaurus Rex outside your school! But without proof of his age - he can't come in! We need to make one VARIABLE called [age] and add some easy code to guess his age! A Tyrannosaurus is NOT included, but maybe you can add one later...

(Start of code) - type in the code in BLACK as shown. Ignore '#' marks are for code COMMENTS only.

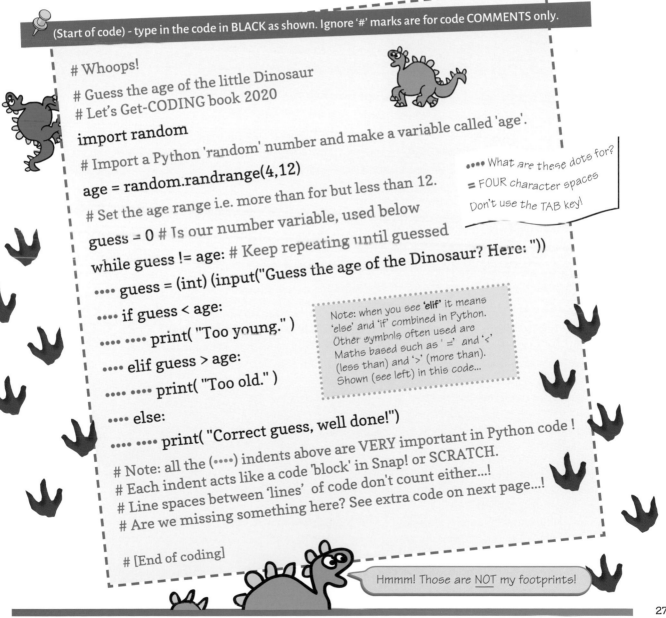

```
# Whoops!
# Guess the age of the little Dinosaur
# Let's Get-CODING book 2020
import random
# Import a Python 'random' number and make a variable called 'age'.
age = random.randrange(4,12)
# Set the age range i.e. more than for but less than 12.
guess = 0 # Is our number variable, used below
while guess != age: # Keep repeating until guessed
•••• guess = (int) (input("Guess the age of the Dinosaur? Here: "))
•••• if guess < age:
•••• •••• print( "Too young." )
•••• elif guess > age:
•••• •••• print( "Too old." )
•••• else:
•••• •••• print( "Correct guess, well done!")
# Note: all the (••••) indents above are VERY important in Python code !
# Each indent acts like a code 'block' in Snap! or SCRATCH.
# Line spaces between 'lines' of code don't count either...!
# Are we missing something here? See extra code on next page...!

# [End of coding]
```

•••• What are these dots for?
= FOUR character spaces
Don't use the TAB key!

Note: when you see **'elif'** it means 'else' and 'if' combined in Python. Other symbols often used are Maths based such as '=' and '<' (less than) and '>' (more than). Shown (see left) in this code...

Hmmm! Those are NOT my footprints!

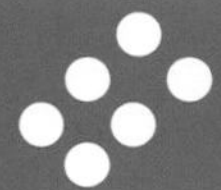

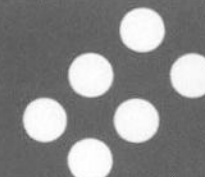

Options to try:

Sidney

Harry

Georgina

Bruce

You can easily make changes to your Dinosaur game by making more Dinosaurs (names) and make them different colours. Easy enough in Snap! and Scratch to make. Simply duplicate your Sprite (and all the code will also be duplicated), change the Dino colour and then change the random age to an age you prefer. Don't forget to change the 'Go' button to 'when pressed' - so only when you press that exact DINOSAUR colour, or they will all answer at once (not a good idea). When pressed, is the best way here for Snap! and Scratch.

Python Coding: a wee bit different but not-a-lot different...

To show you how to do the same in Python I have made four Dinosaurs (above) with names (above). Each has a a secret 'age' (random) and he (or she) will answer either 'Too young' or 'Too old'. Its really so easy, even a very small dinosaur could make it. Now its your turn!

(Start of code) - type in the code in BLACK as shown. Ignore '#' marks are for code COMMENTS only.

```
# Lets get Coding book - extra code.  Guessing and Counting!

import random
counter = 0 # Make a counter that starts at zero
Name = input('Enter name of the Dinosaur: ')
age = random.randint(3, 12) # Age is any number between 3 and 12

print('Dinosaur, ' + Name + ', says, hello to you..') # Adds a 'Name' input to our sentence

while counter < 5: # Counts (loop up to 5 times) until a correct age is guessed
•••• guess=int(input('Can you Guess this Dinosaurs age? - in just 5 guesses! Try now...  '))
•••• counter = counter + 1 # Add a 1 to our counter (adds  1 each  time to  the counter)
•••• if guess < age: # Guess is 'less than' the hidden 'random-number 'variable called 'age'
•••• •••• print('Too young, try again...')
•••• if guess > age: # Guess the 'random-number' (variable) called 'age'
•••• •••• print('Too old, try again...')
••••  if guess == age: #  When you guess correct, it breaks out of loop
•••• •••• break

# We break out of the loop and do this instead
if guess == age:  # Following on from break, you can then add 'well-done' or show 'guesses'
•••• counter = str(counter)
•••• print('Dinosaur, ' + Name + ' says, well-done! you guessed in just '+ counter + ' guesses.')
if guess != age: # When all 5 guesses used with no correct answer, add correct number it should be
•••• age = str(age)
•••• print('Dinosaur, ' + Name + ', says; I am aged ' + age)  # Includes Name (input) and age (random) variable.

# [End of coding]
```

•••• What are these dots for?
= FOUR character spaces
Don't use the TAB key!

Tips: Adding a single [spacebar] gap between '+Name' and '+age' in last line of code - (below) helps it read a lot better when you run and test the code. Try it and see!

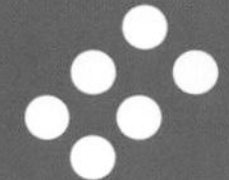

NEXT: Huge Shopping list!

5

Don't forget that thing!

Shopping lists are just so 'B-O-R-I-N-G!'

Some may say, but it all depends on what your shopping list is for. Here is my shopping list for Christmas. Whoopee!

My Christmas list is:

a. Shiny new bike with helmet

b. Toy robot dog with batteries

c. Chocolate Cake with buttons

d. Mince pies with Custard

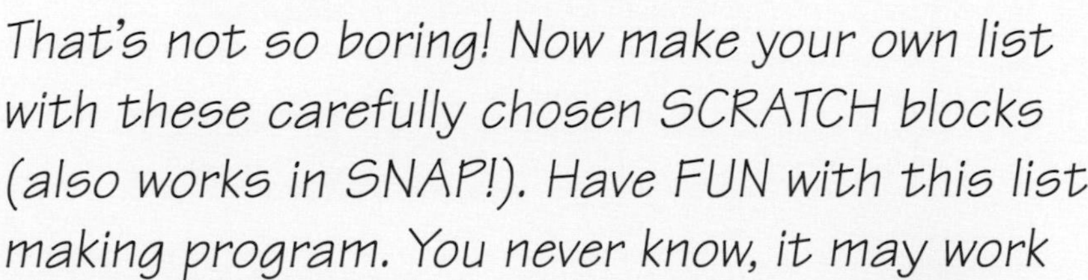

That's not so boring! Now make your own list with these carefully chosen SCRATCH blocks (also works in SNAP!). Have FUN with this list making program. You never know, it may work first time!

The Author (likes Chocolate Cake)

Robodog!

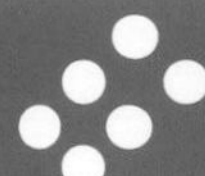

My Shopping list for things!

We create a shopping list for your Mum (or Dad) using this easy-to-make Scratch code to create a working shopping list. We need three icons and and a background image (Scratch only project).

Let's get coding...

MAKE A SHOP! or draw any shop you like. It does not have to be a food shop. Make one VARIABLE called 'number' and make one list called 'shopping-list'. That is all you need to go shopping!

Snap! ✗ SCRATCH ✓

Motion, Looks, Sounds, Pen, Control, Sensing, Operators, Variables

Make a variable

set [ ] to 0

change [ ] by 200

show variable [ ]

hide variable [ ]

Note: 'Make a variable' and call it 'number' then make a List and call it 'shopping'. Both variables are 'clicked' to then display on screen. (as below).

☑ number

Make a list

☑ shopping

The Shopping (Listed)

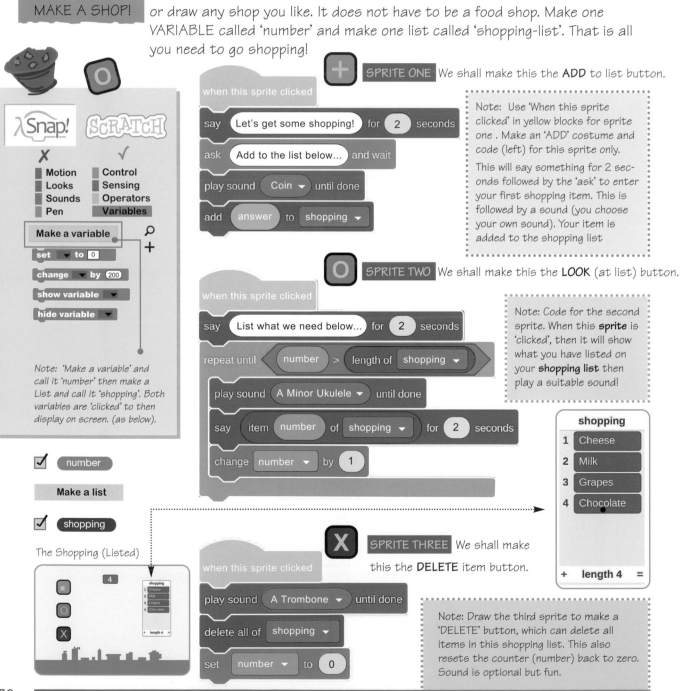

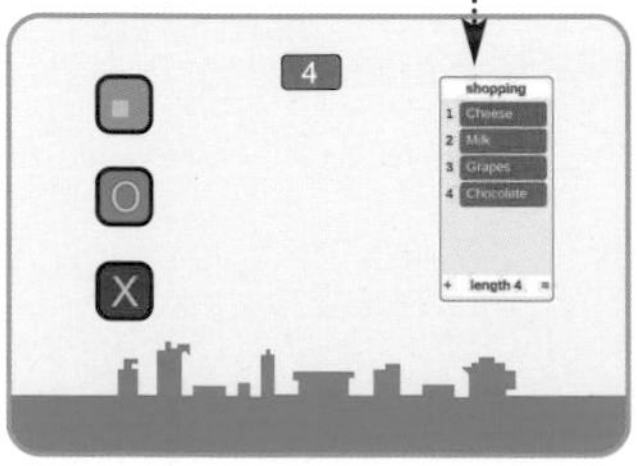

SPRITE ONE We shall make this the **ADD** to list button.

```
when this sprite clicked
say [Let's get some shopping!] for (2) seconds
ask [Add to the list below...] and wait
play sound [Coin ▾] until done
add (answer) to [shopping ▾]
```

Note: Use 'When this sprite clicked' in yellow blocks for sprite one . Make an 'ADD' costume and code (left) for this sprite only.

This will say something for 2 seconds followed by the 'ask' to enter your first shopping item. This is followed by a sound (you choose your own sound). Your item is added to the shopping list

SPRITE TWO We shall make this the **LOOK** (at list) button.

```
when this sprite clicked
say [List what we need below...] for (2) seconds
repeat until < (number) > (length of [shopping ▾]) >
    play sound [A Minor Ukulele ▾] until done
    say (item (number) of [shopping ▾]) for (2) seconds
    change [number ▾] by (1)
```

Note: Code for the second sprite. When this **sprite** is 'clicked', then it will show what you have listed on your **shopping list** then play a suitable sound!

shopping	
1	Cheese
2	Milk
3	Grapes
4	Chocolate
+ length 4 =	

SPRITE THREE We shall make this the **DELETE** item button.

```
when this sprite clicked
play sound [A Trombone ▾] until done
delete all of [shopping ▾]
set [number ▾] to (0)
```

Note: Draw the third sprite to make a 'DELETE' button, which can delete all items in this shopping list. This also resets the counter (number) back to zero. Sound is optional but fun.

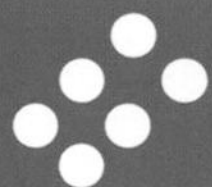

My Shopping in Python!

Shoppers are quite good at making lists. If you don't make a list you will probably end up forgetting whatever you needed and then end-up buying something completely different, (all because you forgot your shopping list).

IMAGINE a Cake. It could be someone you know has a Birthday party and you have been asked to make a program to get all the toy-things listed. What a good idea for a list...

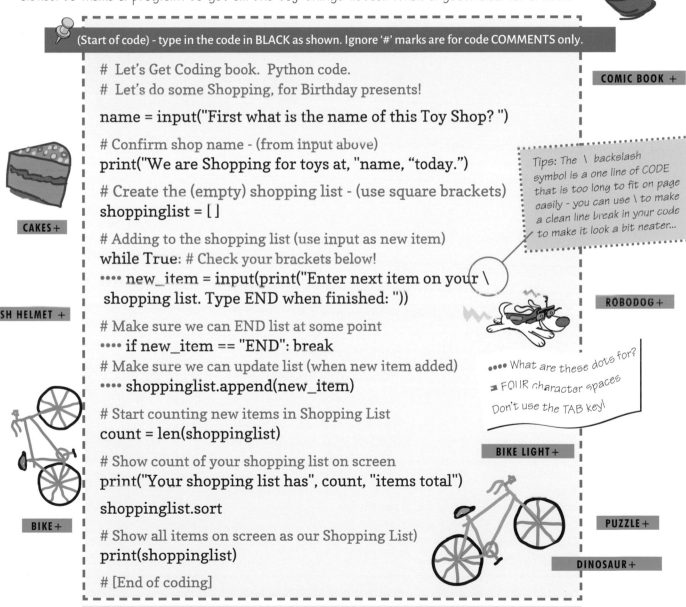

(Start of code) - type in the code in BLACK as shown. Ignore '#' marks are for code COMMENTS only.

```
# Let's Get Coding book. Python code.
# Let's do some Shopping, for Birthday presents!

name = input("First what is the name of this Toy Shop? ")

# Confirm shop name - (from input above)
print("We are Shopping for toys at, "name, “today.”)

# Create the (empty) shopping list - (use square brackets)
shoppinglist = [ ]

# Adding to the shopping list (use input as new item)
while True: # Check your brackets below!
•••• new_item = input(print("Enter next item on your \
 shopping list. Type END when finished: "))

# Make sure we can END list at some point
•••• if new_item == "END": break
# Make sure we can update list (when new item added)
•••• shoppinglist.append(new_item)

# Start counting new items in Shopping List
count = len(shoppinglist)

# Show count of your shopping list on screen
print("Your shopping list has", count, "items total")

shoppinglist.sort

# Show all items on screen as our Shopping List)
print(shoppinglist)

# [End of coding]
```

Tips: The \ backslash symbol is a one line of CODE that is too long to fit on page easily - you can use \ to make a clean line break in your code to make it look a bit neater...

•••• What are these dots for?
= FOUR character spaces
Don't use the TAB key!

COMIC BOOK +

CAKES+

CRASH HELMET +

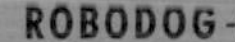

BIKE+

BIKE LIGHT+

PUZZLE+

DINOSAUR+

As an option you can also DOWNLOAD this page of code in the books project RESOURCES pages.

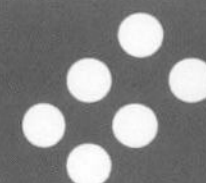

Options to try:

Here you can make interesting changes to your code. In this project you will learn how to use LIST (items list) which when combined with a VARIABLE (count) which can remember all the items in your shopping LIST. We can now add a simple 'roll-over' button effect and add some sounds!

In SCRATCH - think about how your buttons 'look'. To make them visually look more like real 'buttons'. For advanced SCRATCH coders we can make the three buttons change colour when pressed. This is called a button 'rollover' on a web page which uses 'javascript' code *(which is another kind of coding used in web pages)*. Here we do the same, just using Scratch code, to make the same effect.

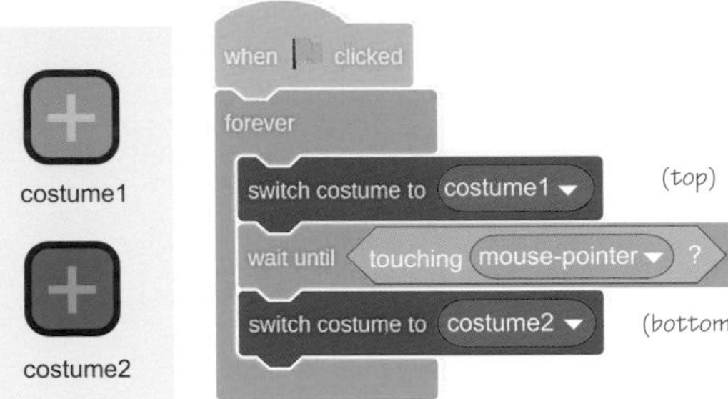

First you need to duplicate your Sprite; *(right click using your mouse) to create two costumes. One Costume is 'top' and the second costume is 'bottom'. Changing the colour of the bottom costume to a darker colours will give the 'roll-over' effect we want. They will automatically 'swap places' -when your mouse hovers over the buttons. Add this code block to each Sprite:*

You can also change the sounds as each button is pressed. *Keep the sounds short or they will stop the program working when the sounds are playing. So keep the sounds short, although you can choose which sounds best!*

In PYTHON, the code is designed to be short and easy to make. To make easy changes to this code (which is entirely text based) we could add images to make buttons and then sounds. But the simplicity of this code is designed around the look of a till receipt. So lets try to make it look better and add some visual lines breaks (as a tear-off strip till receipt) then and add a short beep when done. We do not want to make it over complicated.

Python Code: adding some SOUND!

```
# We need to add a module called PLAYSOUND (in THONNY)
# Add this one line of Python code at line # (1) as below:
from playsound import playsound

# Then add this next line of Python code at line # (2)
playsound('audio.mp3') # Now you will need a 'sound' file, next....
```

SOUNDS

You can ADD any sound as an audio file (**mp3**) - as long as its has an **mp3** ending in the file name. Example: **beep.mp3**. Make and DOWNLOAD your sound (beep) from here: **http://www.orangefreesounds.com/short-beep-noise**

Note: Re-name '**audio.mp3**' to something descriptive such as '**beep.mp3**' or '**blast.mp3**' as our coded example; **playsound('beep.mp3')**. Use a very simple file name with no gap, example: **start-sound.mp3**

Note: Your (**mp3**) sound file must placed in the same folder as your Python code to be played!

```
# Print mock Shopping till receipt perforation, - insert at line # ( 3)
print("--------------------------")
```

Add these lines of code options (shown left) where indicated (numbered 1 to 3).

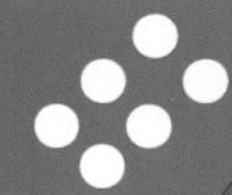

NEXT: A Random Star is born!

6

Create amazing Stars!

Stars are amazing, aren't they?

I have always wondered why we draw stars with so many sides (usually five) sides when I always supposed stars must be a bit 'round' much like our own Sun. But looking at my own picture books and Christmas cards, they always do look better when they have sharp defined edges, so that is what we are going to make today... 'pointy' stars!

To find out what works best, we shall make stars with different colours, sides and sizes. Maybe we can also change the colour of the sky to a dark blue.

After all stars are all different sizes, although I am not so sure all different colours, but they do look great on a dark sky. Let's start.

The Author (likes drawing stars)

Making Random Stars

In this 'star' project we will draw amazing stars and make them appear in the sky with different sizes and colours. It's an amazing simple geometry based on a little bit of Maths.

Let's get coding...

DRAW A BLOB. That's right, your first spirite is a round black circle we'll call a blob. Nothing else required. No VARIABLES, and easy set-up coding by using Random Maths block (in green).

Note: We shall be using the RANDOM function to move our blob (or circle) around the screen. The screen size for Snap! and SCRATCH for this code project is width 400. i.e. from -200 to +200), and height 300 (which is -150 to +150 pixels). The centre point of the screen is y=0 and x=0. We can use that to move our stars around.

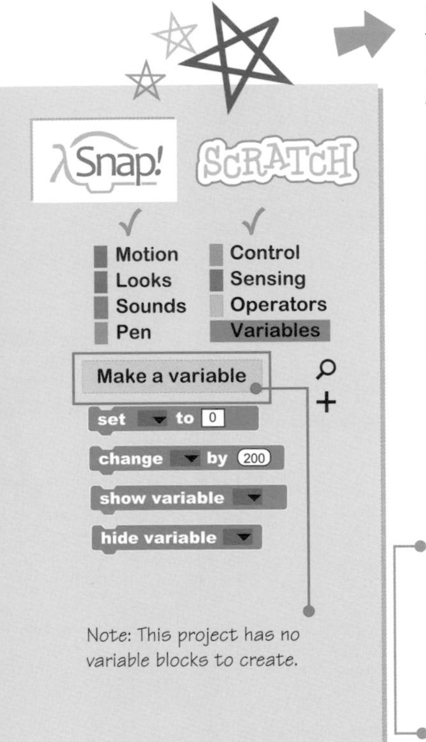

Note: This project has no variable blocks to create.

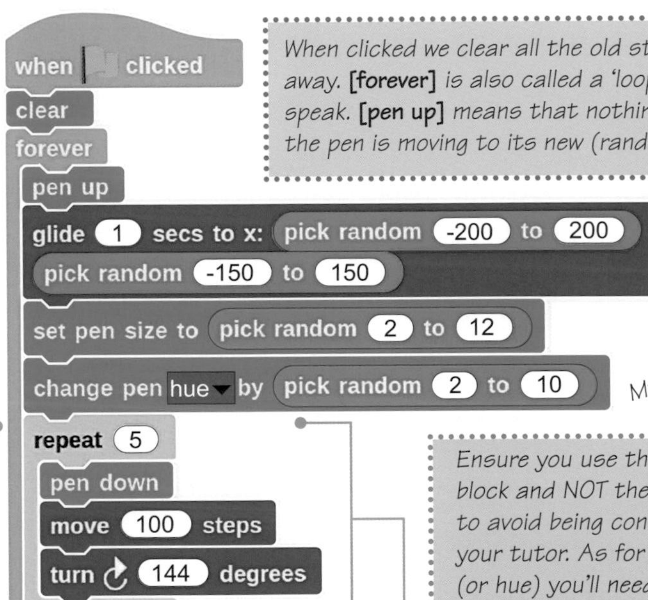

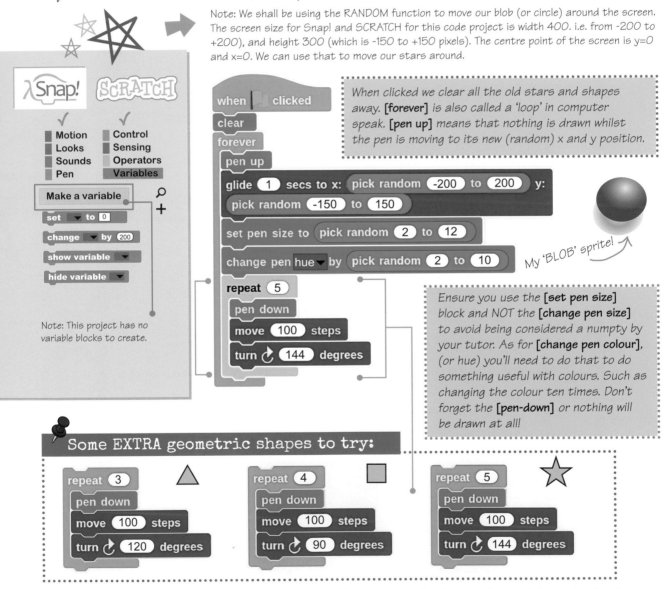

When clicked we clear all the old stars and shapes away. **[forever]** is also called a 'loop' in computer speak. **[pen up]** means that nothing is drawn whilst the pen is moving to its new (random) x and y position.

My 'BLOB' sprite!

Ensure you use the **[set pen size]** block and NOT the **[change pen size]** to avoid being considered a numpty by your tutor. As for **[change pen colour]**, (or hue) you'll need to do that to do something useful with colours. Such as changing the colour ten times. Don't forget the **[pen-down]** or nothing will be drawn at all!

Some EXTRA geometric shapes to try:

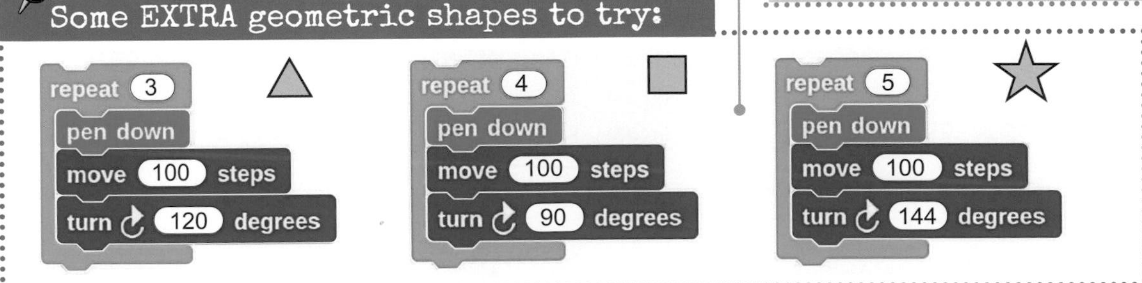

When you have coded all these variations of this code you could try to rotate them by a small amount (by random 1 or 2 degrees). In addition try to combine all shapes into separate code loops (for more advanced students). For tutors and teachers with little time, we do have our page downloads for each project with options. **See book project RESOURCES pages.**

Python: Making Random Stars

Our Python stars are drawn by Turtles. Yes, Turtles are found inside Python (import function) and we shall be making lots of stars using Python code. All in colour with odd sizes.

Let's get coding...

TURTLE BLOB. There are a number of shape options using the import Turtle function. We shall be using the circle option rather than a picture of a Turtle, or square or triangle (see code

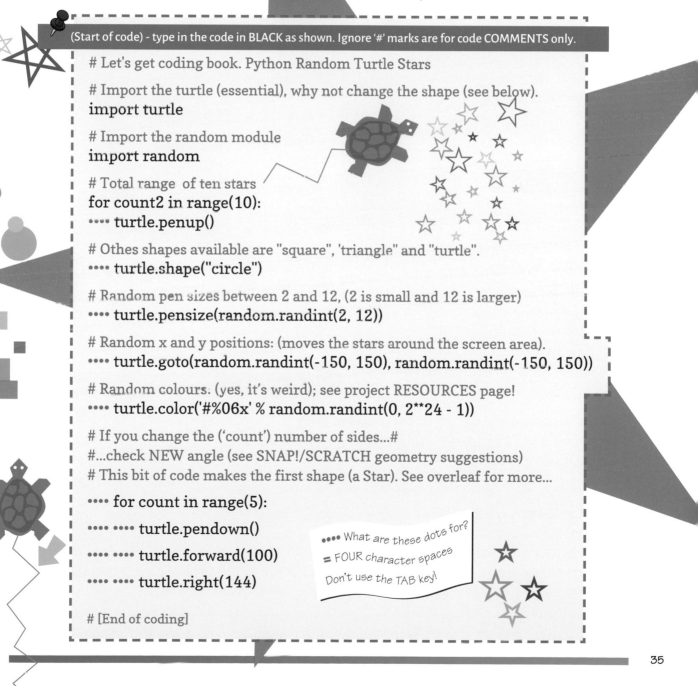

(Start of code) - type in the code in BLACK as shown. Ignore '#' marks are for code COMMENTS only.

```
# Let's get coding book. Python Random Turtle Stars

# Import the turtle (essential), why not change the shape (see below).
import turtle

# Import the random module
import random

# Total range of ten stars
for count2 in range(10):
•••• turtle.penup()

# Othes shapes available are "square", 'triangle" and "turtle".
•••• turtle.shape("circle")

# Random pen sizes between 2 and 12, (2 is small and 12 is larger)
•••• turtle.pensize(random.randint(2, 12))

# Random x and y positions: (moves the stars around the screen area).
•••• turtle.goto(random.randint(-150, 150), random.randint(-150, 150))

# Random colours: (yes, it's weird); see project RESOURCES page!
•••• turtle.color('#%06x' % random.randint(0, 2**24 - 1))

# If you change the ('count') number of sides...#
#...check NEW angle (see SNAP!/SCRATCH geometry suggestions)
# This bit of code makes the first shape (a Star). See overleaf for more...

•••• for count in range(5):

•••• •••• turtle.pendown()

•••• •••• turtle.forward(100)

•••• •••• turtle.right(144)

# [End of coding]
```

•••• What are these dots for?
= FOUR character spaces
Don't use the TAB key!

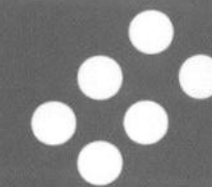

Options to try:

So you have already tried changing the Snap! or SCRATCH code blocks with 'extra' geometric shapes such as Triangle, Square and the five sided Star. With that geometry coding skill you can make other shapes spin as spirals.

As you know by now, the author of this book is a bit oddball, nutty and bonkers. So my shapes are a bit different to yours. My code blocks are going to be the same basic shapes. You only need to add one variable. This is enough to make some amazing geometric shapes and spirals.

Using the coding form Snap! or SCRATCH you can change the previous code blocks to create a totally new geometry shape. First make a new VARIABLE called **line-length**. *When you see the blocks created (as below left) drag them into the coding block to replace the block of code (shown right in blue lines).*

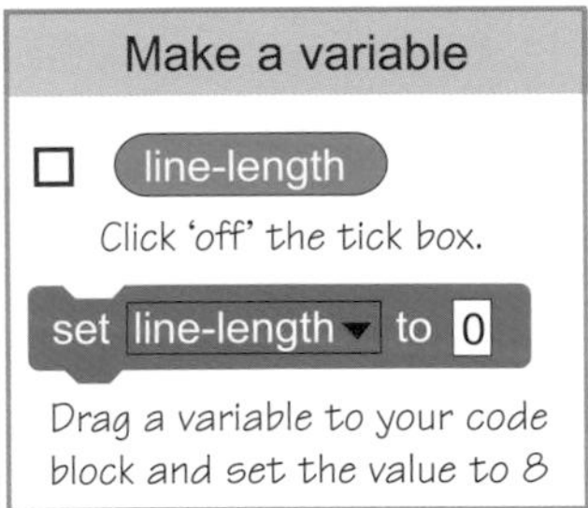

You can also adapt this code block (right) to make two more new shapes by simply changing the angles in 'turn' to either 90, 120 or 144 degress. All will create amazing spiral shapes!

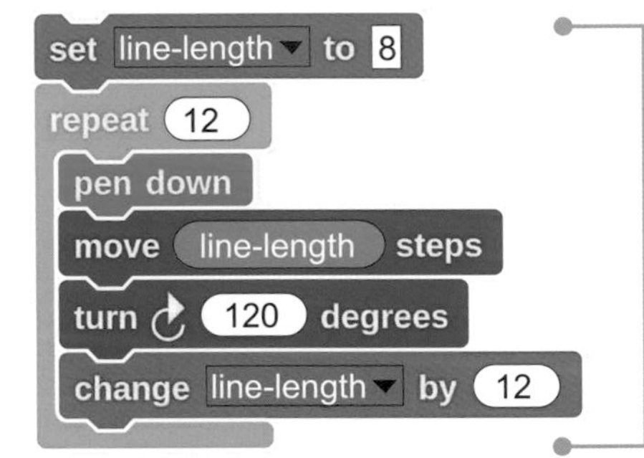

Python code spirals:

Its easy to adjust your Python code by making some small changes. Python follows the same sequence we made in Snap! or Scratch as we only change the end of the code block. We then add a single variable as we show you here to make your spirals. Use the same geometry angles for your Triangles, Square and Star. Angles 120, 90 and 144 degrees can be changed (below).

Have some fun by adding this optional code!

Ignore '#' marks are for code COMMENTS only.

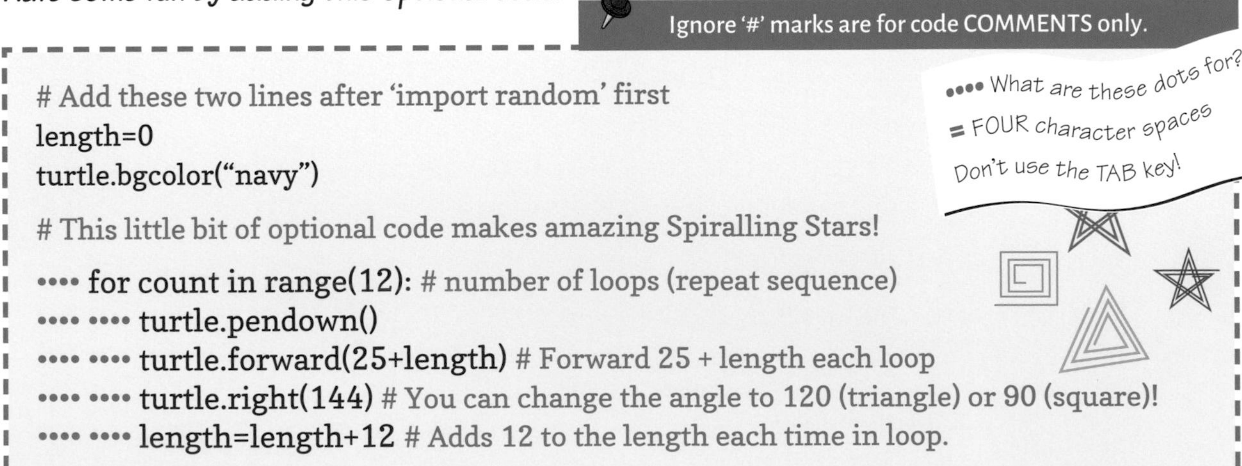

```
# Add these two lines after 'import random' first
length=0
turtle.bgcolor("navy")

# This little bit of optional code makes amazing Spiralling Stars!
•••• for count in range(12): # number of loops (repeat sequence)
•••• •••• turtle.pendown()
•••• •••• turtle.forward(25+length) # Forward 25 + length each loop
•••• •••• turtle.right(144) # You can change the angle to 120 (triangle) or 90 (square)!
•••• •••• length=length+12 # Adds 12 to the length each time in loop.
```


* We ran out of space to explain 'Random Colours' we have used. See **project RESOURCES** page...

NEXT: Trumpet your Silly Stories!

7

Creating a story in code!

We all like a good story and this coding is an 'answer-and-question' style session on how to make your very first story. We start by asking some simple questions and add little bit of imagination to what happens next....

My story is not perfect, it could be better and I shall need you to write the questions a little better than I can. When you start coding it's probably better to follow my story first before you make your own version.

I know you are a better story teller than I am so that is why I have an Elephant in my story, I think that is important, don't you?

The Author (likes Elephants and Stories)

Trumpet your Story!

In this project you get to make your own story. You just need a friend, any old bicycle, some of your favourite food and a place to go. After that some careful typing to avoid errors. Let's get coding...

IMPORT AN ELEPHANT! I am sure you will find the right SPRITE - you will need two ELEPHANTS (on one sprite) so two costumes to import in either Snap! or SCRATCH. Also create a simple background (Stage) scene for your Elephant. Remember: that you need one sprite and two costumes; i.e. **'elephant a'** and **'elephant b'** as shown (below)

Note: Make FIVE VARIABLES to put in your story. Each variable is a key part of your story. Click all tick the variable tick boxes 'off' - you don't want to show them on screen!

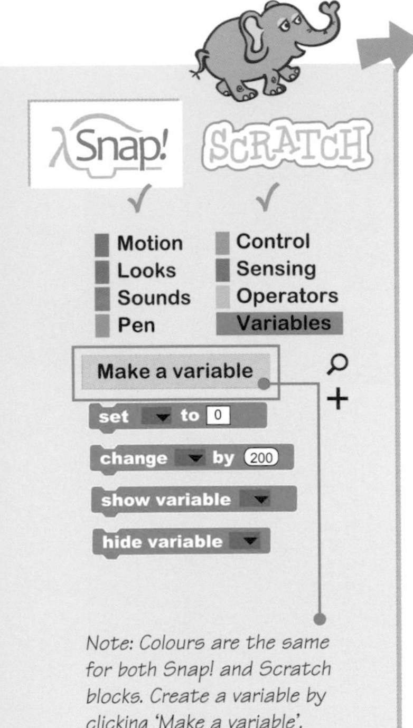

Snap!
SCRATCH
Motion
Looks
Sounds
Pen
Control
Sensing
Operators
Variables
Make a variable
set to 0
change by 200
show variable
hide variable

Note: Colours are the same for both Snap! and Scratch blocks. Create a variable by clicking 'Make a variable'.

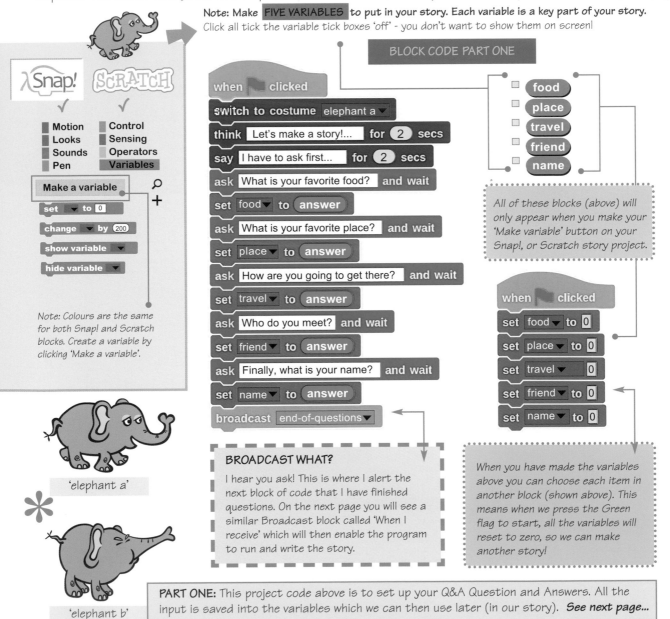

BLOCK CODE PART ONE

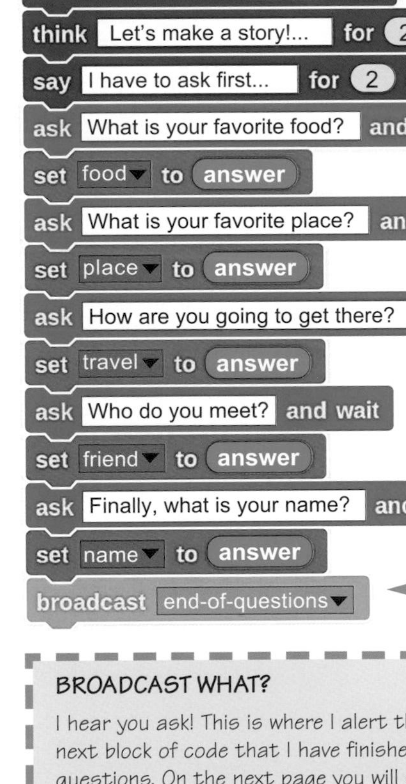

when clicked
switch to costume elephant a
think Let's make a story!... for 2 secs
say I have to ask first... for 2 secs
ask What is your favorite food? and wait
set food to answer
ask What is your favorite place? and wait
set place to answer
ask How are you going to get there? and wait
set travel to answer
ask Who do you meet? and wait
set friend to answer
ask Finally, what is your name? and wait
set name to answer
broadcast end-of-questions

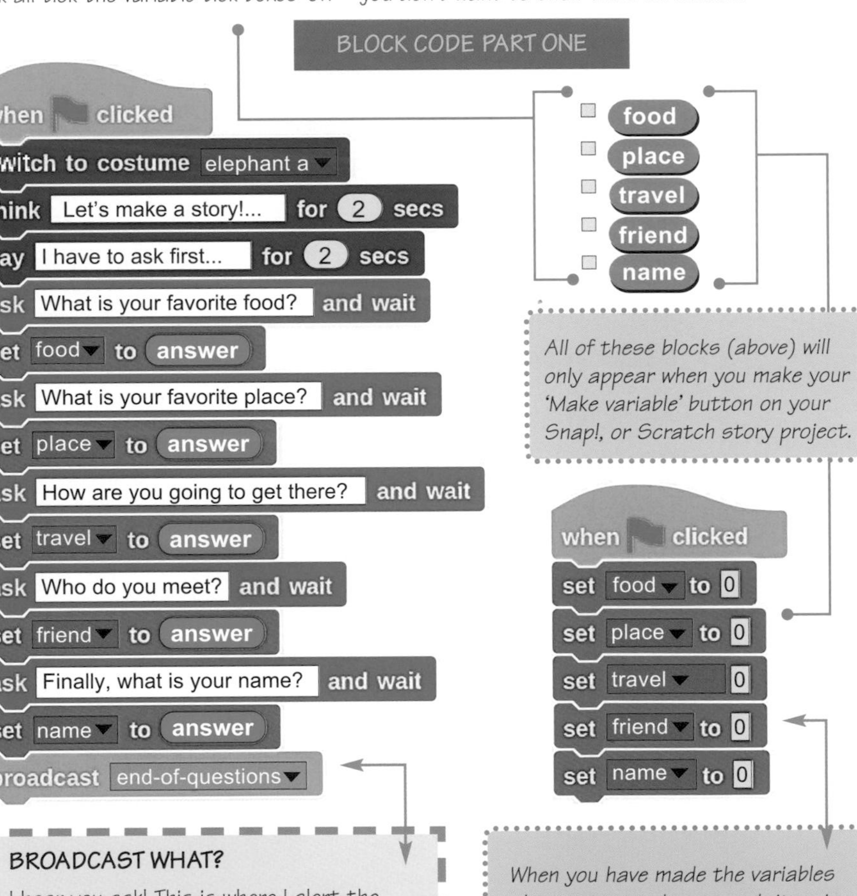

food
place
travel
friend
name
when clicked
set food to 0
set place to 0
set travel 0
set friend to 0
set name to 0

All of these blocks (above) will only appear when you make your 'Make variable' button on your Snap!, or Scratch story project.

'elephant a'

'elephant b'

BROADCAST WHAT?

I hear you ask! This is where I alert the next block of code that I have finished questions. On the next page you will see a similar Broadcast block called 'When I receive' which will then enable the program to run and write the story.

When you have made the variables above you can choose each item in another block (shown above). This means when we press the Green flag to start, all the variables will reset to zero, so we can make another story!

PART ONE: This project code above is to set up your Q&A Question and Answers. All the input is saved into the variables which we can then use later (in our story). ***See next page...***

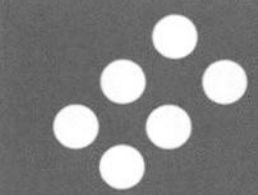

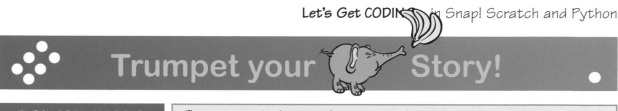

Trumpet your Story!

BLOCK CODE PART TWO

The next page is the part where we write the story. It may look a little different in Scrach but effectively they are the same 'join' blocks found in both.

If you have questions then with your answers, we can now make a story. in this project we input all your answers into a ready prepared story (but you can easily change it), as I am sure you will...

Start a new yellow block 'When i receive' and click on the name you entered previously (you can only do that with the 'broadcast' block) on the previous page.

OK.
This is
my story...

```
when I receive [end of-questions ▾]
think [OK, this is my story ...!] for (2) secs
switch to costume [elephant b ▾]
say (join [There was once an Elephant called] (name) ◂▸) for (2) secs
say
  (join (join [Who met] (friend) ◂▸) (join (join [on the] (travel) ◂▸) [to the zoo.] ◂▸) ◂▸)
for (2) secs
say (join [They both decided to eat some tasty,] (food) ◂▸) for (2) secs
say
  join
  (join (join [Unfortunately the] (food) ◂▸) [was really horrible] ◂▸) (join [in the] (travel) ◂▸)
  ◂▸
for (2) secs
say
  join
  (join (join [Both] (friend) ◂▸) (join [and] (name) ◂▸) ◂▸) [had tummy-ache at Zoo school!]
  ◂▸
for (2) secs
say (join [This is not 'The End' of the story of more Zoo adventures with] (name) ◂▸) for (2)
secs
```

"WHERE IS THE PYTHON CODE PAGE, Mr Zoo keeper?"
Whoops! Too many Elephants on this page! Python code is now on next page...

This may look more difficult than it is. The blocks in Snap! and Scratch are exactly the same and will work the same way. What is more tricky is dropping the right 'variables' into the blocks in all the right places. We are using lots of 'join' blocks to make the story. You may have to insert the odd letterspace between words and phrases to make it read well.

Trumpet your Python Story!

You will find it a lot easier to run text based programs in Python than either Snap! or Scratch but then we have not considered how to run Sprites in Python yet. But this is still great fun to code a story!

Let's get coding...

(start of code) - only type in the code in BLACK shown. # As shown are ignored as being COMMENTS.

```
# Let's Get coding book project. Python Storytime code.
# import a module (as a time delay on creating this story)
import time
print("++Let's write a story!++")
print("Just answer these FIVE questions and I will write a story...!")
# Five questions and (z) save the 'answer' to a variable. i.e.  zfood=(food)
food=input("What is your favorite food?: ")
zfood=(food)
place=input("Where is your favorite place?: ")
zplace=(place)
travel=input("How are you going to get there?: ")
ztravel=(travel)
friend=input("Who do you meet?: ")
zfriend=(friend)
name= input("Finally - what is your name?: ")
zname=(name)
print("Thinking...about your story... in four seconds!")
# Add four seconds time delay - Zzzzz - to pretend I am thinking..!
time.sleep(4)
# Story -- start (with a dotted line spacer to show Start )
print("- - - - - - - - - - - - - - - - - - - - - ")
print("There was once a young Elephant called, "zname)
print("Who met", zfriend, "on his", ztravel, "to the Zoo.")
print("They both decided to eat some tasty,", zfood)
print("Unfortunatly the", zfood,  "was really horrible in the,", zplace)
    print( "Both,", zfriend, "and", zname, "had tummy-ache at the \
    Zoo school!")
print("This is not 'The End' of the Zoo adventures with,", zname, ".")
print("- - - - - - - - - - - - - - - - - - - - - ")
# [End of coding]
```

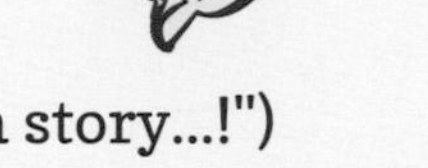

Text in RED are Python VARIABLES: We have added a simple 'z' letter to the important key words in our story. key-words are *'food', 'place', 'travel', 'friend'.* are inserted as: **zfood=food or zname=name....** The 'z' is just a symbol to the various questions. Text highlighted in RED is totally ignored in Python, along with # comments, we also show in BLUE.

This is one line of code The ' \ ' backslash symbol indicates a line break of CODE - it will work - but it's easier for you to make one long line of code.

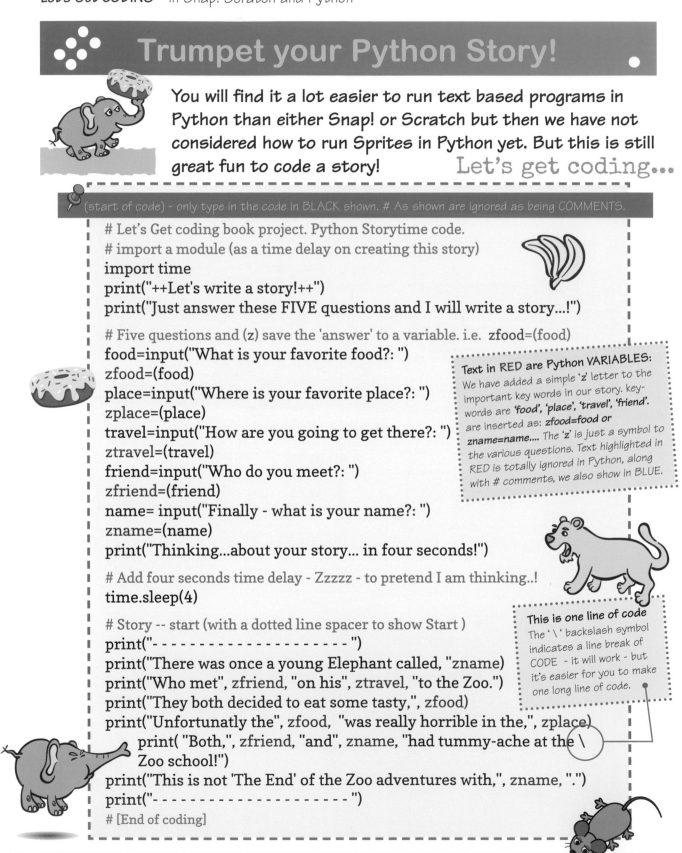

Next: The Train your Brain quiz!

8

Train your Brain with a Quiz!

I.Q.

Q & A ?

!

If you don't use it - you lose it (so they say), teachers mainly, I think. So lets start a Quiz that anyone with a 'Brain' can play.

I have decided that you need more MATHS, but make it more of a memory game; adding up and subtracting, and make it a quiz style.

We are going to use the blocks to work out the answer, but we have to guess the right answer to each question when we play.

Such as: subtract 16 from 24 = 8

How hard can that be? Take care with the blocks as I am putting blocks-into-blocks into blocks to create (using Maths) the answer.

The Author (creates Maths Quizzes)

(Spare Brain not included)

Add 8 to 16!

4/5 ths of this?

The Brain Trainer Quiz

If you don't use your Brain, you lose it! So in this coding project we are making a quiz to train your Brain. It does help if you can add up, take away and multiply before you start! Let's get coding...

IMPORT ABBY she is your host for this quiz who will either be happy or sad as you answer the Questions. Make one **VARIABLE** called 'SUM'. Import a sprite called 'Abby' who has three costume options: **Abby a, Abby b and Abby c**. (Choose a costume in response to the question).

Snap! ✓ SCRATCH ✓

- Motion
- Looks
- Sounds
- Pen
- Control
- Sensing
- Operators
- Variables

Make a variable

set [ ] to 0
change [ ] by 200
show variable [ ]
hide variable [ ]

Note: There is one variable used in this project. It should appear on screen orange block set SUM *

One sprite using all three Abby costumes!

Let Abby ask and respond to the questions. When she answers you just change the costume for each answer using; abby a, abby or abby c.

1.

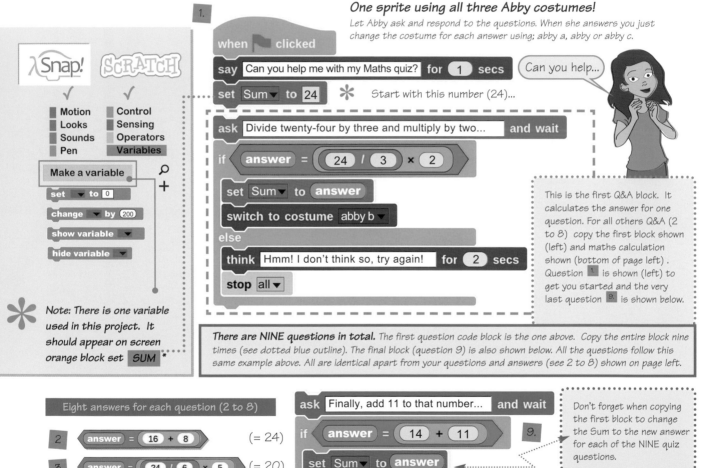

```
when [flag] clicked
say [Can you help me with my Maths quiz?] for (1) secs
set [Sum] to [24]            * Start with this number (24)...
ask [Divide twenty-four by three and multiply by two...] and wait
if <(answer) = ((24) / (3)) × (2)>
if answer = 14 + 11
    set [Sum] to (answer)
play sound trumpet-blast
think That was really cool! for 2 secs
    switch to costume [abby b]
else
    think [Hmm! I don't think so, try again!] for (2) secs
    stop [all]
Don't forget when copying the first block to change the Sum to the new answer for each of the NINE quiz questions.
The the final block 9. (left) shown includes sound which you can import later.
You can add sounds for all questions with answers!
```

Can you help...

This is the first Q&A block. It calculates the answer for one question. For all others Q&A (2 to 8) copy the first block shown (left) and maths calculation shown (bottom of page left) . Question 1. is shown (left) to get you started and the very last question 9. is shown below.

There are NINE questions in total. *The first question code block is the one above. Copy the entire block nine times (see dotted blue outline). The final block (question 9) is also shown below. All the questions follow this same example above. All are identical apart from your questions and answers (see 2 to 8) shown on page left.*

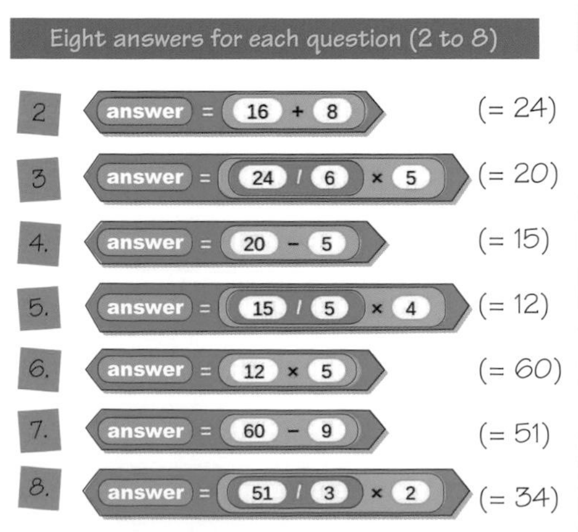

Eight answers for each question (2 to 8)
2 answer = 16 + 8 (= 24)
3 answer = 24 / 6 × 5 (= 20)
4. answer = 20 − 5 (= 15)
5. answer = 15 / 5 × 4 (= 12)
6. answer = 12 × 5 (= 60)
7. answer = 60 − 9 (= 51)
8. answer = 51 / 3 × 2 (= 34)

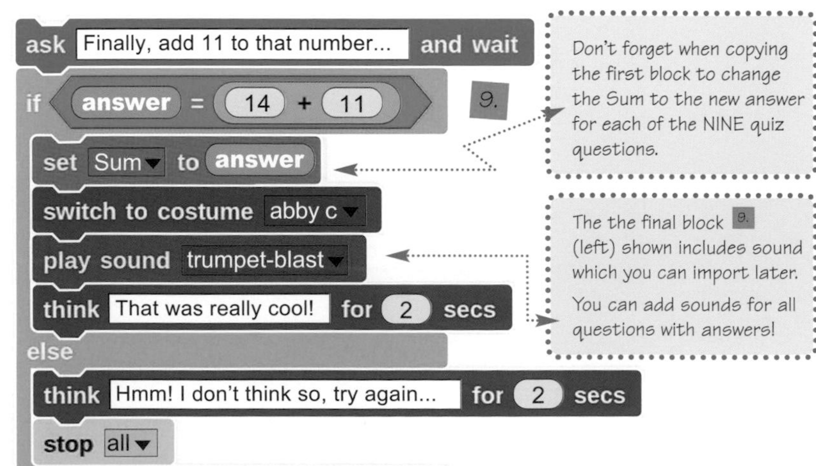

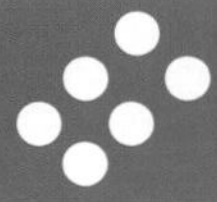

The Python Brain Trainer

In Python we create a coding Calculator. It is basic but you can see how it works and build on that. Making a basic calculator is not as hard as you may think as this calculator can make an easy Quiz game!

(Start of code) - type in the code in BLACK as shown. Ignore '#' marks are for code COMMENTS only.

```
# Brain Trainer quiz calculator. Let's Get Coding book - 2020
# Not so much a quiz as a calculator! See how this Python code works!
# Make a choice MENU (1 to 5 options)
print("** Simple Brain Trainer Calculator **")
print (" ") # line Spacer only
print("[1] Add numbers")
print("[2] Substract numbers")
print("[3] Multiply numbers")
print("[4] Divide numbers")
print("[5] Quit and close calculator")
print (" ") # line Spacer only

# Set up a repeat loop
loop = 1
while loop == 1: #  Forever loop through all menu items.
# Choose Menu item
••• choice=int(input("Press a [x] key number to choose a calculation: "))
•••• print ("Enter your first number below followed by what you want to calculate!") # Instructions
•••• if choice ==1:
•••• •••• a=int(input("> Enter first number:")) # first number is called 'a'
•••• •••• b=int(input("> Enter second number:")) # second number is 'b'
•••• calc=a+b # Calculation is 'a' + 'b' (similar for all other maths calculation)
•••• •••• print("Sum = ",calc)
•••• elif choice ==2: # If menu 2 chosen do this
•••• •••• a=int(input("> Enter first number:")) #  I have added a '>' symbol to message - its not code, just text.
•••• •••• b=int(input("> Enter second number:"))
•••• •••• calc=a-b
•••• •••• print("Difference = ",calc)
•••• elif  choice ==3: # If menu 3 chosen do this
•••• •••• a=int(input("> Enter first number:"))
•••• •••• b=int(input("> Enter second number:"))

# Continued...
```

4/5 ths of this?

Find 5/6th of that?

Add 8 to 16!

Add 11 to that number!

I need to be so careful typing in all this code!

•••• What are these dots for?
= FOUR character spaces
Don't use the TAB key!

Options to try:

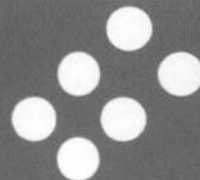

(Continued- code) - type in the code in BLACK as shown. Ignore '#' marks are for code COMMENTS only.

Python does not worry about gaps between lines or how long those lines of code might be.

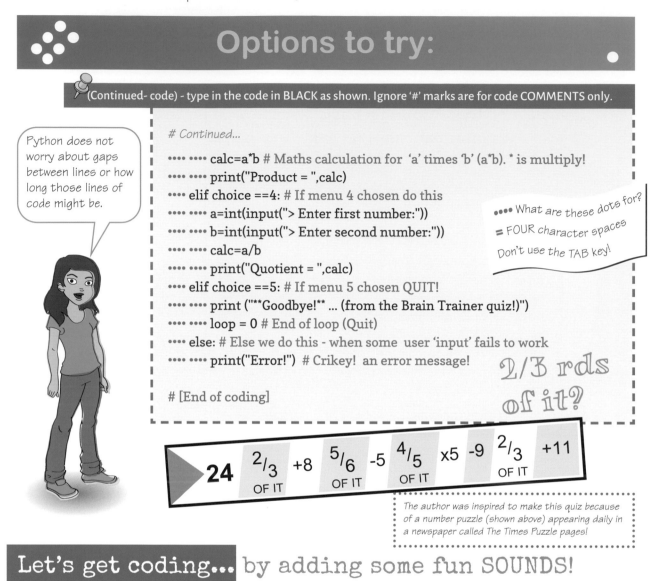

```
# Continued...
•••• •••• calc=a*b # Maths calculation for 'a' times 'b' (a*b). * is multiply!
•••• •••• print("Product = ",calc)
•••• elif choice ==4: # If menu 4 chosen do this
•••• •••• a=int(input("> Enter first number:"))
•••• •••• b=int(input("> Enter second number:"))
•••• •••• calc=a/b
•••• •••• print("Quotient = ",calc)
•••• elif choice ==5: # If menu 5 chosen QUIT!
•••• •••• print ("**Goodbye!** ... (from the Brain Trainer quiz!)")
•••• •••• loop = 0 # End of loop (Quit)
•••• else: # Else we do this - when some user 'input' fails to work
•••• •••• print("Error!") # Crikey! an error message!

# [End of coding]
```

•••• What are these dots for?
= FOUR character spaces
Don't use the TAB key!

2/3 rds of it?

24	2/3 OF IT	+8	5/6 OF IT	-5	4/5 OF IT	x5	-9	2/3 OF IT	+11

The author was inspired to make this quiz because of a number puzzle (shown above) appearing daily in a newspaper called The Times Puzzle pages!

Let's get coding... by adding some fun SOUNDS!

Both Scratch and Snap! can be made more interesting in a quiz; by making Abby's voice to be part of the 'questions and answers'. I have made a voiceover for each question ***(which you can use*)*** but you may prefer to add your own voices using a a web page to create Abby's voice using any text you type-in and then save it as an **'mp3'** file. Import that Mp3 in your sound files for each question or answer you have. **Mp3** is a typical sound file that works in Snap! and Scratch.

Web Resource: http://www.voicemaker.in

Type in your text (suitable words) choose a suitable 'voice' and type of accent if you would like something different to mine. I have used a voice 'English, British, using Emma, female, Convert to Speech and then 'Download to Mp3' and save to your download folder. In schools this may be disabled, ask your Tutor when you have completed all your coding. Have fun with that option.

* See project RESOURCES for full code to download and my custom voices for this project!

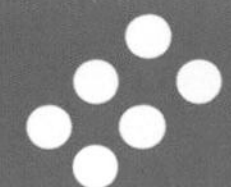

Next: Random number dice!

9

Win or Loose... Start spinning your dice!

If you spin a penny, what are the chances that it will land face up? Some say that its 50:50 and others disagree. It matters how many spins you make, It seems, as you can get a long series of 'heads-up' sometimes.

On another level, I always find my buttered toast (with Jam) always seems to land face down if I drop it on the floor.

To prove you have better luck than me; you will find (on next page) that I have made a super spinning roller dice for you to try. With luck you can give it a spin and you may find that you have won two sixes... If you're really lucky!

The Author (is in a spin again)

Random Number Dice

Two dice are better than one! Who said that? - no idea! ... but you do get more numbers and more unpredictable dice numbers. We just need to find out how to make the coding easily in Snap! or Scratch. Let's get coding...

NO IMPORTS! *No dice found to import! so we must make our own.... A spinning dice has six sides, so we must make our six costume 'Sprite'.*

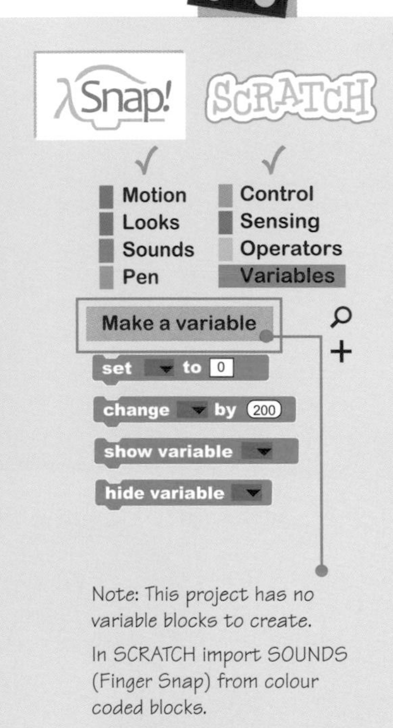

Note: This project has no variable blocks to create.

In SCRATCH import SOUNDS (Finger Snap) from colour coded blocks.

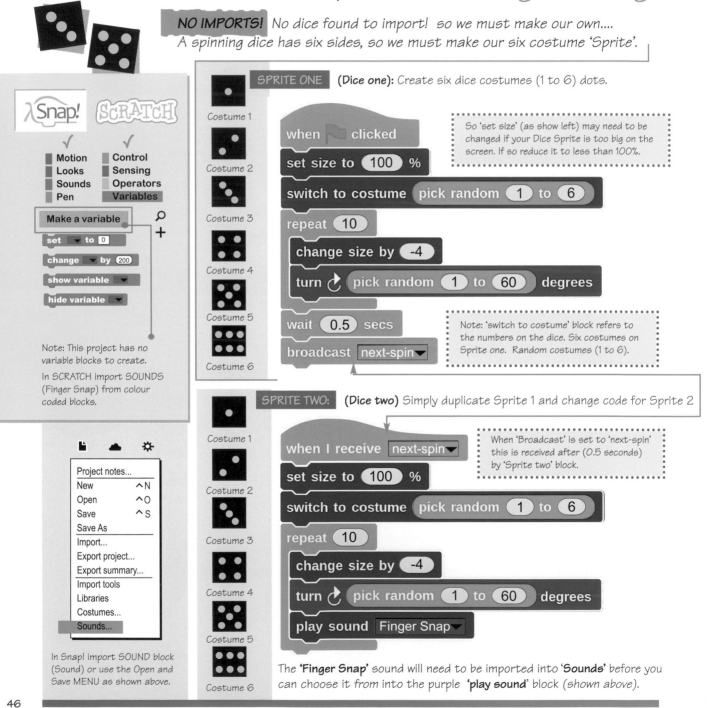

SPRITE ONE **(Dice one):** Create six dice costumes (1 to 6) dots.

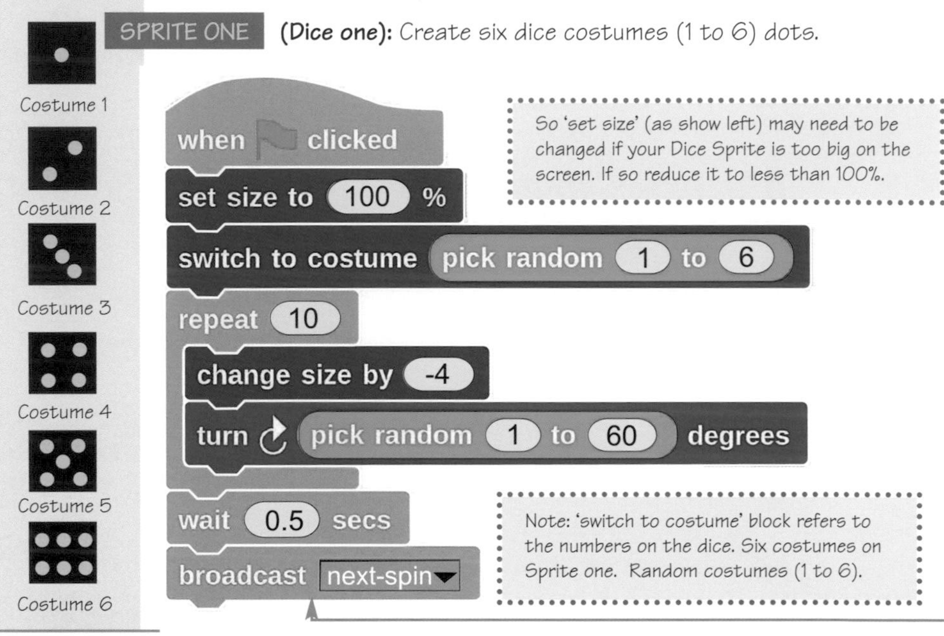

So 'set size' (as show left) may need to be changed if your Dice Sprite is too big on the screen. If so reduce it to less than 100%.

Note: 'switch to costume' block refers to the numbers on the dice. Six costumes on Sprite one. Random costumes (1 to 6).

SPRITE TWO: **(Dice two)** Simply duplicate Sprite 1 and change code for Sprite 2

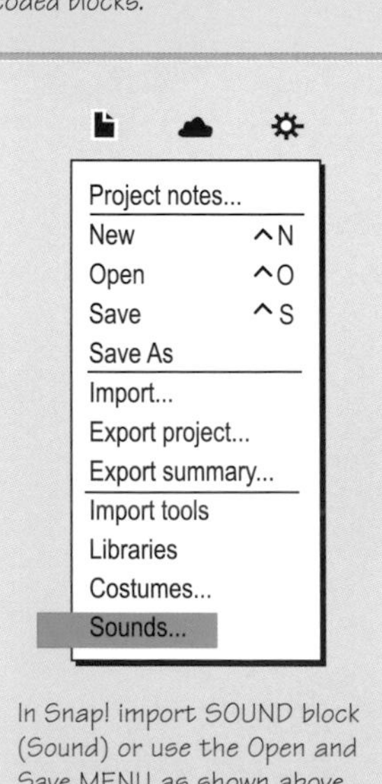

In Snap! import SOUND block (Sound) or use the Open and Save MENU as shown above.

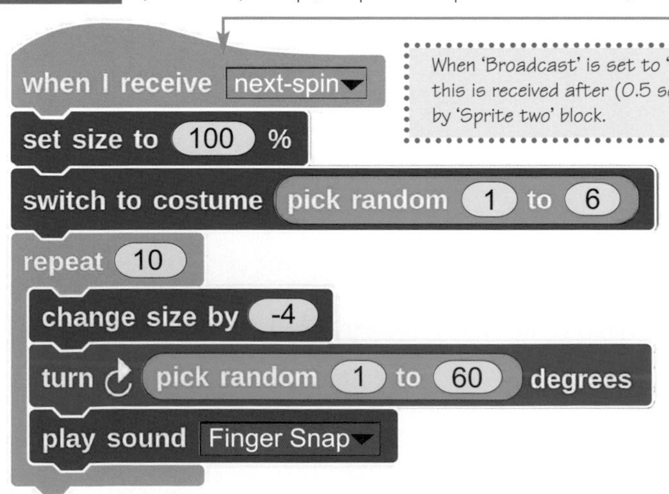

When 'Broadcast' is set to 'next-spin' this is received after (0.5 seconds) by 'Sprite two' block.

The **'Finger Snap'** sound will need to be imported into **'Sounds'** before you can choose it from into the purple **'play sound'** block (shown above).

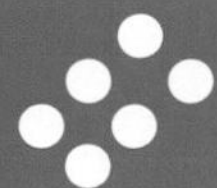

The spinning Python Dice

We shall be making a simple program to create our dice numbers. Random numbers allow us to make all kinds of games. This game is for two dice, but you can add more, when you see how it works. Let's get coding...

RANDOM numbers? It could be a high number or it could be low. But on a dice there are only six numbers, so it's an easy project to code. Remember to import a random module (which means we can make a random number from one to six)...

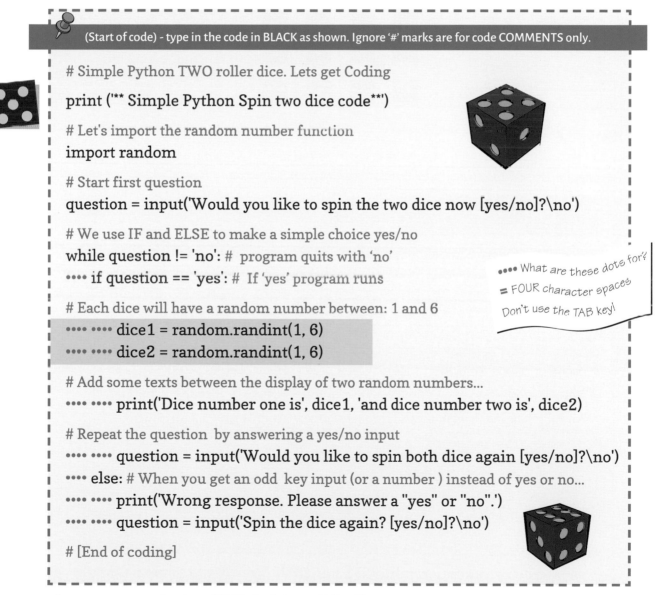

(Start of code) - type in the code in BLACK as shown. Ignore '#' marks are for code COMMENTS only.

```
# Simple Python TWO roller dice. Lets get Coding
print ("** Simple Python Spin two dice code**")
# Let's import the random number function
import random
# Start first question
question = input('Would you like to spin the two dice now [yes/no]?\no')
# We use IF and ELSE to make a simple choice yes/no
while question != 'no': #  program quits with 'no'
•••• if question == 'yes': #  If 'yes' program runs
# Each dice will have a random number between: 1 and 6
•••• •••• dice1 = random.randint(1, 6)
•••• •••• dice2 = random.randint(1, 6)
# Add some texts between the display of two random numbers...
•••• •••• print('Dice number one is', dice1, 'and dice number two is', dice2)
# Repeat the question  by answering a yes/no input
•••• •••• question = input('Would you like to spin both dice again [yes/no]?\no')
•••• else: # When you get an odd  key input (or a number ) instead of yes or no...
•••• •••• print('Wrong response. Please answer a "yes" or "no".')
•••• •••• question = input('Spin the dice again? [yes/no]?\no')
# [End of coding]
```

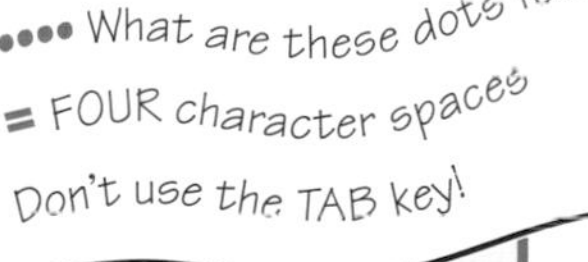

•••• What are these dots for?
= FOUR character spaces
Don't use the TAB key!

Can you see a way of making THREE dice? Just add 'dice3' and then copy that to the print function.

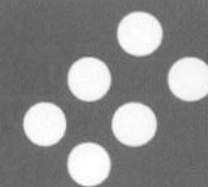

Options to try:

This is a very easy game to make. You can also learn what makes a RANDOM number. Its fun to make in either Snap! and Scratch with very similar coding for each. Try some of these options for both Snap!, Scratch and PYTHON.

Costumes are all the same, just change the colours for each new sprite!

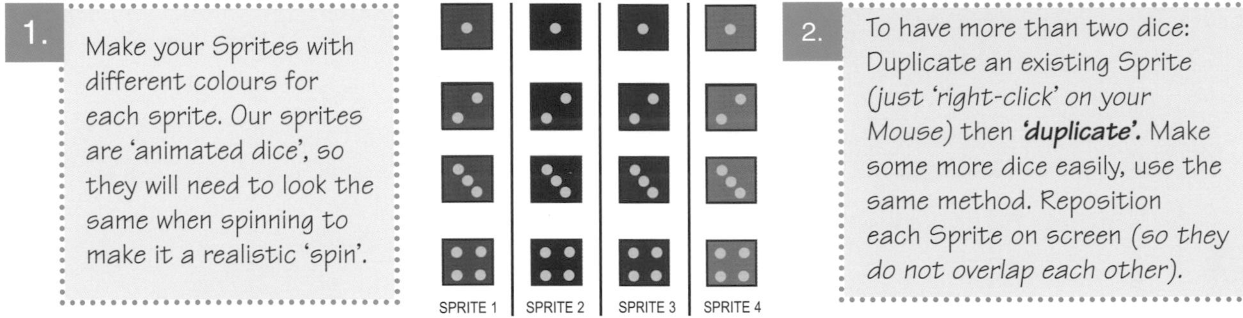

1. Make your Sprites with different colours for each sprite. Our sprites are 'animated dice', so they will need to look the same when spinning to make it a realistic 'spin'.

2. To have more than two dice: Duplicate an existing Sprite (*just 'right-click' on your Mouse*) then ***'duplicate'.*** Make some more dice easily, use the same method. Reposition each Sprite on screen (*so they do not overlap each other*).

Another option you can try: *is making your dice have twelve faces (12 sides). You need to make twelve costumes and change the block code from random (1-6) to random (1-12). Duplicating your dice is also easy with a right click of your mouse. You choose how many there will be!*

Let's get coding... using Python code options...

It's even easier in Python! We can easily edit your code you made earlier and make simple changes. We can ADD more dice and then we can ADD more SIDES to the dice (*so we can extend the random numbers to TWELVE or more*). You could choose a really big RANDOM number for example! ***See how fast you can make your multiple dice with multiple Random numbers run!***

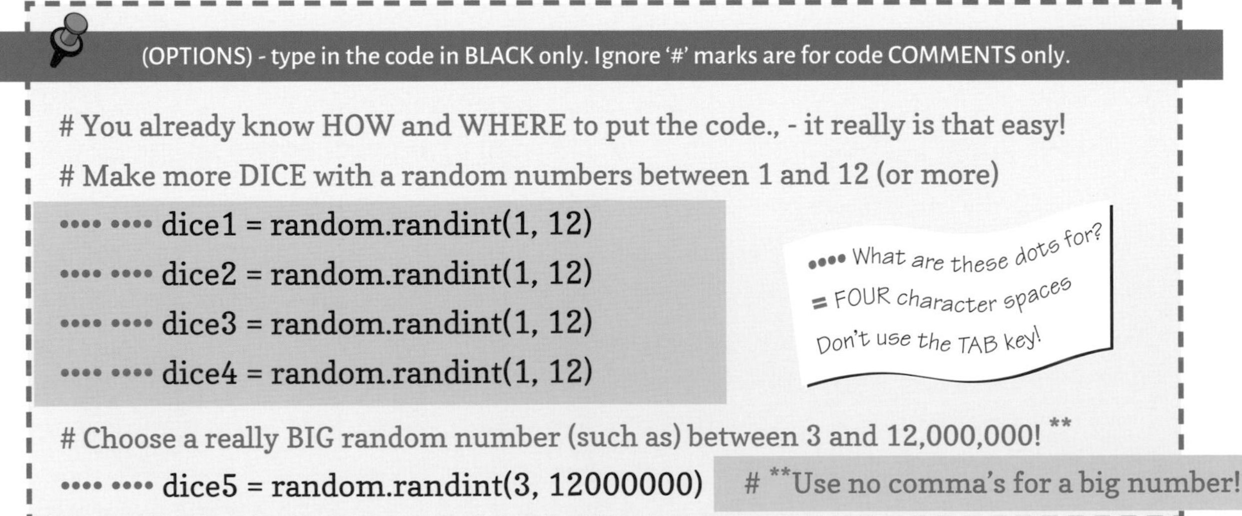

(OPTIONS) - type in the code in BLACK only. Ignore '#' marks are for code COMMENTS only.

```
# You already know HOW and WHERE to put the code., - it really is that easy!
# Make more DICE with a random numbers between 1 and 12 (or more)
•••• •••• dice1 = random.randint(1, 12)
•••• •••• dice2 = random.randint(1, 12)
•••• •••• dice3 = random.randint(1, 12)
•••• •••• dice4 = random.randint(1, 12)
# Choose a really BIG random number (such as) between 3 and 12,000,000! **
•••• •••• dice5 = random.randint(3, 12000000)    # **Use no comma's for a big number!
```

•••• What are these dots for?
= FOUR character spaces
Don't use the TAB key!

See project RESOURCES for more information on this project with examples from this book!

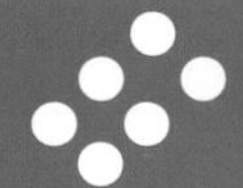

Next: Sprout eating Chomp!

10

Hate EATING your Sprouts?

Get CHOMP to EAT your sprouts!

Well in this game, you can or eat Jelly instead, - and you can avoid all the Sprouts! The Jelly is not very nice either but you can choose which you prefer to eat in school or at home.

In my game you can get 1,000 points for eating Sprouts and only 10 points for eating Jelly. But as you are the coder, I suspect you will swop them around.

You just have to avoid getting any 'tummy-ache' in this game. Get CHOMP! to eat all the things you don't like!

The Author (likes Sprouts, not Jelly)

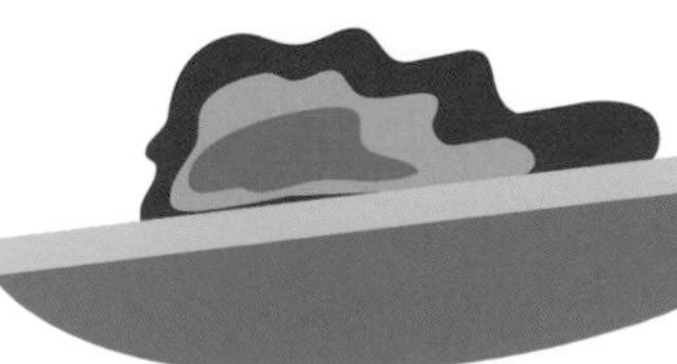

The 'Chomp' is hungry!

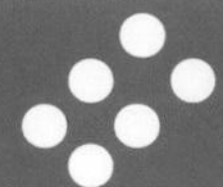

In this game we use an animated 'Pac-man' to munch his way around the screen scoring points for eating 'Jelly' and losing when he's eating rotten 'Sprouts' and Custard. This game is fun to make. Let's get coding...

DRAW CHOMP! Chomp has a mouth wide open or closed - just like a pac-man game! We will use one VARIABLE to keep a simple score of his favourite eats (a plus score) and things he should avoid (a minus score).

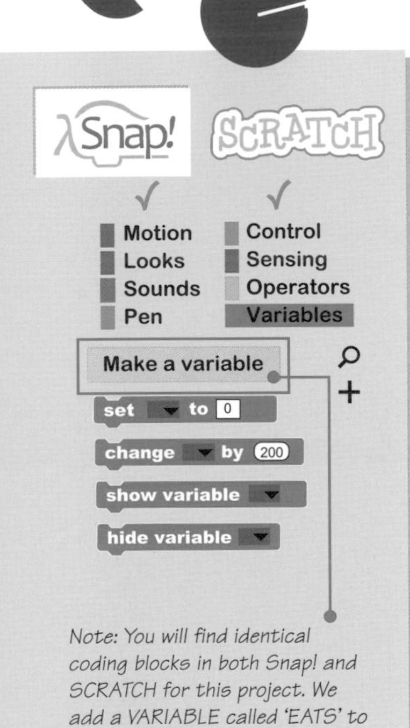

Snap!
SCRATCH
Motion
Looks
Sounds
Pen
Control
Sensing
Operators
Variables
Make a variable
set to 0
change by 200
show variable
hide variable

Note: You will find identical coding blocks in both Snap! and SCRATCH for this project. We add a VARIABLE called 'EATS' to keep score of the food eaten.

Costumes: One Sprite and TWO costumes:

Pac-a

Pac-b

'Pac-a' and 'Pac-b' will open and shut mouth in a loop (forever) when we start the game.

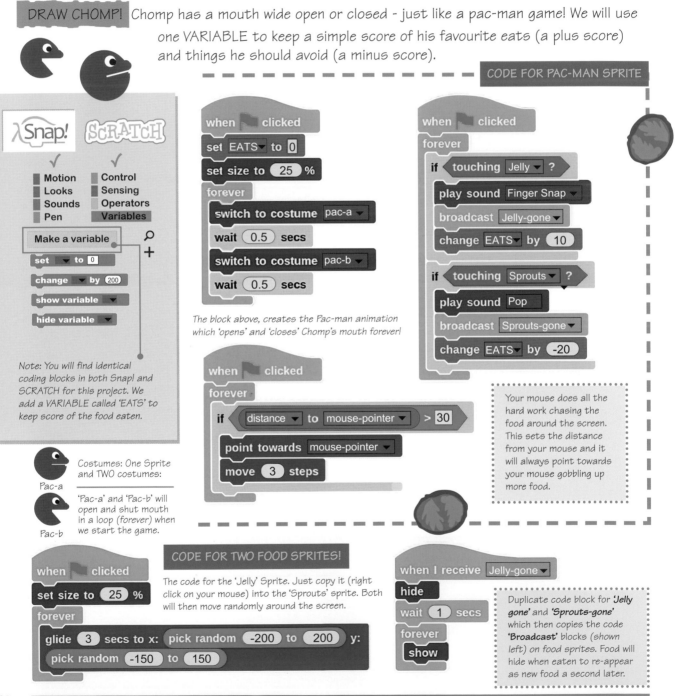

CODE FOR PAC-MAN SPRITE

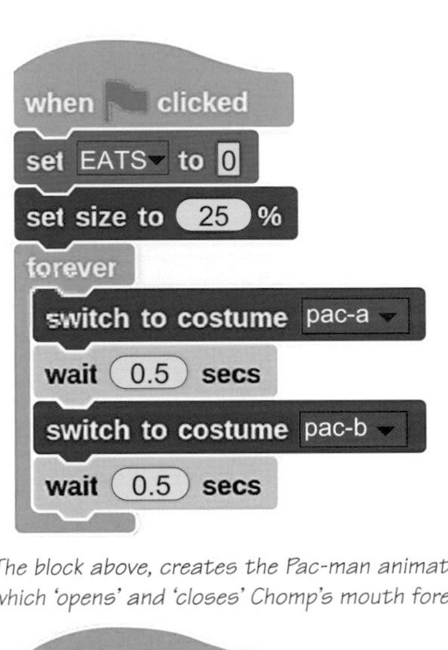

when clicked
set EATS to 0
set size to 25 %
forever
switch to costume pac-a
wait 0.5 secs
switch to costume pac-b
wait 0.5 secs

The block above, creates the Pac-man animation which 'opens' and 'closes' Chomp's mouth forever!

when clicked
forever
if touching Jelly ?
play sound Finger Snap
broadcast Jelly-gone
change EATS by 10
if touching Sprouts ?
play sound Pop
broadcast Sprouts-gone
change EATS by -20

when clicked
forever
if distance to mouse-pointer > 30
point towards mouse-pointer
move 3 steps

Your mouse does all the hard work chasing the food around the screen. This sets the distance from your mouse and it will always point towards your mouse gobbling up more food.

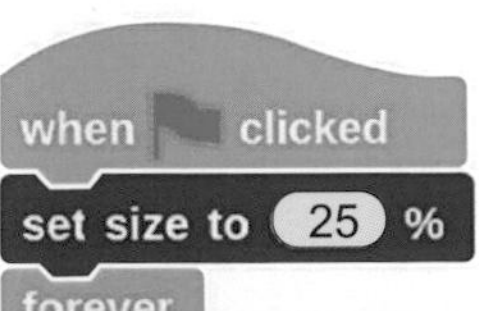

when clicked
set size to 25 %
forever

CODE FOR TWO FOOD SPRITES!

The code for the 'Jelly' Sprite. Just copy it (right click on your mouse) into the 'Sprouts' sprite. Both will then move randomly around the screen.

glide 3 secs to x: pick random -200 to 200 y:
pick random -150 to 150

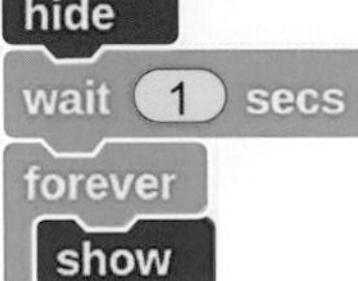

when I receive Jelly-gone
hide
wait 1 secs
forever
show

Duplicate code block for **'Jelly gone'** and **'Sprouts-gone'** which then copies the code **'Broadcast'** blocks (shown left) on food sprites. Food will hide when eaten to re-appear as new food a second later.

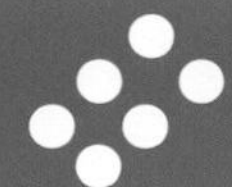

The Python Turtle is hungry!

Using our friendly Python Turtle we shall try to code a similar game that Chomp will recognise. He still has to eat his Sprouts, but only one at a time. Remember that only the code in BLACK type needs to be typed.

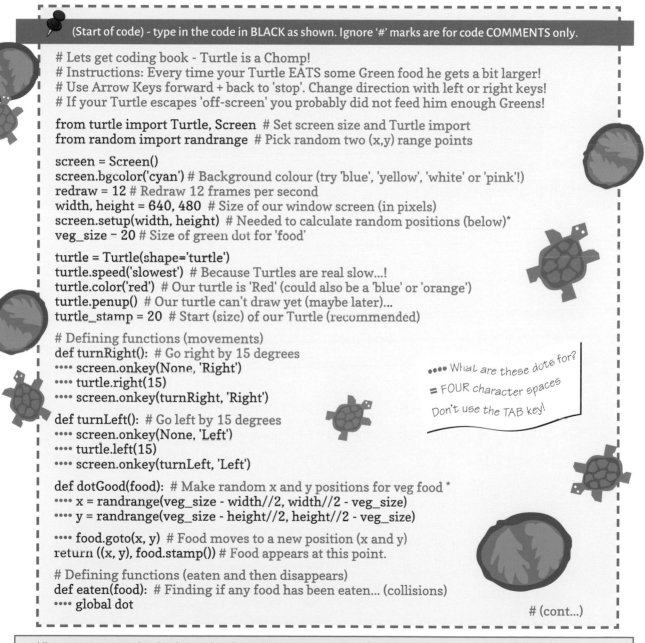

(Start of code) - type in the code in BLACK as shown. Ignore '#' marks are for code COMMENTS only.

```
# Lets get coding book - Turtle is a Chomp!
# Instructions: Every time your Turtle EATS some Green food he gets a bit larger!
# Use Arrow Keys forward + back to 'stop'. Change direction with left or right keys!
# If your Turtle escapes 'off-screen' you probably did not feed him enough Greens!

from turtle import Turtle, Screen  # Set screen size and Turtle import
from random import randrange  # Pick random two (x,y) range points

screen = Screen()
screen.bgcolor('cyan') # Background colour (try 'blue', 'yellow', 'white' or 'pink'!)
redraw = 12 # Redraw 12 frames per second
width, height = 640, 480  # Size of our window screen (in pixels)
screen.setup(width, height)  # Needed to calculate random positions (below)*
veg_size = 20 # Size of green dot for 'food'

turtle = Turtle(shape='turtle')
turtle.speed('slowest') # Because Turtles are real slow...!
turtle.color('red')  # Our turtle is 'Red' (could also be a 'blue' or 'orange')
turtle.penup()  # Our turtle can't draw yet (maybe later)...
turtle_stamp = 20  # Start (size) of our Turtle (recommended)

# Defining functions (movements)
def turnRight():  # Go right by 15 degrees
•••• screen.onkey(None, 'Right')
•••• turtle.right(15)
•••• screen.onkey(turnRight, 'Right')

def turnLeft():  # Go left by 15 degrees
•••• screen.onkey(None, 'Left')
•••• turtle.left(15)
•••• screen.onkey(turnLeft, 'Left')

def dotGood(food):  # Make random x and y positions for veg food *
•••• x = randrange(veg_size - width//2, width//2 - veg_size)
•••• y = randrange(veg_size - height//2, height//2 - veg_size)

•••• food.goto(x, y)  # Food moves to a new position (x and y)
return ((x, y), food.stamp()) # Food appears at this point.

# Defining functions (eaten and then disappears)
def eaten(food):  # Finding if any food has been eaten... (collisions)
•••• global dot
```

•••• What are these dots for?
= FOUR character spaces
Don't use the TAB key!

(cont...)

All our projects in this book are downloadable in three working formats. You can use our examples or custom the code supplied to create a new class project. See project RESOURCES for this project code and graphics.

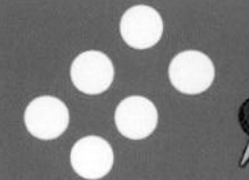

The Python Turtle is hungry!

```
# (cont...)
•••• ((x, y), stamp_id) = dot  # dot is a dot (food) and moves x and y random
•••• if abs(turtle.xcor() - x) < veg_size and  abs(turtle.ycor() - y) < veg_size:
•••• •••• food.clearstamp(stamp_id)  # Food disappears when eaten
•••• •••• dot = dotGood(food)  # (required to make new food)

•••• •••• return True

•••• return False

# Defining functions (food not moving)
def move():
•••• global score
•••• if not moving:  # When food stops moving, do this...
•••• •••• return

•••• if eaten(food):  # When our Turtle eats food he gets BIGGER by five sizes!
•••• •••• score += 1
•••• •••• turtle.shapesize((turtle_stamp + 5 * score) / turtle_stamp)

•••• turtle.forward(3) # Moves turtle forward

•••• screen.ontimer(move, 12 // redraw) ; # Update (screen) 12 times per second

# Defining move functions: Turtle keeps moving until  back arrow key pressed!
def start():
•••• global moving

•••• moving = True
•••• move()

def stop():
•••• global moving

•••• moving = False

food = Turtle(shape='circle', visible=False)
food.speed('fastest')  # Our food moves 'fastest' to re-appear in new position
food.color('green')  # Because Brussel Sprouts are green!
food.penup() # Because food can't draw!

moving = False

dot = dotGood(food)  # Used to place good food on screen

score = 0  # Score shows food Eaten (score = +1). Nothing else!

screen.onkey(turnRight, 'Right')
screen.onkey(turnLeft, 'Left')
screen.onkey(start, 'Up')
screen.onkey(stop, 'Down')

screen.listen() # Keep listening for any keyboard  arrow keys pressed

# [End of coding]
```

Optional) changes to make:
Try changing the colour of the background!
Try changing the colour of the turtle!

•••• What are these dots for?
= FOUR character spaces
Don't use the TAB key!

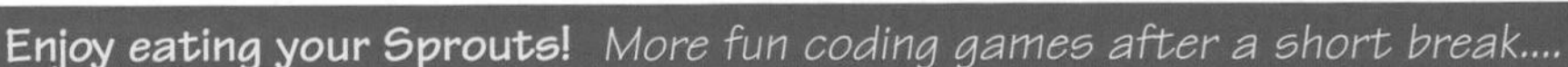

Enjoy eating your Sprouts! *More fun coding games after a short break....*

Snap! v SCRATCH compared

What's the difference? Both are block based programs based on the original concept of LEGO bricks. However NO LEGO is going to be used in any of the constructions we are going to make in this book. But we take the bright colours and take the shapes that [click] together easily, this works by copying the code (script) into blocks. Coding is mostly following a recipe.

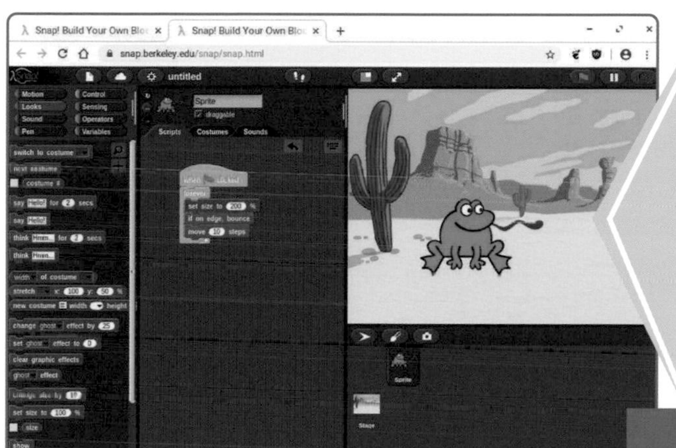

Using Snap!

Based on Scratch v 1.4 concept (and looks much the same in layout), and has major functional improvements and is a lot 'sharper' then the original Scratch. Now fills the entire screen. Scratch v 1.4 is suitable for smaller screens. Secondly Snap! was originally called BYOB (Build Your Own Blocks) a new concept of making custom code blocks. In this book, we only use the standard (easy) Snap! or Scratch blocks found.

https://snap.berkeley.edu

Using Scratch 3

Scratch 3 (right) now has a new ability to 'Build You-Own-Blocks', much like Snap! but this book's author has avoided all 'custom blocks' for simplicity of the book. There are some differences between the two programs which you can learn by using them both. Our code will work on both with very minor changes and you can also find which program works for you.

https://scratch.mit.edu

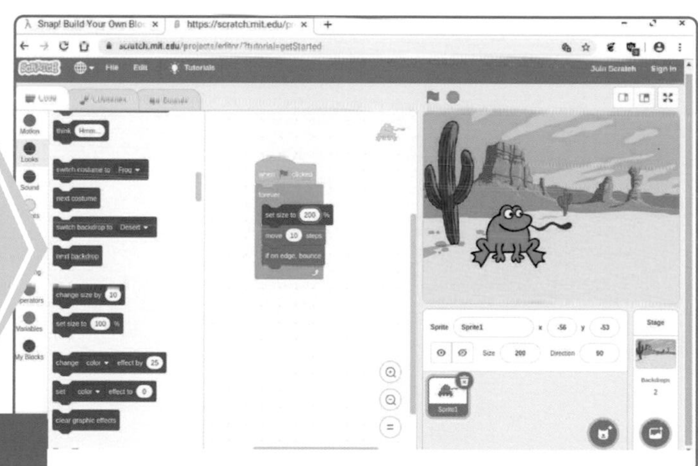

Hopefully in this book you can see how they work in both - the book code is ***hot swappable*** in that you can use them in both - but you cannot **'save'** (*say using SNAP!*) and then open it in Scratch. ***You should try both and save to its own file format***. This is usually done 'online'. Cloud computing is a way of saving your work to another computer (a Server) on the internet. All you really need is an internet connection and good browser. Save your work with a 'free' account with either **Snap!** or **Scratch 3** (*online*) then save your programs. When you **'log-in'** with your chosen name (*don't use your real name*), create a password based on something you like *i.e.* ***Name:*** *Peanuts-the-dog*, ***Password:*** *bonkers (chose an unforgettable password and coding name).*

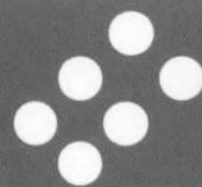

Snap! v SCRATCH compared

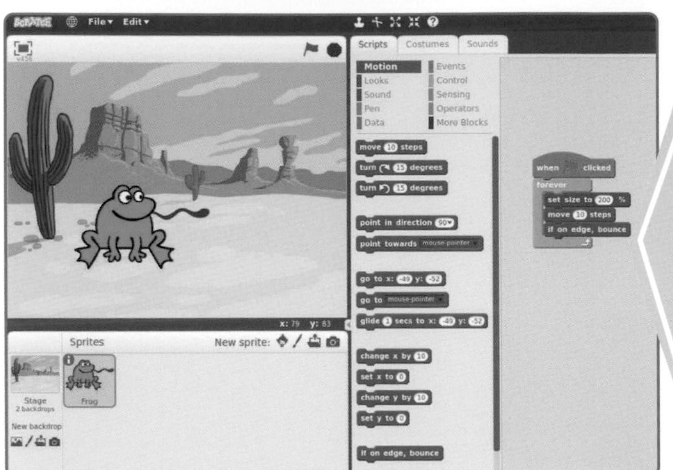

Using Scratch 2

This is Scratch 2 (left) and is installed by default on all Raspberry pi mini computers along with Scratch 1.4 (picture below). This version does not need any internet connection to work. All of the images are 'built-in' (we call them SPRITES) and float over a background layer called the STAGE. You can edit the images by clicking the paintbrush. You can edit images and change backgrounds and even add sounds (maybe we will do that later in the book on a project).

Using Scratch 1.4

This is original Scratch v 1.4 (which is installed on the raspberry pi, along with newer Scratch 2, so you can use both and compare. You do not need any internet connection to start and it is ideal for starting programming. Unfortunately anything you create in Scratch 1.4 (files) are not copied across to Scratch 2, they are not compatible formats. Both work well enough, but you then cannot swop files between the two.

Your choice is to what kind of computer you have. The Author often uses **Scratch 1.4** as it works well on very old computers and is easy to try out at first. It also works well on the smaller raspberry pi computers in the same way. That is why I test the code on all three **Scratch** versions, *(on different computers you may have at home).* My favourite is **Snap!** but most children, at school, may prefer **Scratch 2**, but now we have **Scratch 3** for the block code in this book. All projects should work in exactly the same on any type of computer you may have!

*The Python projects in this book are tested using **Python 3** and not Python 2. **Python 3 is the standard to use in this book.** I have chosen **THONNY** a Python editor (IDE) as it's easier to use (for children) than many others to edit Python text and when adding basic Python modules found later in this book. The author recommends **THONNY** as it is easier to run Python code -- not just on a raspberry pi, but is also available for most modern computers.* **You may need THONNY installed and Python 3 to run all twenty projects found in this book!**

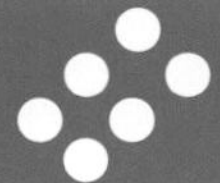

Next: Secret Morse-Code!

11

S.O.S
Why learn MORSE-CODE?

Because you can then become a TOP SECRET AGENT! and send secret messages that only somebody at the other end can understand!

There are two ways to send a message, one is writing it out and trying to remember all the codes and then telling someone over the telephone a 'dot-dot-dash-dash' message or get a computer to type it a lot faster.

Before telephones were invented, there was only a Morse-code 'Telegraph'. Even after the Telephone, Morse-code was used for Radio transmissions to identify individual Ships at Sea (and SOS) and as Navigation beacons at all harbour entrances. Aeroplanes can also find the correct Airport runway using specially morse-coded runway beacons.

The Author (likes '—-— —-- —-- -- —- --')
('coding')

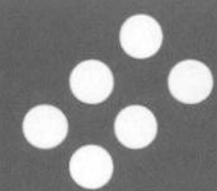

Secret Morse-Code...sshhh!

We are using Scratch (any version) today and enabling two LISTS that we can use to write Morse-code. You can transmit secret 'dots and dashes' messages by radio or even a flashlight.

Let's get coding...

IMPORT AGENT. *You are going 'import' a TOP secret agent to convert your secret message to dots-and-dashes. We need VARIABLES and a LIST to do that. Snap! and Scratch both have LISTS, but we found it a bit easier to code a LIST in Scratch. So use Scratch for this.*

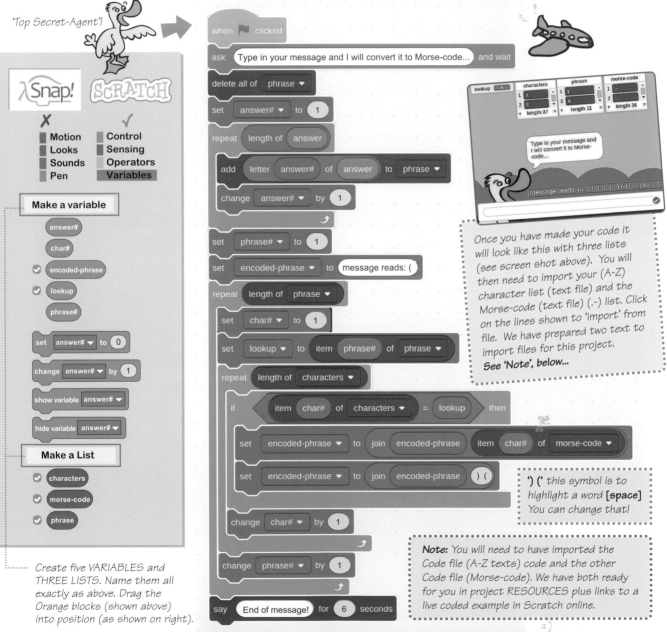

'Top Secret-Agent'!

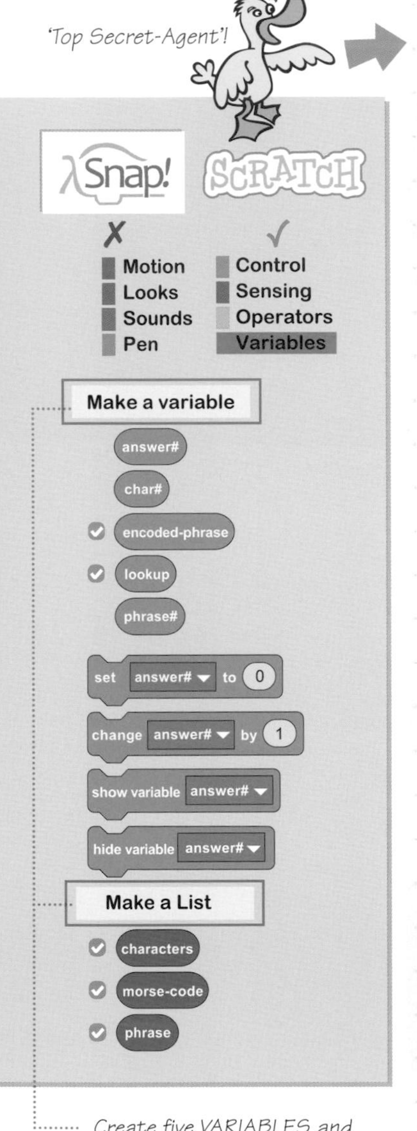

Create five VARIABLES and THREE LISTS. Name them all exactly as above. Drag the Orange blocks (shown above) into position (as shown on right).

```
when [flag] clicked
ask [Type in your message and I will convert it to Morse-code...] and wait
delete all of [phrase]
set [answer#] to (1)
repeat (length of (answer))
    add (letter (answer#) of (answer)) to [phrase]
    change [answer#] by (1)
set [phrase#] to (1)
set [encoded-phrase] to [message reads: (]
repeat (length of [phrase])
    set [char#] to (1)
    set [lookup] to (item (phrase#) of [phrase])
    repeat (length of [characters])
        if <(item (char#) of [characters]) = (lookup)> then
            set [encoded-phrase] to (join (encoded-phrase) (item (char#) of [morse-code]))
            set [encoded-phrase] to (join (encoded-phrase) [) (])
        change [char#] by (1)
    change [phrase#] by (1)
say [End of message!] for (6) seconds
```

Once you have made your code it will look like this with three lists (see screen shot above). You will then need to import your (A-Z) character list (text file) and the Morse-code (text file) (.-) list. Click on the lines shown to 'import' from file. We have prepared two text to import files for this project. **See 'Note', below...**

') (' this symbol is to highlight a word **[space]** *You can change that!*

Note: *You will need to have imported the Code file (A-Z texts) code and the other Code file (Morse-code). We have both ready for you in project RESOURCES plus links to a live coded example in Scratch online.*

Python Code for Secret Agents!

There are a lot less lines of coding with Python on this project. Compare the speed and functionality, now you are the TOP coding 'Secret-Agent' - both speed and coding functionality is your TOP priority!

S.O.S

Let's get coding...

(Start of code) - type in the code in BLACK as shown. Ignore '#' marks are for code COMMENTS only.

(L) .-.. (E) . (T) - (S) ... (G) --. (E) . (T) - (C) -.-. (O) --- (D) -.. (I) .. (N) -. (G) --.

```
# International Morse Coder - Lets get coding (2020)
import time  # Time delay used in final output...
print" ++Amazing secret Morse coder+ +" # Title
print(" ") # Make a new line space (" ")

MORSE = { # Type a letter and get a coded symbol
•••• 'A': '.-',          'B': '-...',        'C': '-.-.',
•••• 'D': '-..',         'E': '.',           'F': '..-.',
•••• 'G': '--.',         'H': '....',        'I': '..',
•••• 'J': '.---',        'K': '-.-',         'L': '.-..',
•••• 'M': '--',          'N': '-.',          'O': '---',
•••• 'P': '.--.',        'Q': '--.-',        'R': '.-.',
•••• 'S': '...',         'T': '-',           'U': '..-',
•••• 'V': '...-',        'W': '.--',         'X': '-..-',
•••• 'Y': '-.--',        'Z': '--..' ,       " ": " "
•••• }

def main(): # Convert to code from your input text...
•••• message = input("ENTER YOUR SECRET MESSAGE: ")')
•••• for char in message:
•••• •••• print(MORSE[char.upper()], end=" ")

# Simple delay timer for our Morse-code message...
•••• •••• time.sleep(0.5)

if __name__ == "__main__": # Defines a special class to use
•••• main()

print" " # Makes a visual line space (" ")
print"Secret Message has been sent"

# Quit program (system quit)
def main():
•••• eval(input("Press [Enter] and exit"))

# [End of coding]
```

MORSE = *is a simple function that swops the letters (that you key in) for matching* **morse-code** *symbols. This can display CAPITALS letters only!*

print MORSE[char.upper()] *allocates each letter you type in to automatically converted to CAPITAL letters. See project RESOURCES to download all resources including this Python code!*

•••• What are these dots for?
= FOUR character spaces
Don't use the TAB key!

'dot-dot-dot, dash-dash-dash, dot-dot-dot'

Repeated by a Ship's Telegraph in distress!

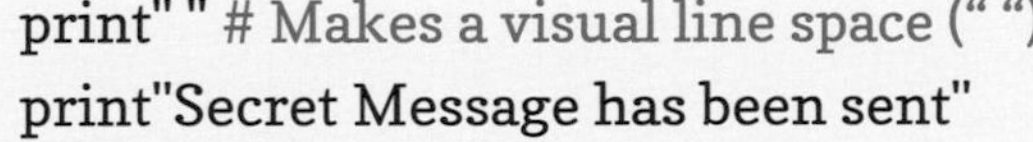

Note: *Check your 'syntax'. i.e a missing dot or colon and the code won't work. Avoid the 'tab' key as Python indents are always four spaces (press* **[spacebar]**) *four times. To assist there is a lot of RESOURCES to help young and old coders like myself, and you will find everything you need to know in the resource weblinks at the back of this book. See project RESOURCES at back of book for helpful code links.*

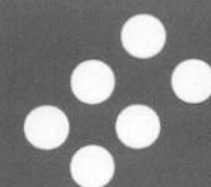

Morse coder SOS'ssss!

One of the safest and fastest ships ever built is now at the bottom of the ocean. The TITANIC was un-sinkable - it was said at the time. When it was sinking, Morse-code was the ONLY radio communication. S.O.S. is still when all else fails, it's a vital alert. You can relay all sorts of messages in Morse-code. Ideal for secret communications. You can do a lot with Morse-code.

Try out your morse-coding skills, you never know when you may need them!

Why is this code in SCRATCH and not SNAP?

Rather than leave this code out altogether, and I did try, I could not get the same functions working easily in Snap! *(as I could Scratch)*. In this code we need to create 'lookup' tables we call **LISTS**. Both Scratch and Snap! have lists, but only Scratch has a dedicated LIST entry which is the easier of the two. In Snap! you need to create a list by inserting it into a variable, as shown below. Even knowing how its done, it's not always easy to do, so this is a Scratch only project for children, with an option to try and get it working in Snap!

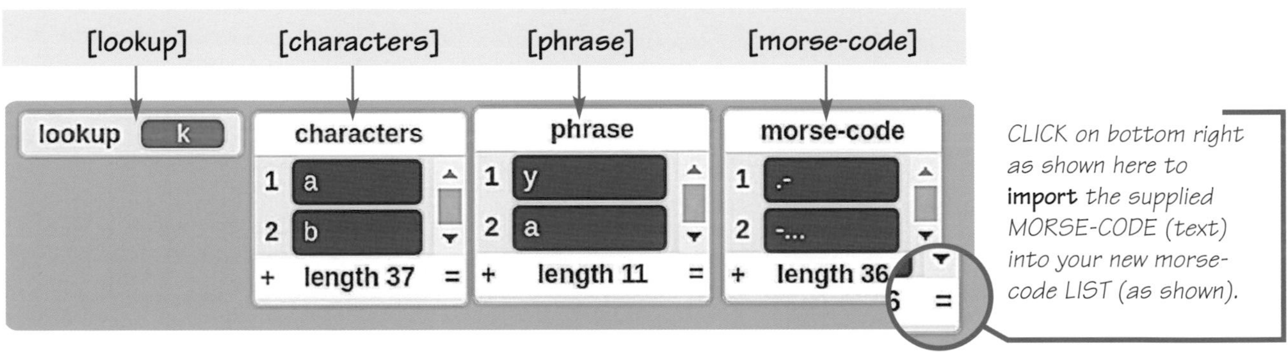

CLICK on bottom right as shown here to ***import*** *the supplied MORSE-CODE (text) into your new morse-code LIST (as shown).*

The **LISTS** *for this project can be imported into Scratch only after you have created all the* **VARIABLES** *in the code. Those you should see on Screen above, (you can tick 'on' and 'off' each variable to display on the screen as shown above).*

See above Scratch Lists: **[lookup], [characters], [phrase], [morse-code].**

Morse Code in Python could not get any easier.

All the Python Morse-code is held in a 'lookup' table that we use for each and every keyboard entry. ***There is not a lot to change.*** I would consider changing each keyboard pressed into a dot-dash sound that can be made using Blocks and Python. There will be something like that in the Project resources page at the end of this book. The Python script is there too.

See project RESOURCES for code and information on this and all twenty projects in this book.

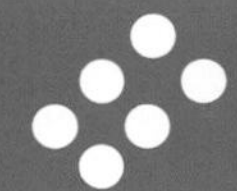

Next: The Bouncing Turtles!

12

Make TURTLES bounce...

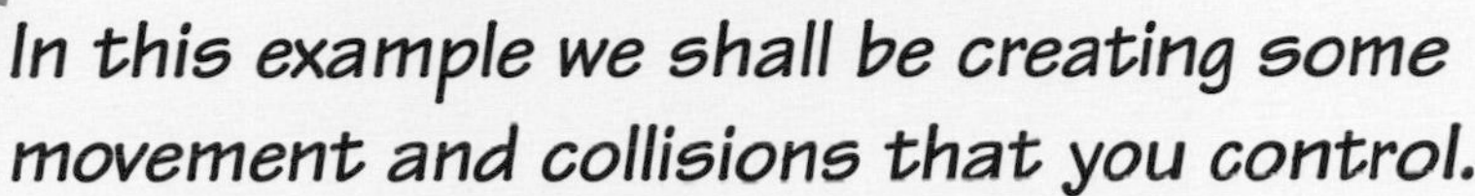

In this example we shall be creating some movement and collisions that you control.

You may think it's all about Tortoises bouncing about the screen but it is far more than that. You will be learning and observing 'partial collisions' (whilst ignoring all the high-end science stuff about momentum, bounce-elasticity and the effects of gravity), you can see how things collide (and what happens if they don't) in this simple demonstration of fun bouncing Turtles.

I had fun making this one. You can have as many Turtles on screen as you like, and then speed them up and slow them down!

The Author (avoids such collisions)

The Bouncing Turtles

We will be using a simple drawing of a turtle to bounce around the screen, but this time for a change we will import it as a graphic. This Turtle must be exactly like this Turtle (as we have shown here). Let's get coding...

IMPORT a Turtle. Not any old Turtle, it has to be this one. Learn how to import the exact turtle for this project*.

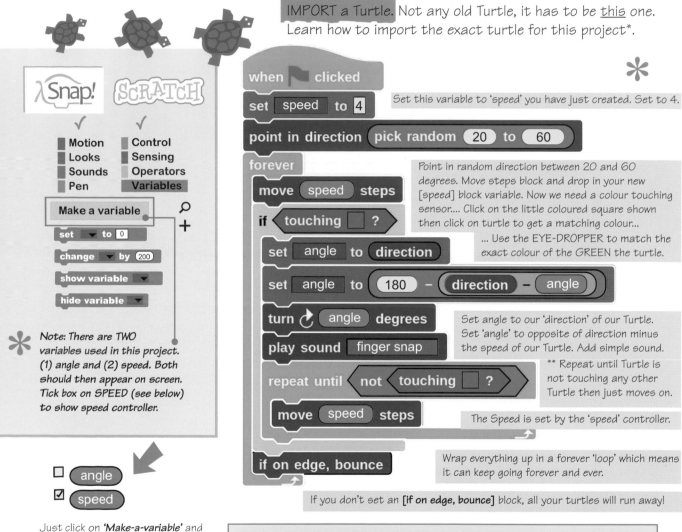

Snap! ✓ SCRATCH ✓

- Motion
- Looks
- Sounds
- Pen
- Control
- Sensing
- Operators
- Variables

Make a variable

set [ ] to 0
change [ ] by 200
show variable [ ]
hide variable [ ]

Note: There are TWO variables used in this project. (1) angle and (2) speed. Both should then appear on screen. Tick box on SPEED (see below) to show speed controller.

☐ angle
☑ speed

Just click on **'Make-a-variable'** and name it (1) angle and (2) speed. These are your two speed and angle controllers. They will ONLY work if you 'double-click' them (both) on the display screen see 'scoreboards' to show a small sliding control. You may have to click them more than once to see the handles.

```
when [flag] clicked
set [speed] to 4
point in direction (pick random 20 to 60)
forever
    move (speed) steps
    if <touching [ ] ?>
        set [angle] to (direction)
        set [angle] to (180 - ((direction) - (angle)))
        turn ↻ (angle) degrees
        play sound [finger snap]
        repeat until <not <touching [ ] ?>>
            move (speed) steps
    if on edge, bounce
```

Set this variable to 'speed' you have just created. Set to 4.

Point in random direction between 20 and 60 degrees. Move steps block and drop in your new [speed] block variable. Now we need a colour touching sensor.... Click on the little coloured square shown then click on turtle to get a matching colour...

... Use the EYE-DROPPER to match the exact colour of the GREEN the turtle.

Set angle to our 'direction' of our Turtle. Set 'angle' to opposite of direction minus the speed of our Turtle. Add simple sound.

** Repeat until Turtle is not touching any other Turtle then just moves on.

The Speed is set by the 'speed' controller.

Wrap everything up in a forever 'loop' which means it can keep going forever and ever.

If you don't set an **[if on edge, bounce]** block, all your turtles will run away!

You can play this straight away. You will soon find out that you don't have another Turtle to collide with. That is easily solved! When you have one working turtle you can simply duplicate the entire Sprite *(see sprites costumes block)* and use your mouse to 'right-click' on the sprite. This will copy the Turtle and code. You can repeat this until your screen is full of Turtles. However you also need to make some important adjustments to each Turtle. To do this click on 'costumes' and change the 'size' and 'angle' of each image. That will make more realistic collisions. To avoid image overlap collisions, reset angle or your speed and they will soon clear themselves.

* To import this turtle you will need to use your browser to download our turtle graphic. **See project RESOURCES pages.**

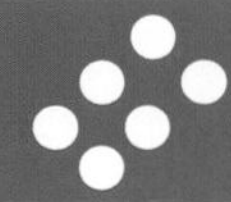

Python Turtle bounce!

Turtle graphic is built right into Python(all versions), we just call it up when needed. Here you can make lots of adjustments and see the Turtles bouncing around the screen in six colours.

Let's get coding...

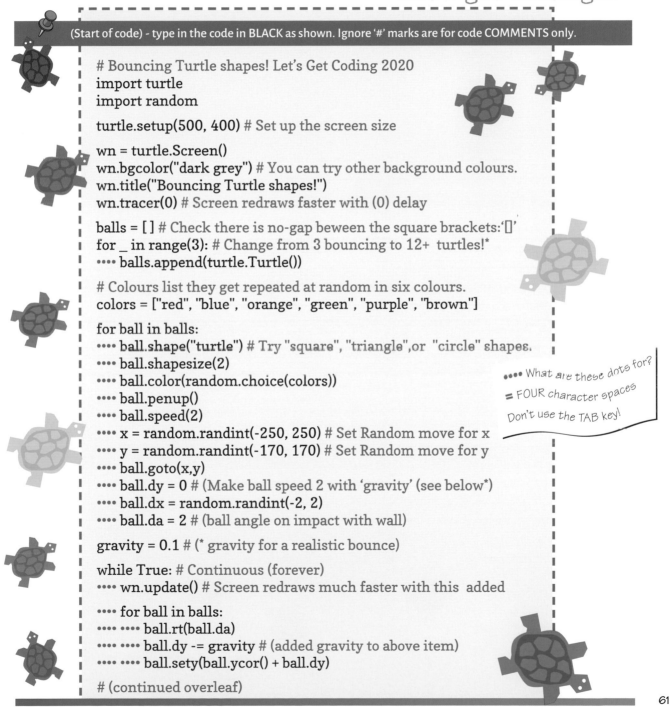

(Start of code) - type in the code in BLACK as shown. Ignore '#' marks are for code COMMENTS only.

```
# Bouncing Turtle shapes! Let's Get Coding 2020
import turtle
import random

turtle.setup(500, 400) # Set up the screen size

wn = turtle.Screen()
wn.bgcolor("dark grey") # You can try other background colours.
wn.title("Bouncing Turtle shapes!")
wn.tracer(0) # Screen redraws faster with (0) delay

balls = [ ] # Check there is no-gap beween the square brackets:'[]'
for _ in range(3): # Change from 3 bouncing to 12+ turtles!*
•••• balls.append(turtle.Turtle())

# Colours list they get repeated at random in six colours.
colors = ["red", "blue", "orange", "green", "purple", "brown"]

for ball in balls:
•••• ball.shape("turtle") # Try "square", "triangle",or "circle" shapes.
•••• ball.shapesize(2)
•••• ball.color(random.choice(colors))
•••• ball.penup()
•••• ball.speed(2)
•••• x = random.randint(-250, 250) # Set Random move for x
•••• y = random.randint(-170, 170) # Set Random move for y
•••• ball.goto(x,y)
•••• ball.dy = 0 # (Make ball speed 2 with 'gravity' (see below*)
•••• ball.dx = random.randint(-2, 2)
•••• ball.da = 2 # (ball angle on impact with wall)

gravity = 0.1 # (* gravity for a realistic bounce)

while True: # Continuous (forever)
•••• wn.update() # Screen redraws much faster with this  added

•••• for ball in balls:
•••• •••• ball.rt(ball.da)
•••• •••• ball.dy -= gravity # (added gravity to above item)
•••• •••• ball.sety(ball.ycor() + ball.dy)

# (continued overleaf)
```

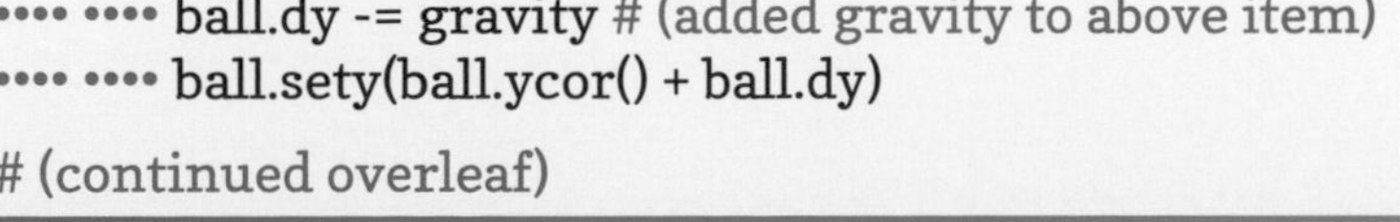

•••• What are these dots for?
= FOUR character spaces
Don't use the TAB key!

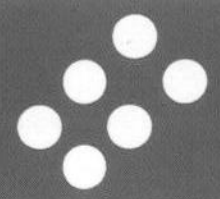

Options to try:

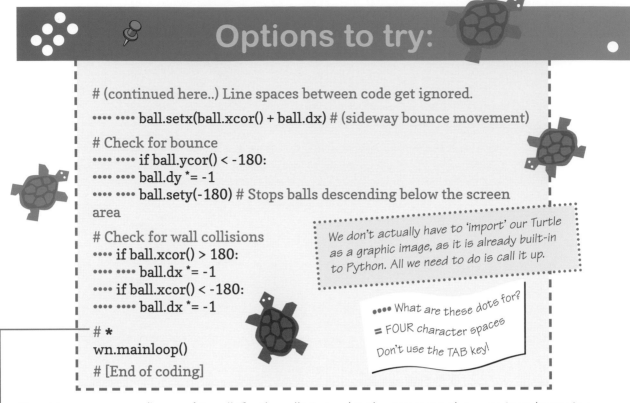

```
# (continued here..) Line spaces between code get ignored.
•••• •••• ball.setx(ball.xcor() + ball.dx) # (sideway bounce movement)

# Check for bounce
•••• •••• if ball.ycor() < -180:
•••• •••• ball.dy *= -1
•••• •••• ball.sety(-180) # Stops balls descending below the screen
area

# Check for wall collisions
•••• if ball.xcor() > 180:
•••• •••• ball.dx *= -1
•••• if ball.xcor() < -180:
•••• •••• ball.dx *= -1

# *
wn.mainloop()
# [End of coding]
```

We don't actually have to 'import' our Turtle as a graphic image, as it is already built-in to Python. All we need to do is call it up.

•••• What are these dots for?
= FOUR character spaces
Don't use the TAB key!

To add some proper 'bounce' to all Turtle collisions. At the moment they are just bouncing around a lot of the edges. When you add collisions it will be more frantic and you may have to reduce the number of turtles on screen (suggest no more than twelve).

```
# insert this code for collisions: (marked in code with a red * asterisk)
if turtle.ycor() >= 200 or turtle.ycor() <=-200 or  turtle.xcor() >= 200 or turtle.xcor <= -200
```

As usual you have more options in Python with a few lines of well placed code. You can easily change the 'gravity' (**gravity = 0.1**) (i.e. if you're on another planet for example, the gravity will change a little or a lot). Change it to zero to see what happens!

Scratch or Snap! (import) a Turtle drawing:

One easy option is to add a line - use **[pen-down]** for one (or each) of your Turtles. You probably know how to do this already *(see Etch-a-Sketch page)*. Turtles can create some random line drawing, or a 'bit-of- a-mess' if you leave the Turtles long enough. Place a **[clear]** *(green block)*, to clean-up afterwards place under the **[Green flag]** start block. ***Turtles can draw too!***

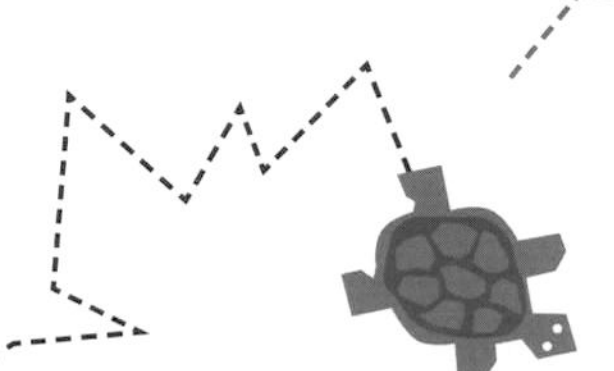

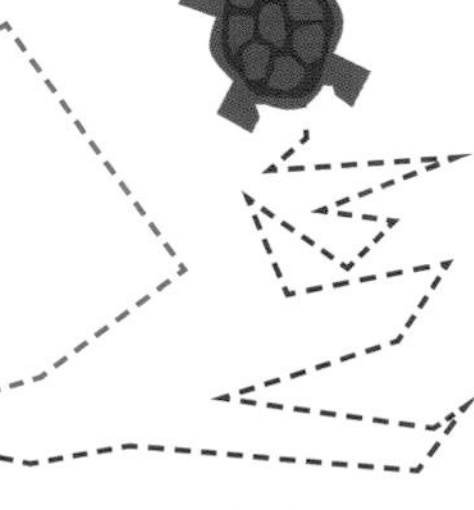

** See project RESOURCES for code and information on this and all twenty projects in this book.*

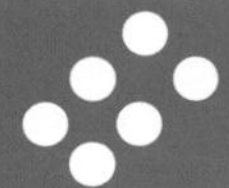

Next: Nice Knitting patterns!

13

Knitting a JUMPER badly!

This project I have called Knitting patterns has nothing to do what-so-ever with actual 'Knitting' but a lot to do with Sewing. Not that I am good at either but I like to look at how the patterns work. Sewing is usually made up of a series of straight lines.

So I was wondering if I could make a project that just used 'straight-lines' and then make that into a knitting pattern...

Sounds easy but making this as good as your School jumper, or embroidered on your school hat, was too much of a challenge for me. Nothing seemed to work, until I played around with this code, and thought, 'yup!' that's about right. I do hope you like it.

The Author (likes making Polygons)

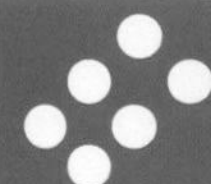

Knitting in Polygons

We shall be making a pattern from a Triangle. A triangle can make a Hexagon. Hexagons can make other Polygons, and ours looka as if they are all made of straight lines, but really - it's a Triangle!

Let's get coding...

DRAW a Tent, I mean a Triangle that looks like a tent. Do not import anything. I want you to draw like I have done it here (see picture right).

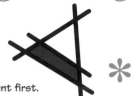

Draw this Tent first.

Then make two **variables** called **'size'** and **'spin'**. Take care to EDIT your tent drawing by (*right click on mouse*) and follow the instructions** at bottom of this page.

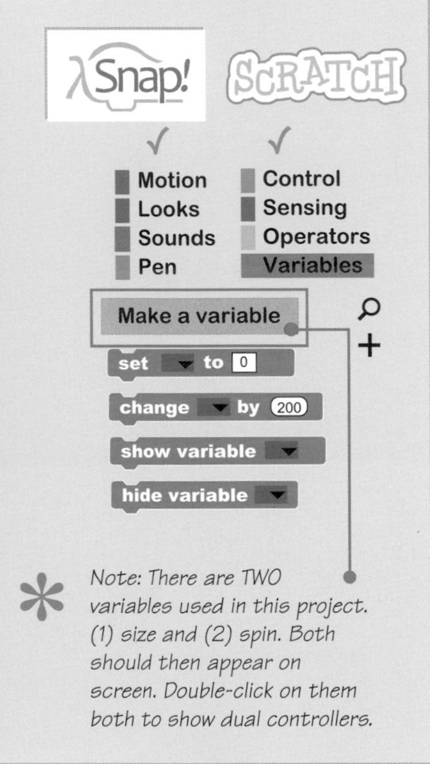

Note: There are TWO variables used in this project. (1) size and (2) spin. Both should then appear on screen. Double-click on them both to show dual controllers.

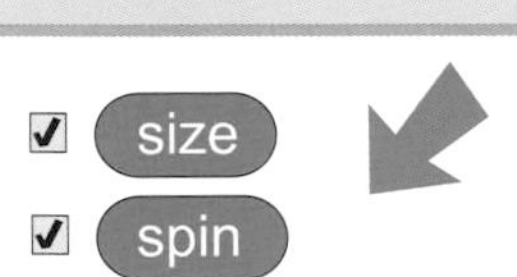

Just click on ***'Make-a-variable'*** and name it (1) size and (2) spin. There are two screen controllers. You will need to 'double-click' them to show a small sliding control below as seen below. Snap! and Scratch are both similar.

Spin is set at (1) and the Size is set (150). Change by dragging the sliders left or right.

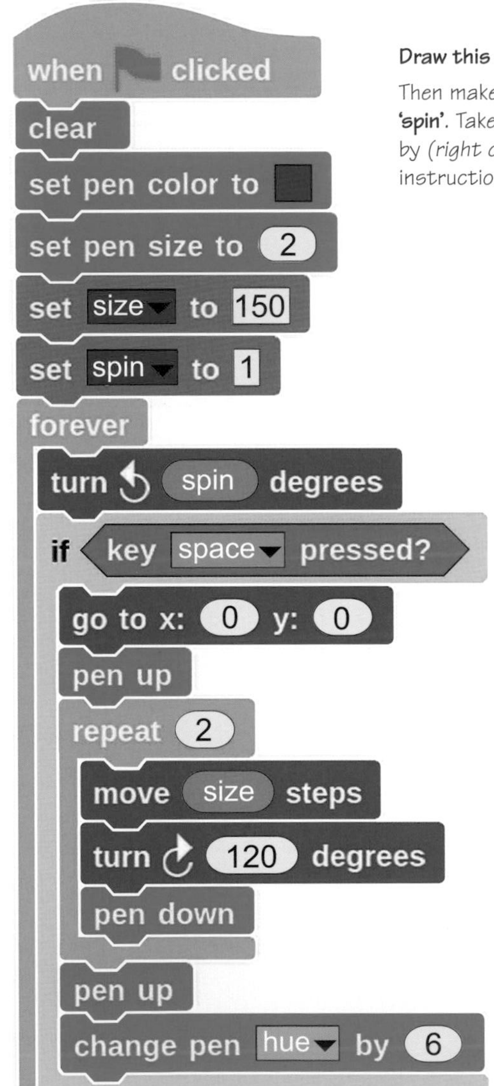

From start Green Flag) block.
Clear (all screen patterns)

Set pen colour to red

Set pen size from 50 to 200. (See size control sliders)*.

Set spin to 1 control. (See size control sliders)*.

Forever loop (keeps on going).

Blue **turn degrees** block with Orange control variable (drag and drop inside the blue block).

IF block operates only when the SPACE bar (big key on your keyboard) is clicked.

Pen up (no drawing)

That starts a series of operations: **go to** the centre of screen (xO, yO) then ***repeat*** twice the MOVE steps which are controlled by the **spin** variable. See controllers at bottom left. **Pen down** (start drawing). pattern.

Finally **Pen up** and change pen hue (hue is a colour) that will repeat all of which is inside the forever loop.

Get Knitting that pattern!

*** Note: A diagram showing on how to re-set the centre of our tent drawing is shown on the Options to try page 66.*

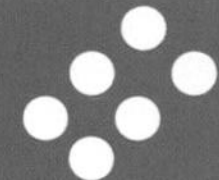

Knitting in Python

This bit of Python code was the inspiration for making a block code knitting pattern. Something so simple hides a great deal of Maths complexity. Making this in Snap! or SCRATCH is possible but it is way above the level of this Let's Get Coding book. This code may look simple, but it is very powerful and wonderfully decorative code. A bit like my Knitting patterns!

(Start of code) - type in the code in BLACK as shown. Ignore '#' marks are for code COMMENTS only.

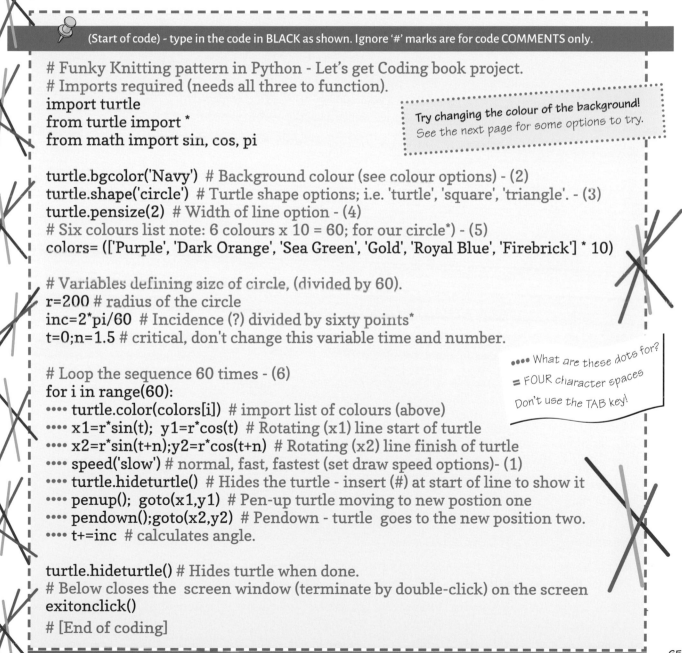

```
# Funky Knitting pattern in Python - Let's get Coding book project.
# Imports required (needs all three to function).
import turtle
from turtle import *
from math import sin, cos, pi

turtle.bgcolor('Navy') # Background colour (see colour options) - (2)
turtle.shape('circle') # Turtle shape options; i.e. 'turtle', 'square', 'triangle'. - (3)
turtle.pensize(2) # Width of line option - (4)
# Six colours list note: 6 colours x 10 = 60; for our circle*) - (5)
colors= (['Purple', 'Dark Orange', 'Sea Green', 'Gold', 'Royal Blue', 'Firebrick'] * 10)

# Variables defining size of circle, (divided by 60).
r=200 # radius of the circle
inc=2*pi/60 # Incidence (?) divided by sixty points*
t=0;n=1.5 # critical, don't change this variable time and number.

# Loop the sequence 60 times - (6)
for i in range(60):
•••• turtle.color(colors[i]) # import list of colours (above)
•••• x1=r*sin(t); y1=r*cos(t) # Rotating (x1) line start of turtle
•••• x2=r*sin(t+n);y2=r*cos(t+n) # Rotating (x2) line finish of turtle
•••• speed('slow') # normal, fast, fastest (set draw speed options)- (1)
•••• turtle.hideturtle() # Hides the turtle - insert (#) at start of line to show it
•••• penup(); goto(x1,y1) # Pen-up turtle moving to new postion one
•••• pendown();goto(x2,y2) # Pendown - turtle goes to the new position two.
•••• t+=inc # calculates angle.

turtle.hideturtle() # Hides turtle when done.
# Below closes the screen window (terminate by double-click) on the screen
exitonclick()
# [End of coding]
```

Try changing the colour of the background!
See the next page for some options to try.

•••• What are these dots for?
= FOUR character spaces
Don't use the TAB key!

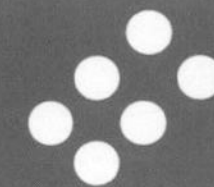

Options to try:

A triangle has three straight lines and we are drawing with just one part of that triangle in our code. Effectively stamping a line every time we press the SPACE bar (key). To get this to work and align itself to your drawing, (which is our tent drawing), we need to change the costume centre...

If you don't align your tent then it won't work as it should. Make sure you have aligned it to the top of the tent as shown below. You can edit your drawing at any time to do this. Better earlier than later as it's part of learning code project, whilst other shapes may not work as well.

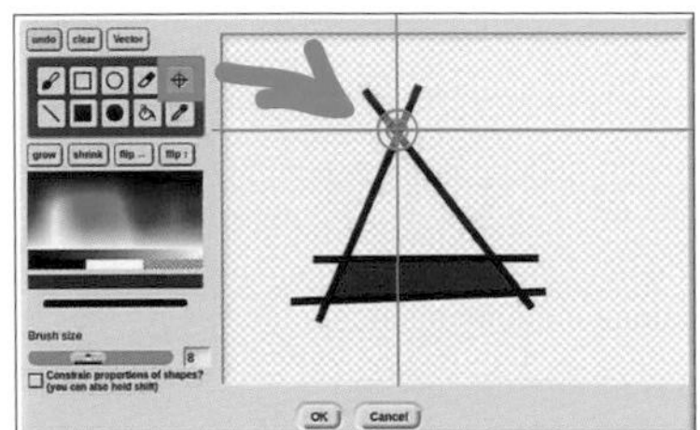

Snap! (make centre point)

Click on 'EDIT' Click on costume sprite and EDIT by using second button on your mouse to 'EDIT". Re-set the drawing centre as shown above. Move the cross-hairs to where I have indicated. If you make a mistake you can undo it. Just press where you see the cross-hair symbols.

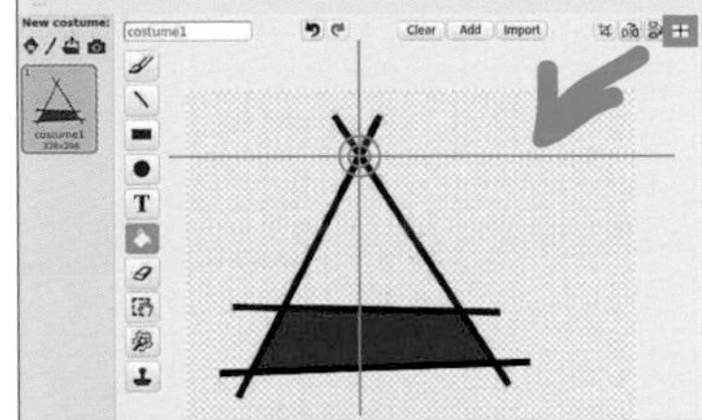

Scratch (make centre point)

For Scratch 3 - see book page 14 *(finding the centre point was changed in Scratch 3)*. For Scratch 1.4 users, use the button called ***'Set costume center'***. For Scratch 2 *(see image left)*. Drag and drop the 'cross-hairs' into the new position of your drawing.

Python: Hack your own code!

(Start of code) - type in the code in BLACK as shown. Ignore '#' marks are for code COMMENTS only.

```
# (1) Change the spin speed from 'slow', to 'normal', 'fast' or 'fastest'!
speed('slow')

# (2) Change the background colour. Not all colours are supported but there is a huge list to
# choose from... see: https://ecsdtech.com/8-pages/121-python-turtle-colors
turtle.bgcolor('Navy') # Background colour (see colour options below)

# (3) Don't like my turtle? Change it! try another...
turtle.shape('circle') # Turtle shape options; i.e. 'turtle', 'square', 'triangle'

# (4) Pensize can be from zero (0) to (6 )you can change size as an option.
 turtle.pensize(2) # Width of line option

# (5) Change the colour sequence list. There are six colours but you don't have to have six in list.
colors= (['Purple', 'Dark Orange', 'Sea Green', 'Gold', 'Royal Blue', 'Firebrick'] * 10)

# (6) Change the loop function: I have it set at sixty (for my pattern). Try less (or more) loops.
for i in range(60):
```

Options are Numbered 1 to 6.
See comments in Blue on previous coding Page 65
Place your code hack according to my numbers 1 to 6... Go try!

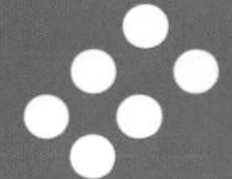

Next: The Famous Five (game)

Guess the:

This project is a book guessing game. You have to name five characters from a famous book. It's my choice of book, so it should be your choice of book if you wish. So now you have read a lot of children's books, I suspect, what was the best one?

Was it Harry Potter or Treasure Island? Go to the school library, take out a book that others have already read, and then make your book guessing game. Quiz your friends on the same book you have read to set the questions.

Hopefully, they will have forgotten all the characters from the book. This is one way to make a Quiz from any book you have all read.

The Author (likes Enid Blyton books)

We shall be making a guessing game of your favourite book. We have then chosen five characters from The Famous Five (a book by Enid Blyton). Create two lists; one to ask the 'questions' and the other holds the 'answers'.

This is a SCRATCH project based on the LIST function which is easier to show and use for younger readers*.

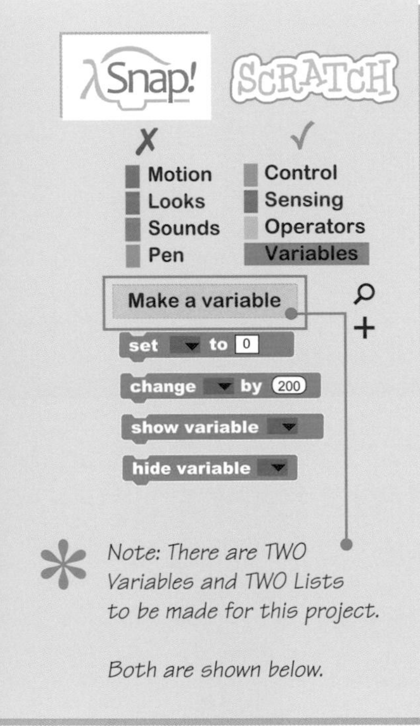

Note: There are TWO Variables and TWO Lists to be made for this project.

Both are shown below.

The light Orange blocks (you create and name when you 'add a variable'. Same with List (Make a list). You can hide your List of Names and questions by un-ticking box shown above.

Let's get coding...

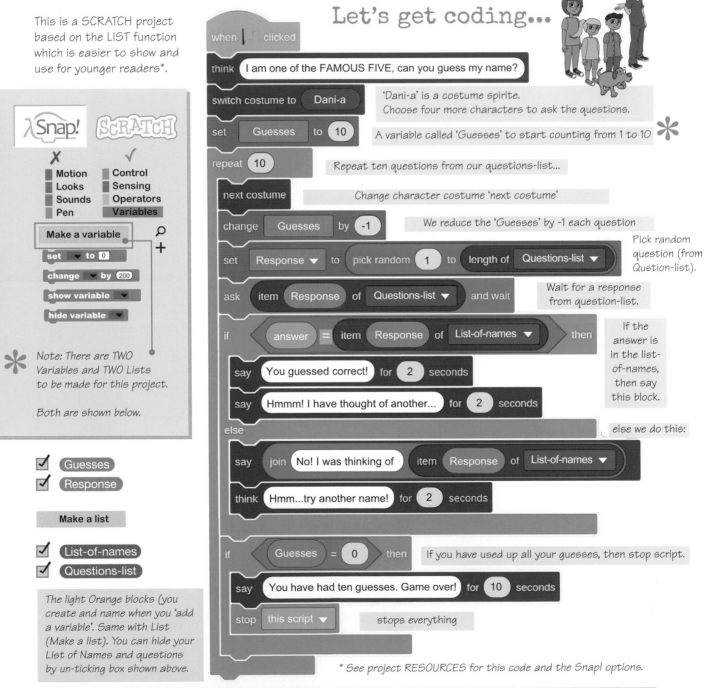

```
when [flag] clicked
think [I am one of the FAMOUS FIVE, can you guess my name?]
switch costume to [Dani-a]
set [Guesses] to (10)
repeat (10)
    next costume
    change [Guesses] by (-1)
    set [Response] to (pick random (1) to (length of [Questions-list]))
    ask (item (Response) of [Questions-list]) and wait
    if <(answer) = (item (Response) of [List-of-names])> then
        say [You guessed correct!] for (2) seconds
        say [Hmmm! I have thought of another...] for (2) seconds
    else
        say (join [No! I was thinking of] (item (Response) of [List-of-names]))
        think [Hmm...try another name!] for (2) seconds
    end
    if <(Guesses) = (0)> then
        say [You have had ten guesses. Game over!] for (10) seconds
        stop [this script]
    end
end
```

'Dani-a' is a costume spirite. Choose four more characters to ask the questions.

A variable called 'Guesses' to start counting from 1 to 10 *

Repeat ten questions from our questions-list...

Change character costume 'next costume'

We reduce the 'Guesses' by -1 each question

Pick random question (from Qustion-list).

Wait for a response from question-list.

If the answer is in the list-of-names, then say this block.

else we do this:

If you have used up all your guesses, then stop script.

stops everything

** See project RESOURCES for this code and the Snap! options.*

Guess names with Python

This bit of Python code does almost the same thing as the SCRATCH blocks but we can add some help along the way. We have ten guesses to find all the names in the book. It can be any book, such as a book on Astronomy, (name all seven planets), or a book on animals at the Zoo. It all works the same way.

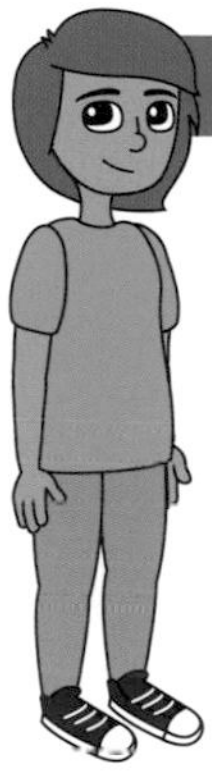

(Start of code) - type in the code in BLACK as shown. Ignore '#' marks are for code COMMENTS only.

```
# Guess names in The Famous Five book. Let's get Coding!
# The (import) 'random' module  is used to 'mix-up' the words in our LIST
import random

NAME_LIST = ["dick", "george", "julian", "timmy", "anne"]  # Any number of names in your list.
named = random.choice(NAME_LIST)

def startGuessing():
•••• triesLeft = 10 # Up to 10 guesses allowed.
•••• answer = "-" * len(named)

•••• while triesLeft > -1 and not answer == named:
•••• •••• print("\n" + answer)
•••• •••• print(str(triesLeft) + " tries left")
•••• •••• guess = input("Guess a single letter:") # Useful to help guess a difficult  word or name!

•••• •••• if len(guess) != 1:
•••• •••• •••• print("You can only enter one letter at a time.") # Instructions
•••• •••• elif guess in named:  # if letter is guessed
•••• •••• print("Yup! that is a letter in the name I was thinking of.")
•••• •••• answer = updateAnswer(named, answer, guess)
•••• •••• else:
•••• •••• print("Sorry, that letter does not appear in the name, I am thinking of.")
•••• •••• triesLeft -= 1

•••• •••• if triesLeft < 0: # When your guesses are at zero do this or (else) do that
•••• •••• print("You have had ten guesses. Game over! The name was: " + named)
•••• else:
•••• •••• print("Well done!, you are very well-read on Enid Blyton. That name was: " + named)

def updateAnswer(word, ans, guess): # Update answers and if result = word answer) in NAME_LIST...
•••• result = " "

•••• for i in range(len(word)):  # Repeat until all thewords (in our NAME_LIST) are guessed.
•••• if word[i] == guess:
•••• •••• result = result + guess
•••• •••• else:
•••• •••• result = result + ans[i]
•••• return result

# This is the main START message of the quiz (and how to play the guessing game).
print("Guess which of the children's names I am 'THINKING' about. Each name appears in the \
'The Famous Five' book, by Enid Blyton. Enter each letter (one-at-a-time) to guess the name!")

startGuessing()

# [End of coding]
```

•••• What are these dots for?
= FOUR character spaces
Don't use the TAB key!

When you see a Python backslash; \ this means that this is line code break and is just a longer line of code than the rest.

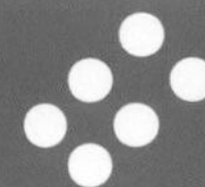

Options to try:

As we have FIVE characters I am going to make FIVE costumes on one sprite. You can choose (import) your own characters but it does help - if you have a favourite children's book. Use that book for your guessing game.

Choose any costume and in any order for your Sprite! See the image costume library in Snap! or Scratch.

Import any image (as a costume), and in any order you think is best. You do that by clicking on a sprite and 'import' a costume. Then 'add' another costume, to the same sprite. Do that for each character in your book. This works in any version of Scratch or Snap! .

Making Scratch Lists:

When you 'add' a word such as a name to the list just click on the first entry on **'List-of-names'** and enter name. Add another name in the same way. You should have at least three names and there is no limit to the names you can add. Five is good enough for my Famous Five book.

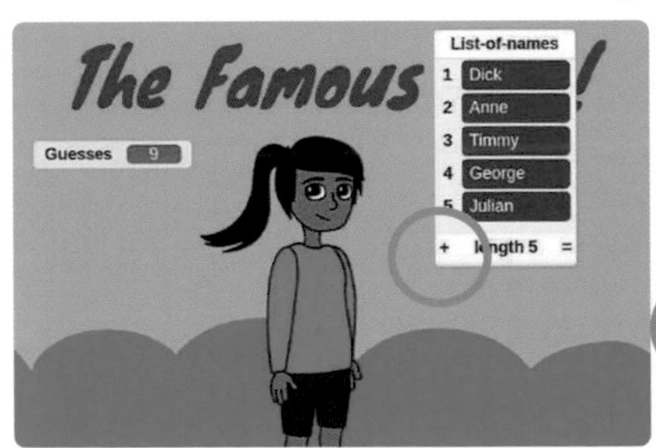

List-of-names:
Add names by clicking on + button

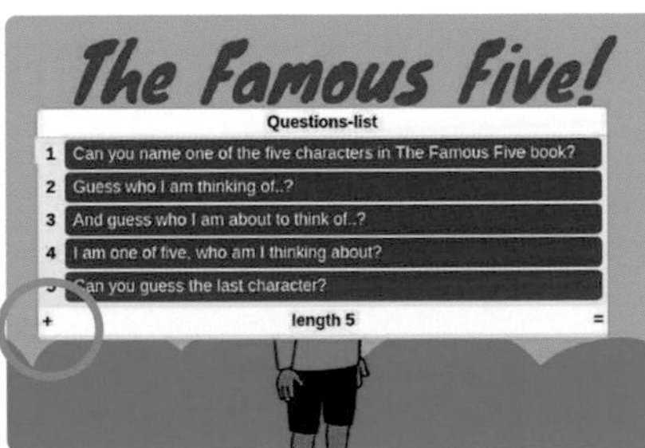

Questions-list
Add questions by clicking on + button

When we add questions you need to 'add' a question to the 'Questions-list'. Just click on the first entry on list to make the first question. After that repeat, you may spot a small plus on the list. In our program, the questions are picked at random, so I suggest you make three or more questions to start.

Python Code options:

The Python code is not identical but works much the same way. It's easier and faster to try out Python code but also easier to make mistakes. So keep the list of names short and questions few. Don't expect your code to work the first time. Missing out one colon (:) , *a ( ) bracket* or indent (*shown in this book as •••• of four character spaces*) can sometimes be difficult to spot on your own. Ask someone to check your code against the working code we supply on our PROJECTS resources page. We have code for each and every project in this book. But only use that if you really need to. You'll learn more by making some small mistakes. Some coding programs like THONNY will suggest what is missing and where you should look (*usually a line number*), is a good indicator of the error. **** See project RESOURCES for this project.***

Next: Mirror Reflections in code

15

Mirror Mad REFLECTIONS in code

This project is one of my favourites because you will (probably) get a little confused. Remember earlier in this book when coding 'Etch-A-Sketch' you knew your 'right' from 'left' and your 'Ups' from your 'Downs' directions?

But what if 'Ups' was 'Down' and 'Left' and 'Right' were swopped (just like in a mirror?) If you look at your reflection in a mirror, your left is now on your right, (although I know you're not upside down!)

So now you're all a bit confused, its time to make a simple reflection game. All you have to do is know which way up you are, (and then) do the opposite... (without getting into trouble at school). Lets get coding!

The Author (is now upside down)

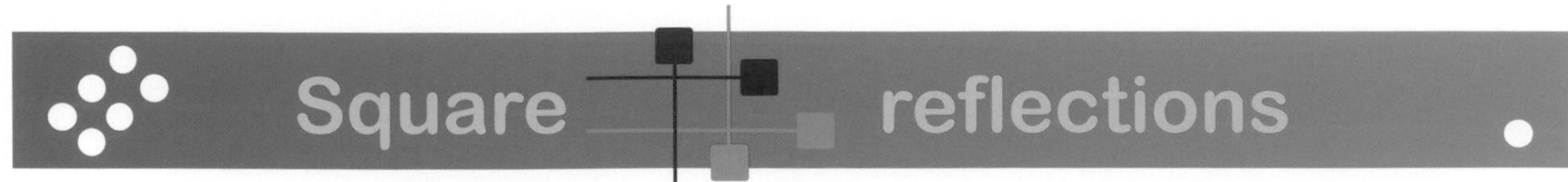
Square reflections

This is going to be simpler than you think! We shall be drawing a square as our Costume. Don't import anything, just make a square and call it RED. Our Sprite will be called RED. Follow the code below and 'Click right' with your Mouse and duplicate that sprite three times. Total four Sprites...

RED, GREEN, BLUE and ORANGE

Let's get coding...

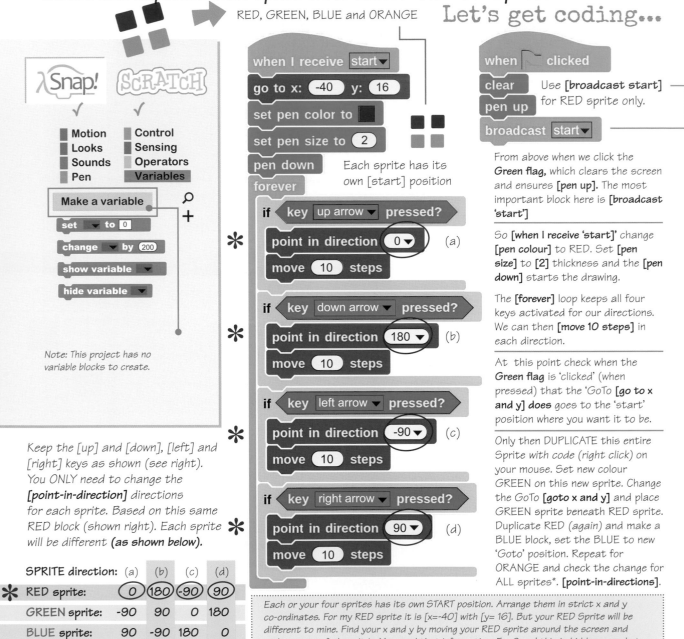

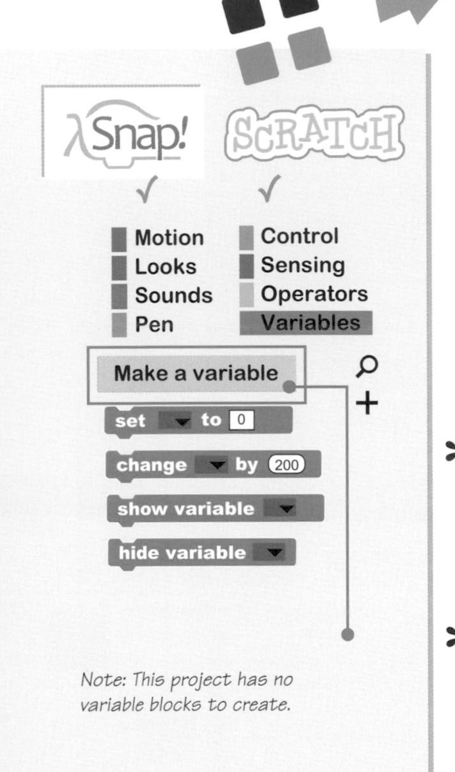
Snap!
SCRATCH
Motion
Looks
Sounds
Pen
Control
Sensing
Operators
Variables
Make a variable
set to 0
change by 200
show variable
hide variable

Note: This project has no variable blocks to create.

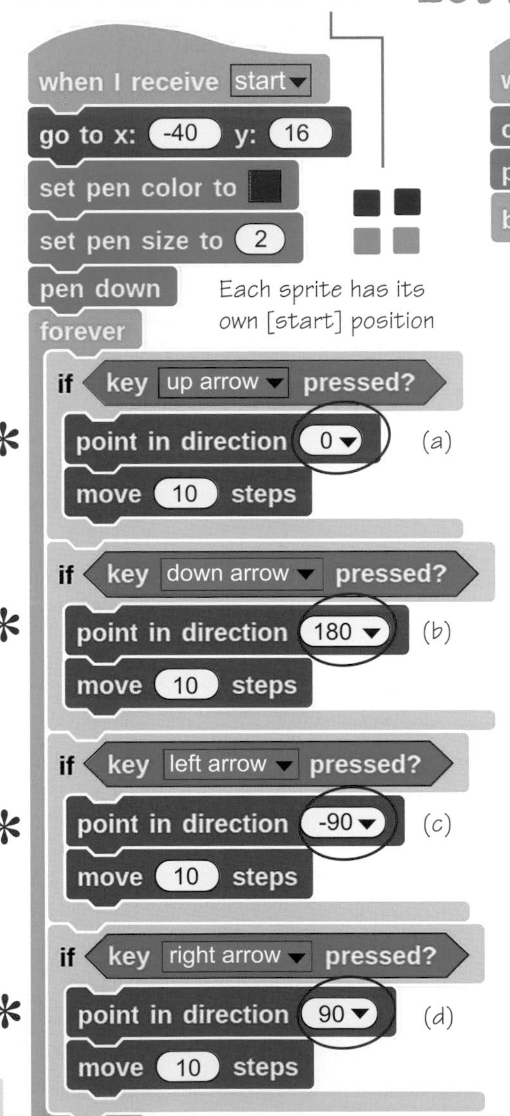
when I receive start
go to x: -40 y: 16
set pen color to
set pen size to 2
pen down
forever
if key up arrow pressed?
point in direction 0
move 10 steps
if key down arrow pressed?
point in direction 180
move 10 steps
if key left arrow pressed?
point in direction -90
move 10 steps
if key right arrow pressed?
point in direction 90
move 10 steps
(a)
(b)
(c)
(d)

Each sprite has its own [start] position

when [flag] clicked
clear
pen up
broadcast start

Use **[broadcast start]** for RED sprite only.

From above when we click the **Green flag,** which clears the screen and ensures **[pen up].** The most important block here is **[broadcast 'start']**

So **[when I receive 'start']'** change **[pen colour]** to RED. Set **[pen size]** to **[2]** thickness and the **[pen down]** starts the drawing.

The **[forever]** loop keeps all four keys activated for our directions. We can then **[move 10 steps]** in each direction.

At this point check when the **Green flag** is 'clicked' (when pressed) that the 'GoTo **[go to x and y] does** goes to the 'start' position where you want it to be.

Only then DUPLICATE this entire Sprite with code (right click) on your mouse. Set new colour GREEN on this new sprite. Change the GoTo **[goto x and y]** and place GREEN sprite beneath RED sprite. Duplicate RED (again) and make a BLUE block, set the BLUE to new 'Goto' position. Repeat for ORANGE and check the change for ALL sprites*. **[point-in-directions]**.

Keep the [up] and [down], [left] and [right] keys as shown (see right). You ONLY need to change the ***[point-in-direction]*** *directions for each sprite. Based on this same RED block (shown right). Each sprite will be different* ***(as shown below).***

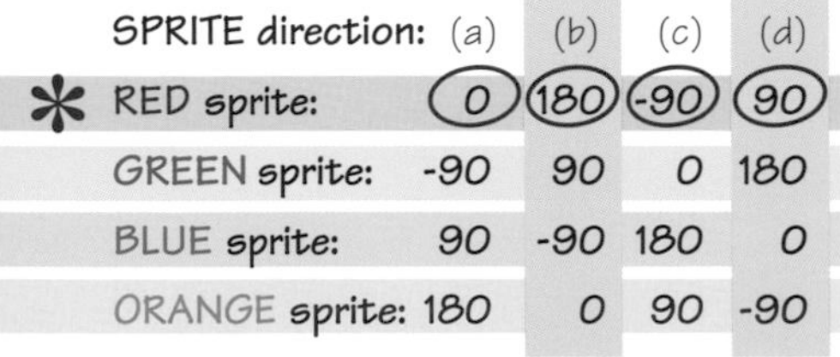

SPRITE direction:	(a)	(b)	(c)	(d)
* RED sprite:	0	180	-90	90
GREEN sprite:	-90	90	0	180
BLUE sprite:	90	-90	180	0
ORANGE sprite:	180	0	90	-90

Each or your four sprites has its own START position. Arrange them in strict x and y co-ordinates. For my RED sprite it is [x=-40] with [y= 16]. But your RED Sprite will be different to mine. Find your x and y by moving your RED sprite around the screen and make a note of where it is. You need that information. For Snap! this is hidden away but you can click it 'on' and find your sprite position. ***See page 74 and project RESOURCES.***

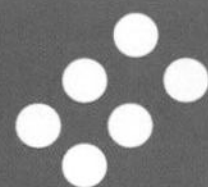

Python mirror Turtles

When you have made the previous page, why then do a Python version? Well why not? It's a lot easier (if you type it in correctly) and it's also a good challenge for the author using just Turtle Code. Good fun for you (as the programme coder) you can change anything you like - to see if it still works...

Note: there are three parts of Python code to join up!

(Start of code) - type in the code in BLACK as shown. Ignore '#' marks are for code COMMENTS only.

Python part one

```
# Turtle Reflections with 4 turtles | Lets get Coding book
# Four drawing turtles on  black screen
from turtle import *
screen = Screen()
move = Turtle()
screen.bgcolor("black") # or White (optional)
# RED turtle (my reference for directions)
red = Turtle()
red.color("red")
red.setheading(180) # Point West
red.shape("turtle") # **
# Change shape to "square" option.
red.shapesize(2) # Default size is small (0)
red.penup() # Remove  unwanted line start
red.goto(-25, 0) # Start position RED
red.pendown()
red.pensize(4) # Thickness of the line

# BLUE turtle
blue = Turtle()
blue.color("blue")
blue.setheading(90)  # Point North
blue.shape("turtle")# **
blue.shapesize(2)
blue.penup()
blue.goto(25, 0) # Start position BLUE
blue.pendown()
blue.pensize(4)
# (cont)...
```

Python part two

```
# GREEN turtle
green = Turtle()
green.shape("turtle") # **
green.shapesize(2)
green.color("green")
green.setheading(270) # Point South
green.penup()
green.goto(-25, -50) # Start position GREEN
green.pendown()
green.pensize(4)

# YELLOW turtle
yellow = Turtle()
yellow.shape("turtle") # **
yellow.shapesize(2)
yellow.color("yellow")
yellow.setheading(0) # Point East (default)
yellow.penup()
yellow.goto(25, -50)
# Start position YELLOW
yellow.pendown()
yellow.pensize(4)

# Timeshares (take turns to move Turtles)
for turn in range(100):
•••• def k1(): # Key 1- ten steps forward
•••• •••• red.forward(10)
•••• •••• blue.forward(10)
•••• •••• green.forward(10)
•••• •••• yellow.forward(10)
•••• def k2(): # Key 2 turn (-90) degrees
# (cont)...
```

•••• What are these dots for?
= FOUR character spaces
Don't use the TAB key!

You can easily change Turtles into 'squares'. I have kept Turtles shapes as you will need to check your coding of Turtle directions. When all working OK you can then change to squares, or keep the Turtles, you choose!

Options to try:

Scratch and Snap!:

The position of your first RED sprite in Scratch is easy to find. However, finding your RED sprite position in Snap! is hidden away at the bottom of the (Blue) Motion blocks. Click the 'tick-box' selection - as shown below [a] . This will create the two indicators as shown [b]. You can switch them 'ON' or 'OFF' by tick-box. You need to know the 'x' and 'y' positions for Green, Blue and Orange sprites in turn. This is essential, see below:

Finding that first RED sprite position (x and y)

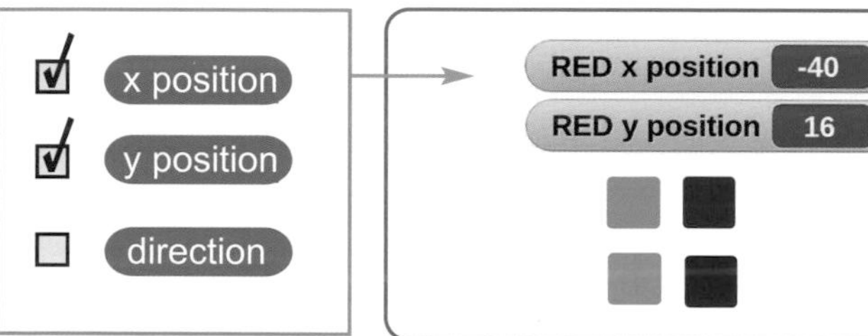

[a] In Snap! Find. then CLICK for the x and y positions (as shown above) will give you the RED sprite position. [b] When you press [Start] (green flag) the RED sprite image will then go to that start position.

Python part three

```
# (cont)...
•••• •••• red.left(90)
•••• •••• blue.left(90)
•••• •••• green.left(90)
•••• •••• yellow.left(90)
•••• def k3(): # Key 3 turn 90 degrees
•••• •••• red.right(90)
•••• ••••  blue.right(90)
•••• •••• green.right(90)
•••• •••• yellow.right(90)
•••• def k4(): # Key 4 - ten steps back
•••• •••• red.backward(10)
•••• •••• blue.backward(10)
•••• •••• green.backward(10)
•••• •••• yellow.backward(10)
# When this arrow key is pressed...
for turn in range(100):
•••• screen.onkey(k1, "Up")
•••• screen.onkey(k2, "Left")
•••• screen.onkey(k3, "Right")
•••• screen.onkey(k4, "Down")
# Keep an ear open for key clicks
listen()
# Click screen to exit
screen.exitonclick()

# [End of coding]
```

•••• What are these dots for?
= FOUR character spaces
Don't use the TAB key!

We can also change our 'Squares' to 'Turtles' to match our Python code 'Turtles'. See project RESOURCES page

PYTHON reflection version

When typed in correctly, the four turtles will move in different directions according to whichever arrow key is pressed. All turtles face different headings and will turn according to left and right keys. Two both heading in different directions each time. Up and Down keys are for forward and backward motion on all turtles. You can play with the speed and headings, but you'll soon get confused as I did. But it was fun to code. I have not changed my turtles to squares but its an easy option to make. See lines marked # ** marked on the code.

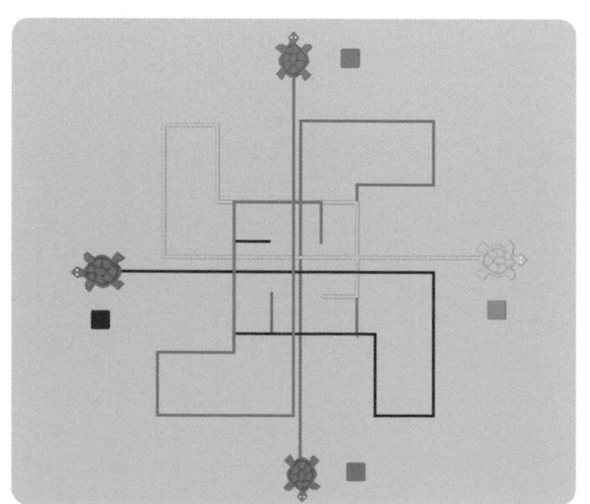

This projects is available in both Scratch and Snap! code formats including Python. **See project RESOURCES pages.**

Next: Coding Polygon pinwheels

16

Making POLYGON shapes

What's the minimum number of sides do you need to form an enclosed shape? The answer is (of course) a Triangle; as it has a minimim three enclosed sides; called a Polygon shape. A Triangle is very useful as it can be used to make all kinds of complex 2D and 3D shapes.

One of those 2D shapes is called a Hexagon (as it's based on creating six arranged Triangles - another Polygon. All three sides being equal length makes it easy to code and arrange in our colour pinwheel spinner.

So this is an easy one for you to code and learn about making Polygons and impress your friends with fun geometry. My friends just think I am nutty about geometry.

The Author (is nuts on geometry)

Triangle to Hexagon Pinwheel

This simple project - is also a challenge to make in Snap! or Scratch. There there is no standard code-block for any 'automatic' FILL of a shape we create in code. We can draw any 'shape' (for a Sprite) and code it but we cannot fill that same shape with a colour automatically. But we have a fun solution!

"■" First meet BLOB! Draw this Sprite costume in grey.

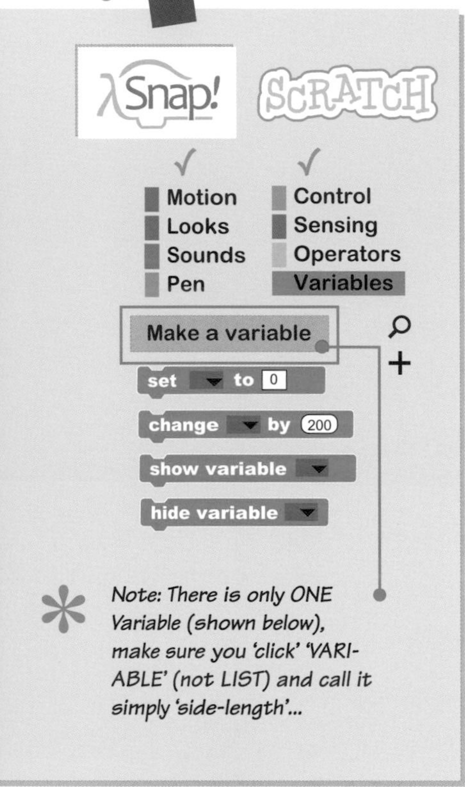

Note: There is only ONE Variable (shown below), make sure you 'click' 'VARIABLE' (not LIST) and call it simply 'side-length'...

To 'click' or not to 'click' tick-box?...

When you create a VARIABLE you will create some more **(Orange)** blocks that you can drag into your code. ***Try it and see.*** When you see a small ***'tick box'*** (as you will see above ***(for both Snap! and Scratch VARIABLES)*** then you choose to show that function ***'on screen'*** or not. I would normally have that clicked 'OFF' (as you don't need to show it), but it may help you see that it works and that it does change the ***'side-lengths'***.

Let's get coding...

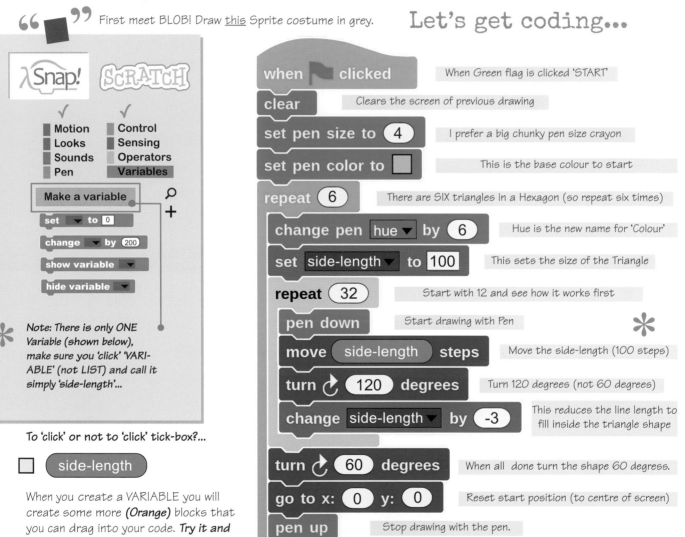

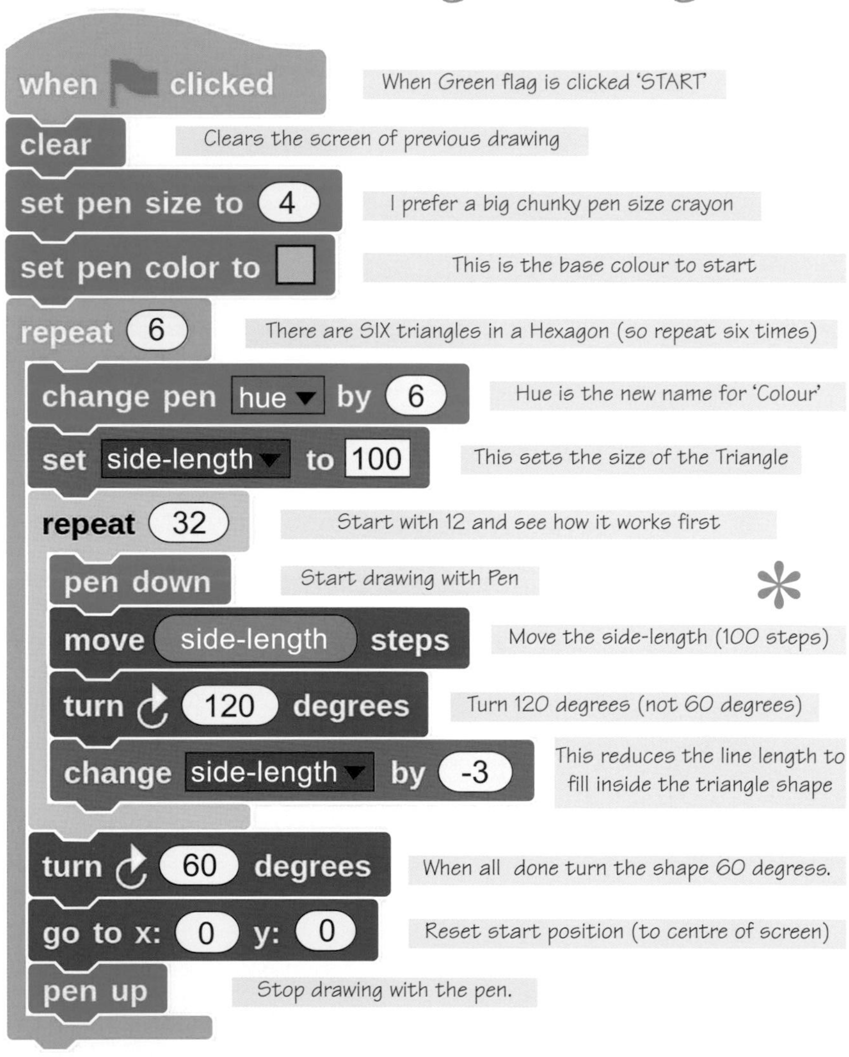

This is a good (but maybe not always practical) way of filling your shape with a colour of your choice. There is no colour 'fill' block code in Scratch that fills a drawn shape easily. Snap! does have a non standard 'fill' colour block, which we could use however.

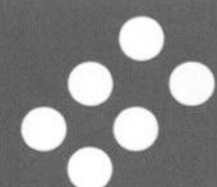

Python to Hexagon Pinwheel

One of the great advantages of Python is that it can do more than block coding can and often (not always) in fewer coding steps. The advantage here for this Python project is that there is already a simple Python code for 'fill' of any enclosed shape (such as a Polygon) or any other shape. This code will draw an outline and fill with a random colour for our Hexagon pinwheel...

Let's get coding...

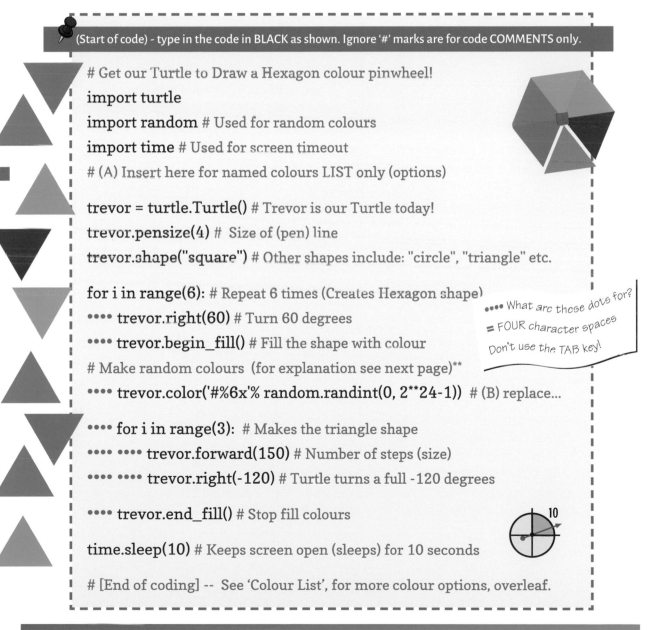

(Start of code) - type in the code in BLACK as shown. Ignore '#' marks are for code COMMENTS only.

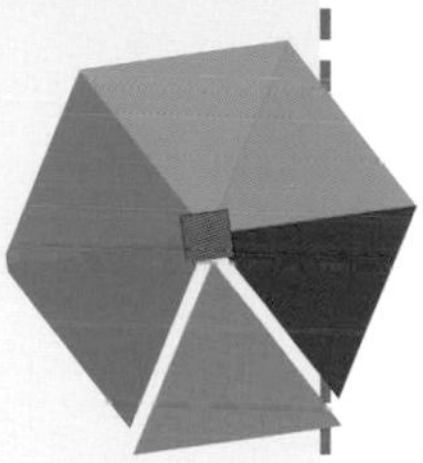

```
# Get our Turtle to Draw a Hexagon colour pinwheel!
import turtle
import random # Used for random colours
import time # Used for screen timeout
# (A) Insert here for named colours LIST only (options)

trevor = turtle.Turtle() # Trevor is our Turtle today!
trevor.pensize(4) #  Size of (pen) line
trevor.shape("square") # Other shapes include: "circle", "triangle" etc.

for i in range(6): # Repeat 6 times (Creates Hexagon shape)
•••• trevor.right(60) # Turn 60 degrees
•••• trevor.begin_fill() # Fill the shape with colour
# Make random colours  (for explanation see next page)**
•••• trevor.color('#%6x'% random.randint(0, 2**24-1)) # (B) replace...

•••• for i in range(3):  # Makes the triangle shape
•••• •••• trevor.forward(150) # Number of steps (size)
•••• •••• trevor.right(-120) # Turtle turns a full -120 degrees

•••• trevor.end_fill() # Stop fill colours

time.sleep(10) # Keeps screen open (sleeps) for 10 seconds

# [End of coding] --  See 'Colour List', for more colour options, overleaf.
```

•••• What are these dots for?
= FOUR character spaces
Don't use the TAB key!

10

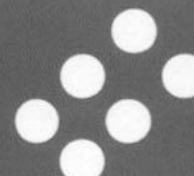

Options to try:

Here are a few options and shapes for you to try in Snap! or SCRATCH

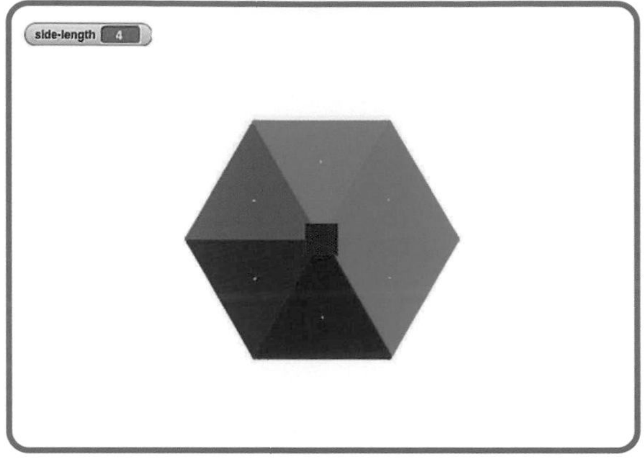

Try and change to a square. A square has four sides and we will have four squares in that square. So we can change the repeat to four, keep **'side-length'** the same and change the angles to 90 degree on each turn. Give that a try. As long as you can work out what angles a shapes is, you should be able to make any polygon sided shape, the same way as my example. Try next a **Pentagon (5), Heptagon (7), or Octagon (8).** I think that will be enough for now. Try to hack some Python code!

Python code: some more options

Well how about changing the name of the Turtle to YOUR own first name? So instead of **trevor.shape("square") try steve.shape("circle").** Don't forget to change every **'trevor'** in the code to the new name, or you will get an error. If you're feeling adventurous in hacking your own code, how about making a five sided polygon *(instead of six sides)*. Think how you would do that. The same rules apply but you need to work out the angles first. Its a question of Maths.

> ***For example: If we were to make a PENTAGON (using the same code shown on page 77).***
> ***Convert to a Pentagon (5 sided shape) will have a repeat of 5, a turn of 72 degrees.***
> ***Repeat same 5 sided shape, which is repeated five times, forward 150, right -108 degrees....***

Finally Colours can be changed to a fixed list of colours instead of using 'Random colours' *(shown below)* which works but is not very descriptive of what it does or how it works. For an explanation on how this odd looking code makes the colours, **see project RESOURCES pages**.

```
# Random Colour generator (as marked in our code), makes all the random colours
trevor.color('#%6x'% random.randint(0, 2**24-1))
```

If you have decided on setting fixed colours from a list *(many to choose from)* you need to set up our Colour list (as seen below) in the exact positions we indicate. You can *choose your own colours (from www.trinket.io/docs/colors).* See project RESOURCES page for coded examples.

```
# Colour LIST (six colour list) options to insert (where marked in code - # (A)
colors = ["blue", "purple", "green", "orange", "red", "olive", "seablue"]
trevor.color(colors[i]) # i.e. repeat in the loop (colors as above) # (B) - replace code line
```

Next: Honey Bees make patterns

17

Coding Busy Bee patterns

The Honey Bee is famous for making honey and that honey is stored in a honeycomb. Not (as you may think) ready to be potted and put on to the shelves of your nearest shop!

If you look at the label on the shelf, there is usually a picture of a Bee and a Hexagon all joined up to make a pattern. The Honey is usually brown, runny and sweet.

A hexagon is a six sided polygon, and in this project we will will make a 'tessellation' which is basically an ordered pattern with no gaps. Honey Bees are quite good at this.

I suspect you will soon be a 'busy-bee', with some coding practice, with (perhaps) a Honey sandwich...

The Author (likes Honey sandwiches)

Honey Bees make patterns

No Bees were harmed in making this Honeybee project! And you can make your Bee draw accurate patterns which is a repeated shape with no gaps between! You can 'import' your Bee as a costume in Scratch but for Snap! you will need to 'import' your Bee - or draw your own 'Bee' if you're really creative. If Bees can draw hexagons, you can too! Let's get coding...

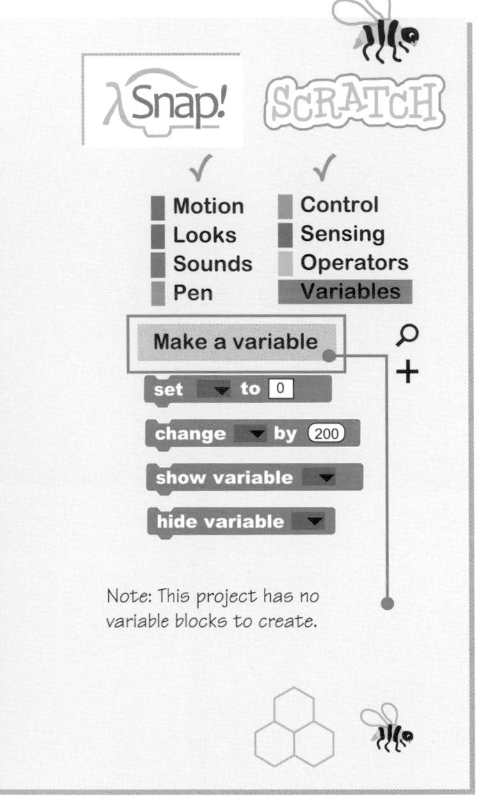
Snap!
SCRATCH
Motion
Looks
Sounds
Pen
Control
Sensing
Operators
Variables
Make a variable
set to 0
change by 200
show variable
hide variable
Note: This project has no variable blocks to create.

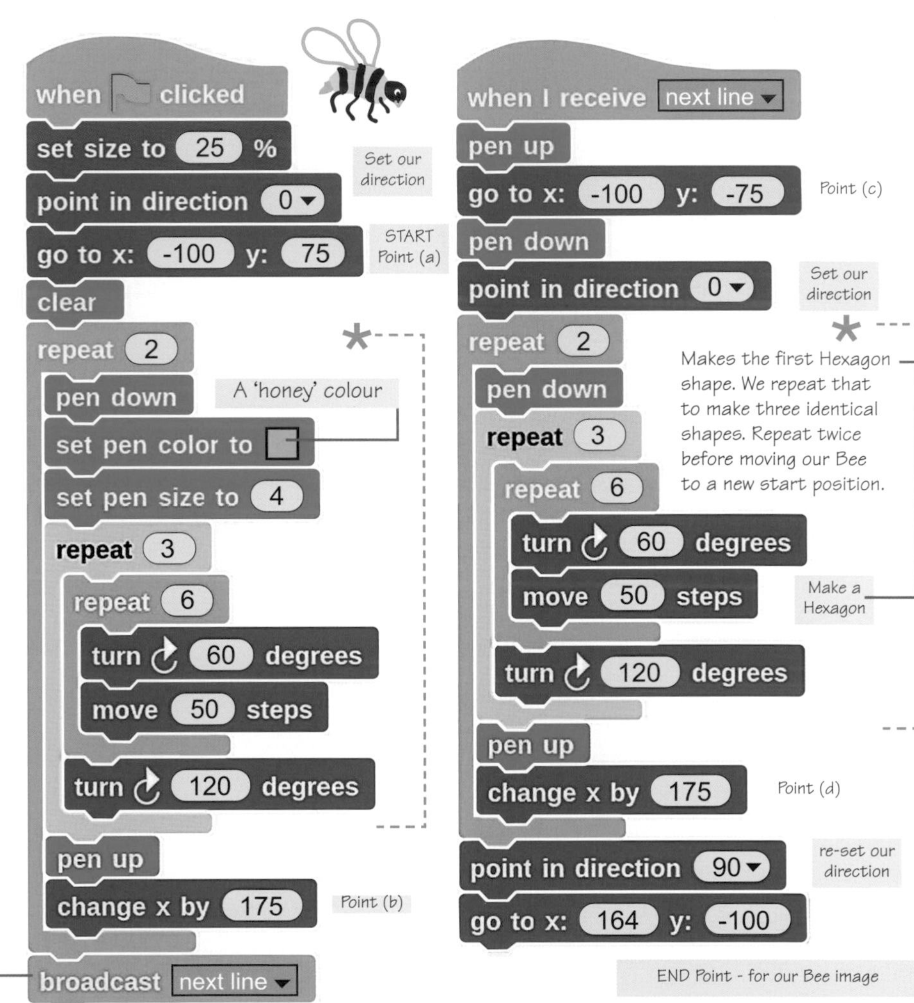
when clicked
set size to 25 %
point in direction 0
go to x: -100 y: 75
clear
repeat 2
pen down
set pen color to
set pen size to 4
repeat 3
repeat 6
turn 60 degrees
move 50 steps
turn 120 degrees
pen up
change x by 175
broadcast next line
Set our direction
START Point (a)
A 'honey' colour
Point (b)
when I receive next line
pen up
go to x: -100 y: -75
pen down
point in direction 0
repeat 2
pen down
repeat 3
repeat 6
turn 60 degrees
move 50 steps
turn 120 degrees
pen up
change x by 175
point in direction 90
go to x: 164 y: -100
Point (c)
Set our direction
Makes the first Hexagon shape. We repeat that to make three identical shapes. Repeat twice before moving our Bee to a new start position.
Make a Hexagon
Point (d)
re-set our direction
END Point - for our Bee image

About that [broadcast] block:

(shown right). You need two blocks, one to 'transmit' ***[broadcast]*** and the other to 'receive' ***[when I receive]***. This is useful to break up your own code blocks to test and compare. Although not essential to code here - it helps me split the code into two blocks so you can compare and see what the ***[change by]*** by and ***'goto'*** position does to start drawing the hexagon(s) in the right position.

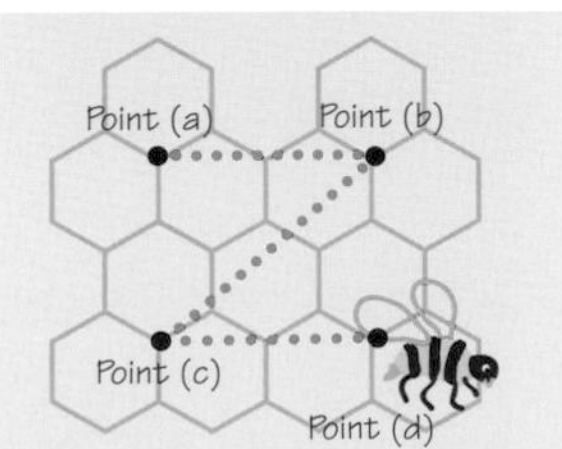
Point (a)
Point (b)
Point (c)
Point (d)

You will learn how to create a 'repeated' image by using a simple technique that you can use on other polygon shapes. The SCRATCH stage (background) is a simple flat 'beige' colour. The Bee is a costume you can draw or import. See our **Project RESOURCES** pages for all graphic files and imported images.

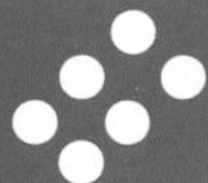

Python to Honeycomb

You will have noticed that Snap! and Scratch are limited in coding shapes that can be filled automatically. In Python it's easy. We can make any shape and simply set it to 'fill' colour of our choice. We can also use the same image we used in Snap! or Scratch and import that image into our Python code to make it more realistic.

Let's get coding...

Python part one

(Start of code) - type in the code in BLACK as shown. Ignore '#' marks are for code COMMENTS only.

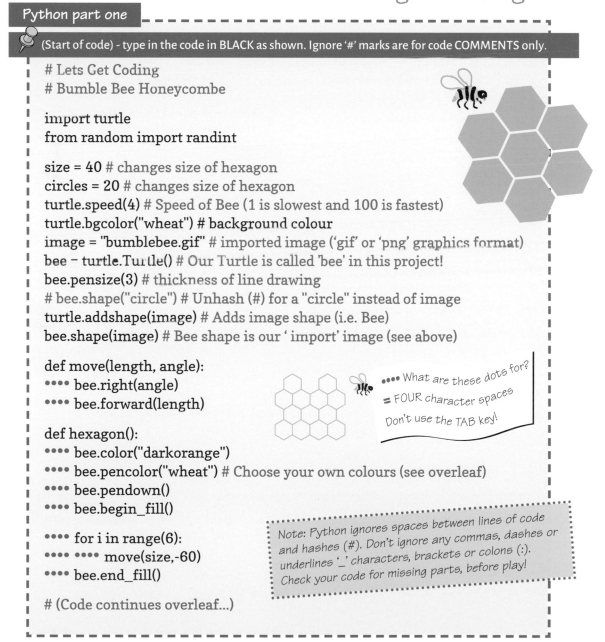

```
# Lets Get Coding
# Bumble Bee Honeycombe

import turtle
from random import randint

size = 40 # changes size of hexagon
circles = 20 # changes size of hexagon
turtle.speed(4) # Speed of Bee (1 is slowest and 100 is fastest)
turtle.bgcolor("wheat") # background colour
image = "bumblebee.gif" # imported image ('gif' or 'png' graphics format)
bee = turtle.Turtle() # Our Turtle is called 'bee' in this project!
bee.pensize(3) # thickness of line drawing
# bee.shape("circle") # Unhash (#) for a "circle" instead of image
turtle.addshape(image) # Adds image shape (i.e. Bee)
bee.shape(image) # Bee shape is our ' import' image (see above)

def move(length, angle):
•••• bee.right(angle)
•••• bee.forward(length)

def hexagon():
•••• bee.color("darkorange")
•••• bee.pencolor("wheat") # Choose your own colours (see overleaf)
•••• bee.pendown()
•••• bee.begin_fill()

•••• for i in range(6):
•••• •••• move(size,-60)
•••• bee.end_fill()

# (Code continues overleaf...)
```

•••• What are these dots for?
= FOUR character spaces
Don't use the TAB key!

Note: Python ignores spaces between lines of code and hashes (#). Don't ignore any commas, dashes or underlines '_' characters, brackets or colons (:). Check your code for missing parts, before play!

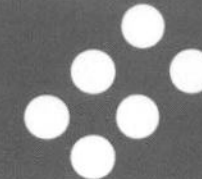

Options to try:

Choose your own Python images:

We shall be learning to import an image into Python on this project. You can use an image from the Scratch costumes library or a web based image (*as long as it is in 'gif' or 'png' image format*). For Snap! you can use the new 'svg' graphics format as well as a 'png'. Note: 'svg' images always look better.

For a Python image that you plan to use you should always place the image (*and import the image*) from the same directory as your Python code. Python cannot 're-size' your graphic as you would in Snap! or Scratch, so check the imported image size is not too big or too small.

You can find all you really need to know about importing graphic images into Python ***(see our 'Web references' box at the bottom of this page).*** *This Bee project is also available for download on our project resources page in three formats for SNAP!, SCRATCH and PYTHON.*

Choose your own Python colours:

You can use **'red, 'green', 'purple', 'blue'** and **'orange'** but it's a bit boring when you want something a bit different to stand out for your project's code.

So go wild and wacky and import your own colours!

I made my own selection for this project using some Bee and honey Python specific colours from Trinket*.

See if you can choose better colours than mine!

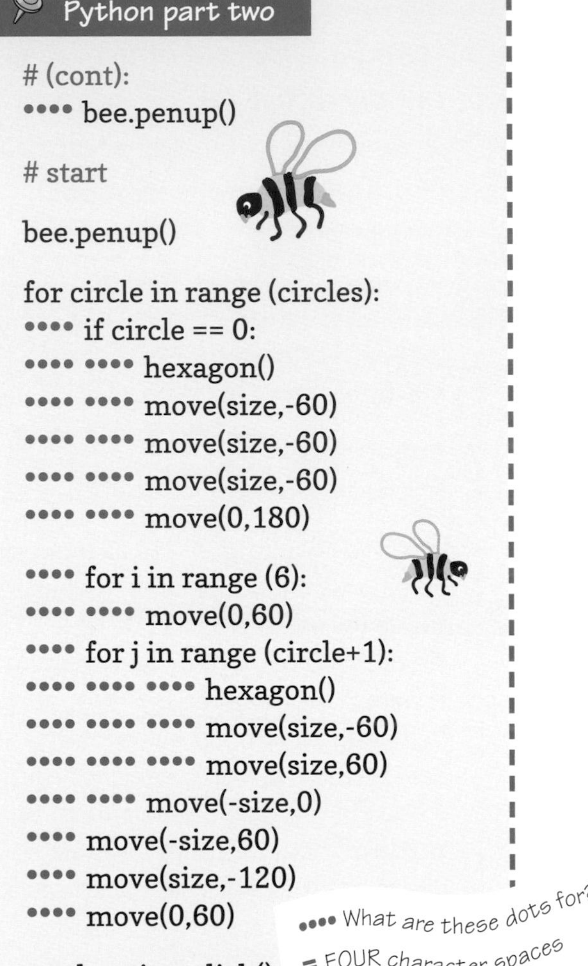

Python part two

```
# (cont):
•••• bee.penup()

# start

bee.penup()

for circle in range (circles):
•••• if circle == 0:
•••• •••• hexagon()
•••• •••• move(size,-60)
•••• •••• move(size,-60)
•••• •••• move(size,-60)
•••• •••• move(0,180)

•••• for i in range (6):
•••• •••• move(0,60)
•••• for j in range (circle+1):
•••• •••• •••• hexagon()
•••• •••• •••• move(size,-60)
•••• •••• •••• move(size,60)
•••• •••• move(-size,0)
•••• move(-size,60)
•••• move(size,-120)
•••• move(0,60)

turtle.exitonclick()

# [End of coding]
```

•••• What are these dots for?
= FOUR character spaces
Don't use the TAB key!

Hexagon code based on: Amélie Anglade - Python workshop from the: opentechschool, Berlin, Germany.

Web references: Using images and colours in Python

How to use images in (Python) Turtle programs:
*https://blog.trinket.io/using-images-in-turtle-programs/

Choose your own 'specific' named colours in Python
https://trinket.io/docs/colors

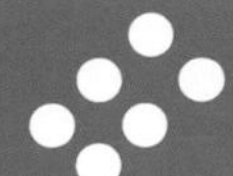

Next: Noughts & Crosses game

18

Coding (probably) the 'oldest' game in the entire world!

If you were thinking of making the oldest game in the world (that is still being played). It has to be Noughts and Crosses. The oldest myth (and the one that I prefer) is that it was played by the ancient Egyptians with shiny stones with Rubies (red) and Sapphires (green) drawn on the desert Sand with a stick. There are few rules and it is simple to play at any age, just for fun.

It not an original idea, but you can make it your own by simply playing and see how it works. You have played the game before, right?

When I first became interested in computers, this was one of the first games I played. Every game has to follow some simple rules. Let's get coding!

The Author (likes playing very old games)

This is the simplest coding game in this book but you still have to work out how it works and how you can improve it yourself. I can only take you so far, to give you the idea and suggest that the best place to start is drawing your own 'funky' game pieces. There are two pieces (x and o) to draw, but there are THREE costumes (on ONE sprite), to draw ('x', 'o' and a 'dot').

Let's gets coding...

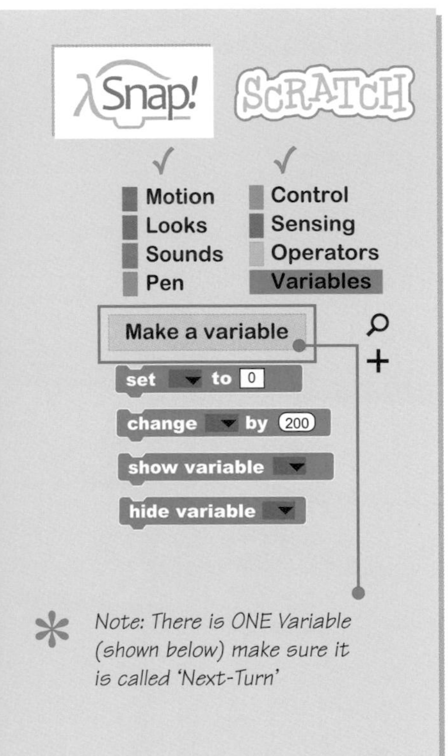

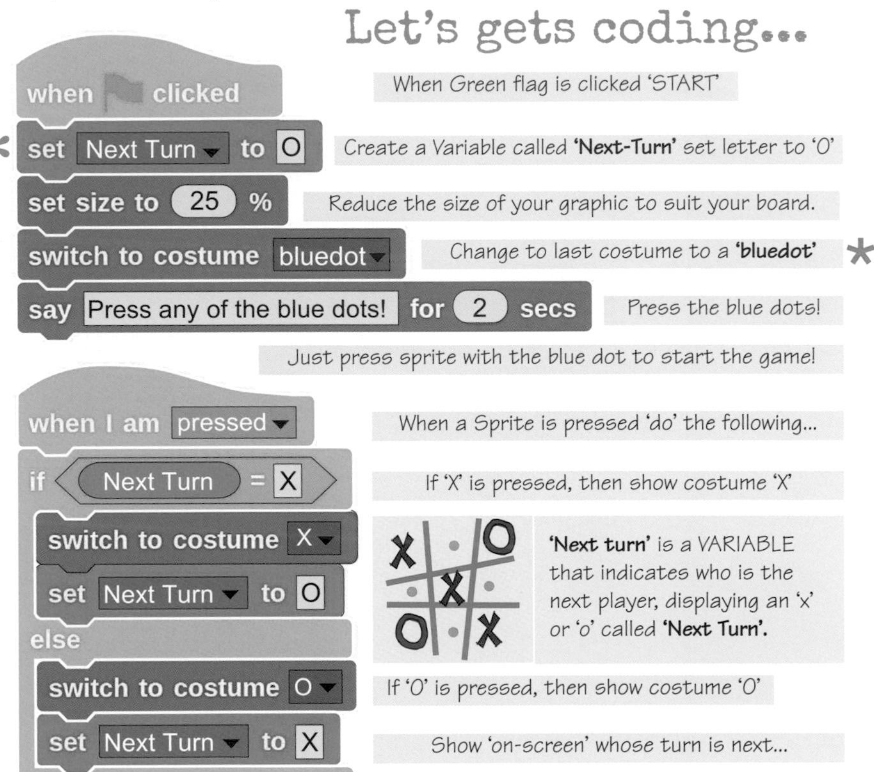

when clicked
When Green flag is clicked 'START'
set Next Turn to O
Create a Variable called 'Next-Turn' set letter to 'O'
set size to 25 %
Reduce the size of your graphic to suit your board.
switch to costume bluedot
Change to last costume to a 'bluedot'
say Press any of the blue dots! for 2 secs
Press the blue dots!
Just press sprite with the blue dot to start the game!
when I am pressed
When a Sprite is pressed 'do' the following...
if Next Turn = X
If 'X' is pressed, then show costume 'X'
switch to costume X
set Next Turn to O
'Next turn' is a VARIABLE that indicates who is the next player, displaying an 'x' or 'o' called 'Next Turn'.
else
switch to costume O
If 'O' is pressed, then show costume 'O'
set Next Turn to X
Show 'on-screen' whose turn is next...

The Variable 'Next-Turn' does not actually 'count' the play moves but indicates whose 'turn' it is to go next. So it's always the opposite to the piece being played. X is opposite to O. We are using CAPITAL 'O' or 'X' Letters (rather than usual numbers) in our simple indicator Variable. It will 'flip- flop' between the two states and change our (X or O) costumes. ***Ensure your SPRITE has three costumes!***

X

O

(bluedot)

This is ONE SPRITE (called xo1) with three 'Costume' changes. Draw each costume as shown here.

Each costumes is an 'x' or 'o' image, the 'blue-dot' costume is necessary to give a button to press when the game starts.

*You only have to make ONE sprite. Simply 'duplicate' that EIGHT TIMES with a simple 'right-click' of your mouse (just click on the same SPRITE you have just drawn). Once duplicated, place on board following the **'bluedots'** position(s) as indicated.*

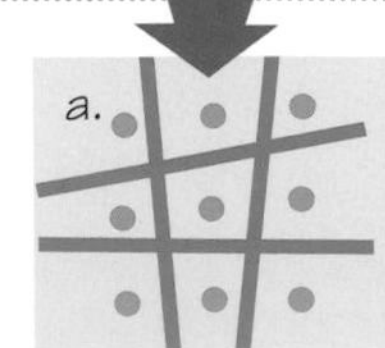

*Drag your Sprite to position a. (right click and duplicate the sprite) place the next sprite to the right, repeat (right click and duplicate the sprite) and then finish the board with each position is as shown left. Press Green flag to **[Start]** button and make sure each **'bluedot'** is the costume we start with. We do that with the **[switch-to-costume-'bluedot']** block.*

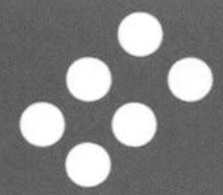

Python: Noughts & Crosses

This Python script duplicates what we have done with block code. It is still playable as it works but, like the Snap! and Scarcth block code we are still missing some vital checking of what is a "Win" situation to someone who had never played the game before. So we need to set the rules of the game. But to start type (key-in) in the following code to get the basics working.

(Start of code) - type in the code in BLACK as shown. Ignore '#' marks are for code COMMENTS only.

```
# Nought & Crosses. Lets Get Coding Book 2020
# Basc code (no colour, no score)

board = [' ',' ',' ',' ',' ',' ',' ',' ',' ',' ']    # Make nine empty 'spaces' on the board
player = 1

# (OPTIONS: insert code block A.)
Running = 0   # Keep game alive
Game = Running   # Game is running
Mark = 'X'  # Indicactor for X and O
# - - - - - - - - - - - - - - - - !!!

# Draw Boardgame with just keyboard symbols
def DrawBoard(): # Nine boards in total (with nine blank spaces + " | " key symbol)
•••• print("---------") # A line of decorative dashes!
•••• print(board[1]," | ",board[2]," | ",board[3])  # Insert input on board 1-3
•••• print("---------")
•••• print(board[4]," | ",board[5]," | ",board[6])  # Insert input on board 4-6
•••• print("---------")
•••• print(board[7]," | ",board[8]," | ",board[9])  # Insert input on board 7-9
•••• print("---------")

# This Function Checks position is empty - or not
def CheckPosition(x):
•••• if(board[x] == ' '):
•••• •••• return True
•••• else:
•••• •••• return False
# - - - - - - - - - - - - - - - - !!!
# (OPTIONS: insert code block B.)
# - - - - - - - - - - - - - - - - !!!

# (Continued overleaf)
```

*Don't forget that all Python code must 'end-with' (.py.) Python is all simple text based. You can use any old text writer but it all must end (saved with) (.py) For example we have called this code, **noughts-cross-game.py***

We are using THONNY as we will need that later on in our coding OPTIONS- if we decide to make it more interactive...

•••• *What are these dots for?*
= FOUR character spaces
Don't use the TAB key!

PLAYER 1 is FIRST!

Know your VERTICALS, HORIZONTALS and DIAGONALS?

Options to try:

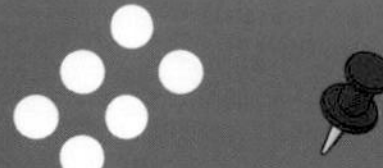

WHO's TURE IS IT?

```
# (Continued...)
print("Player ONE is: [X] and Player TWO is: [O]\n") # On key press
print("[To play: enter a number] - game position shown on board below:")

while(Game == Running):       # Loop game as running
•••• DrawBoard()
•••• if(player % 2 != 0):
•••• •••• print("[Player ONE's turn]")
•••• •••• Mark = 'X'
•••• •••• print() # make line space
•••• else:
•••• •••• print("[Player TWO's turn]")
•••• •••• Mark = 'O'
•••• •••• print()
•••• choice = int(eval(input("Press number between [1-9] then press [ENTER] "))
•••• if(CheckPosition(choice)):
•••• •••• board[choice] = Mark
•••• •••• player+=1
# - - - - - - - - - - - - - - - - !!!
# (OPTIONS: insert code block C.)
# - - - - - - - - - - - - - - - - !!!

DrawBoard()   # Draw the board routine

# [End of Coding]
```

•••• What are these dots for?
= FOUR character spaces
Don't use the TAB key!

RULES!

1	2	3
4	5	6
7	8	9

Boards are numbered 1 to 9 for position placement. A 'Win' is based on certain positions on the board being met. (Horizontally, diagonally or vertically).

The game 'Noughts and Crosses', only works because you know how-the-game-works already!

What if you did NOT know 'how-the-game-works'?

Now we need to extend this Python code to work out how we can count a win horizontally (across board), diagonally (angle across) and vertically (up and down). To do that we need to insert blocks of code where marked as; 'insert code block A', followed by B and C (where marked in our code made previously). It's not any harder to type than the code you have already typed. **Plus we have already done it for you!** *Now you just need to insert the code where marked!*

Try to Insert the code below, into the code above - where marked by #-------!!!!

```
# - - - - - - - - - - - - - - - - !!!
# (OPTIONS: insert code block A.)
# - - - - - - - - - - - - - - - - !!!
```

In your previous keyed in Python code you will see OPTIONS that we can include. It is 'optional' - but the only way to create a 'win' situation is to create rules that the game (and players) will follow.

Shown left is code block A. *(insert where marked)*

For coding (insert blocks A to C). *Find Python coding options, see this* ***project's RESOURCES*** *(on page 127)*

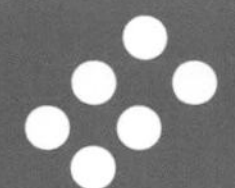

Next: The Colour Mix-up game!

19

Is this an **ORANGE?**

Coding COLOURFUL confusion

Red

Blue

Green

Pink

Black

Yellow

Orange

Do you like a challenge? I hardly dare ask, do you know your colours? Hopefully, YES!

But then what if I swopped them all about and then asked which one you think it is?

You may 'guess' right, but usually most players get it totally wrong! Even if you cannot see all the colours of the rainbow (I think there were seven, - when I last counted!), you can read and write such colours as 'Red', 'Green' and 'Orange' (before I came along and mixed them all up for you), - so be prepared to be confused - for fun of course. You know your colours!

This is my colour 'Mix-up-game'. It looks like a lot of code, so I have extended it over two more pages for you to code and play.

The Author (plays with colours!)

White

Purple

Is this **BROWN?**

Brown

The Colour Mix-up game!

This is the longest coding game in this book - so take care with the coding. I shall be showing you some advanced coding skills using 'Lists' in Scratch which store the 'real' colour as we try to make all the colours 'mixed-up'. That's the game we are about to make...

Let's get coding...

Toucan code block part (A)

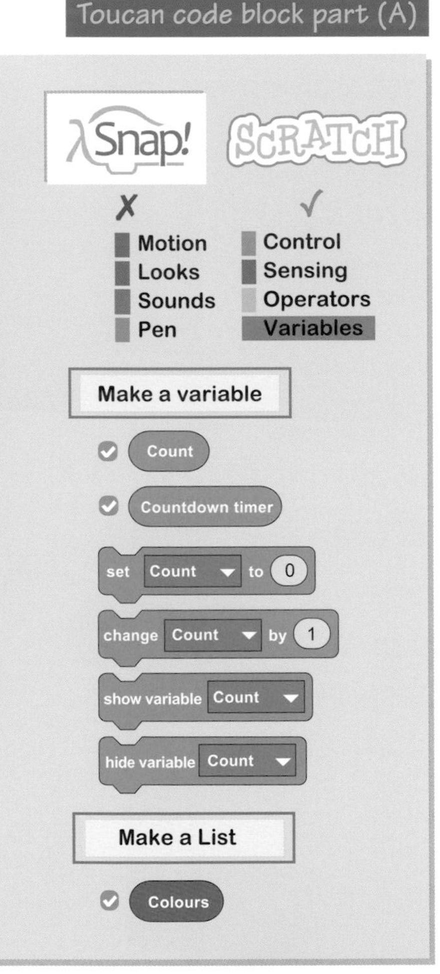


```
when [flag] clicked
go to x: -142 y: 42
switch costume to toucan-a
set Countdown timer to 45
set Count to 1
say There are ten COLOURS to spot, ready? for 3 seconds
change y by -100
forever
    switch costume to toucan-c
    move 30 steps
    ask What does the word say above...? and wait
    if answer = item Count of Colours then
        say Correct! for 1 seconds
        change Count by 1
    else
        think hmm...I don't think so! for 1 seconds
        change Count by 1
    broadcast next word colour
```

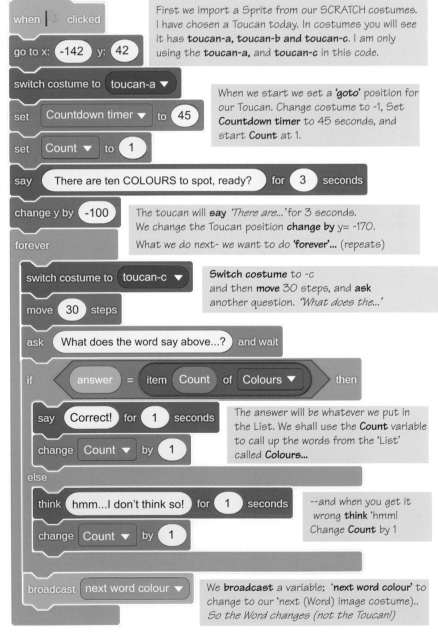

First we import a Sprite from our SCRATCH costumes. I have chosen a Toucan today. In costumes you will see it has **toucan-a, toucan-b and toucan-c**. I am only using the **toucan-a,** and **toucan-c** in this code.

When we start we set a **'goto'** position for our Toucan. Change costume to -1, Set **Countdown timer** to 45 seconds, and start **Count** at 1.

The toucan will **say** *'There are...'* for 3 seconds.
We change the Toucan position **change by** y= -170.
What we do next- we want to do **'forever'...** (repeats)

Switch costume to -c
and then **move** 30 steps, and **ask** another question. *'What does the...'*

The answer will be whatever we put in the List. We shall use the **Count** variable to call up the words from the 'List' called **Colours...**

--and when you get it wrong **think** 'hmm! Change **Count** by 1

We **broadcast** a variable; **'next word colour'** to change to our 'next (Word) image costume)..
So the Word changes (not the Toucan!)

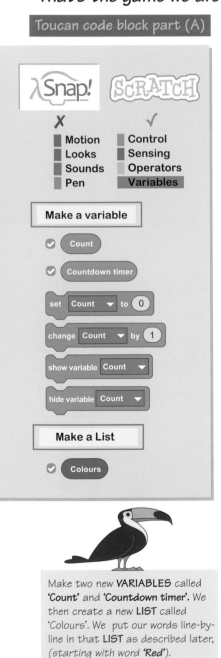

Make two new **VARIABLES** called **'Count'** and **'Countdown timer'.** We then create a new **LIST** called 'Colours'. We put our words line-by-line in that **LIST** as described later, (starting with word **'Red'**).

Note: This is code (part A) for Toucan sprite! See also next page - part [B].

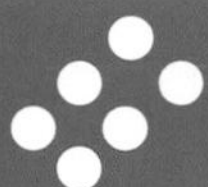

The Colour Mix-up game!

This page continues from the previous page... It is extended as there are two parts to the Toucan Sprite and another for Words Sprite....

WORDS: Costume Sprites:

Make a NEW sprite called 'Words' with TEN costumes. Each Costume has one BIG word on it the first being 'Red'. Choose a big bold Typeface for your first costume. To make new costumes (changing the Words each time to another colour), simply duplicate (right-click) the costume (not the Sprite itself) until you have TEN costumes.

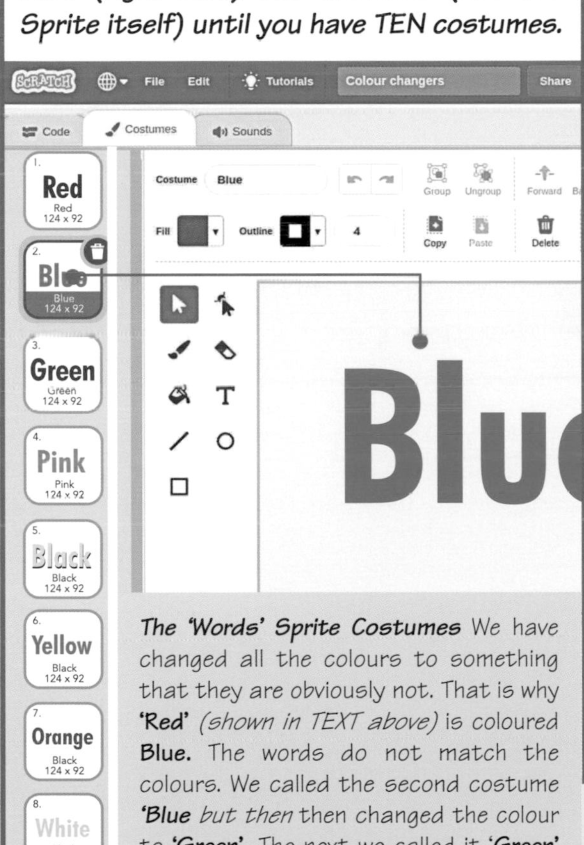

File
Edit
Tutorials
Colour changers
Share
Code
Costumes
Sounds
Red
Blue
Green
Pink
Black
Yellow
Orange
White
Purple
Costume
Fill
Outline
Group
Ungroup
Forward
Copy
Paste
Delete
Blue

The 'Words' Sprite Costumes We have changed all the colours to something that they are obviously not. That is why **'Red'** *(shown in TEXT above)* is coloured **Blue.** The words do not match the colours. We called the second costume **'Blue** *but then* then changed the colour to **'Green'**. The next we called it **'Green'** etc.. This Sprite has TEN costumes. They are all in colour sequence: ***Red, Blue, Green, Pink, Black, Yellow, Orange, White, Purple and Brown.*** In that same order top to bottom *(as shown left). Do NOT change this costume order.*

Toucan code block part (B)

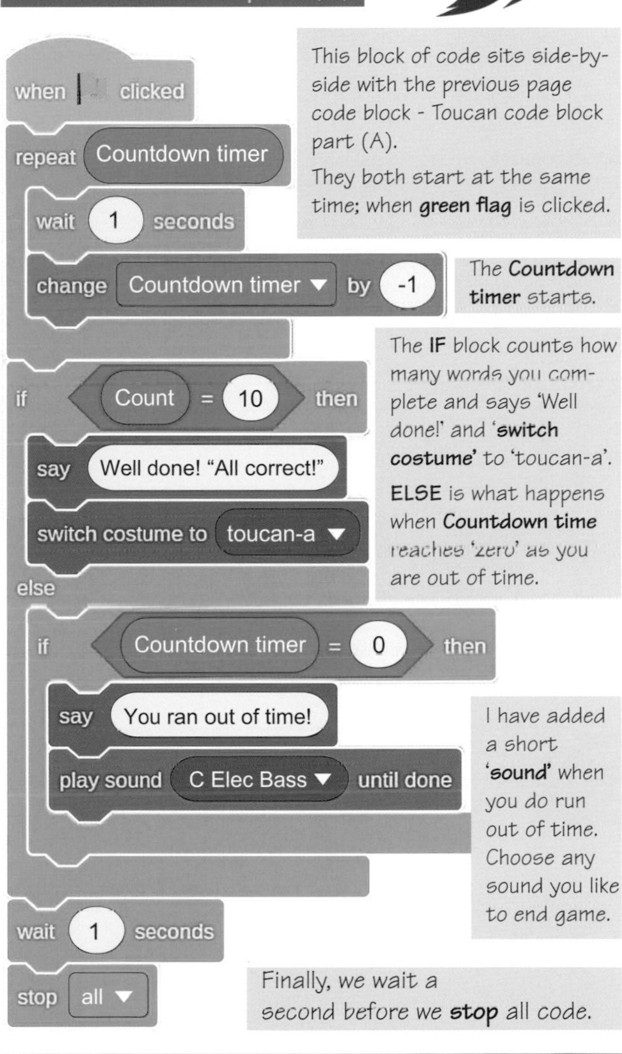

when clicked
repeat Countdown timer
wait 1 seconds
change Countdown timer by -1
if Count = 10 then
say Well done! "All correct!"
switch costume to toucan-a
else
if Countdown timer = 0 then
say You ran out of time!
play sound C Elec Bass until done
wait 1 seconds
stop all
This block of code sits side-by-side with the previous page code block - Toucan code block part (A).
They both start at the same time; when **green flag** is clicked.
The **Countdown timer** starts.
The **IF** block counts how many words you complete and says 'Well done!' and **'switch costume'** to 'toucan-a'.
ELSE is what happens when **Countdown time** reaches 'zero' as you are out of time.
I have added a short **'sound'** when you do run out of time. Choose any sound you like to end game.
Finally, we wait a second before we **stop** all code.

Note: *To get the* **'Words'** *in costumes to change automatically we need to do TWO things at once.... Finally add the last two code blocks (shown below including* ***'broadcast'*** *called* ***'next-word-colour'****, to the* **'Words'** *sprite. Switch costume to* **'Red'**.

when I receive next word colour
next costume
when clicked
switch costume to Red

The Colour Mix-up game!

We are nearly finished... just one more thing to do, it won't work until we have filled in our List of Colours. Find the List on the screen in Scratch and click on the little [+] symbol and enter carefully each word in turn. I mean be 'really careful' here as it's text line-by-line you enter, the exact words (not colours) that you have made already. Your list should look identical to the one shown below called 'Colours'.

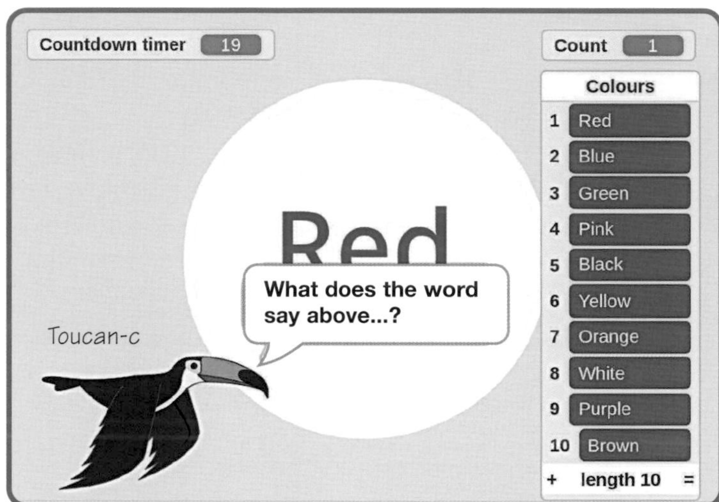

I have *imported* a 'background image to make it look nicer. You will find the exact same image in the SCRATCH 3 backgrounds library, along with many others to choose from.

In our List *'Colours'* we should have in sequence the following: **(1) Red, (2) Blue, (3) Green, (4) Pink, (5) Black, (6) Yellow, (7) Orange, (8) White, (8) Purple and (10) Brown.** It's important that you don't change the sequence of the words in the list.

The Words in our List *(shown left)* are to match the 'Word' *(as images)* we made as Sprite costumes. List and Costumes need to be in exactly the same order to make our game work.

Toucan-b Toucan-a

Lets go over what Sprites you should have right now...

One is a Toucan import (with three costumes) and the other is a Sprite of 'Words' *(which has ten costumes - showing one word each - all showing a different colour word)*. You should have just Two Sprites - as shown below.

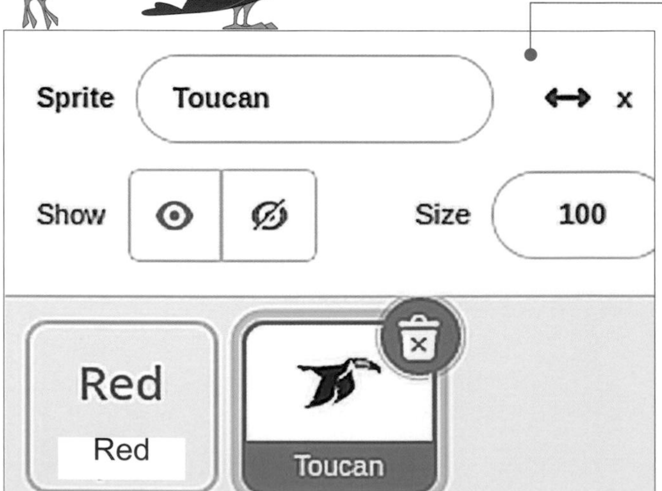

Game complete! The instructions to play the game are *(when Toucan speaks)* then **'answer'** *(type in)* what you think the colour is on the **IMAGE** shown on screen. You should always answer 'Red' *(for word 'Red')* even if the colour shown is Blue. The **Countdown timer** is there to count down from **45** seconds, but you can change that if you wish. To answer all ten questions correctly in 45 seconds is much harder than you think!

As in all the books twenty projects we have a **Project RESORCES** *page to download all projects (complete) in either Snap!, Scratch (created in both the formats with live online examples). We encourage children to try and build all book projects for a* **'hands-on'** *experience.*

Python: Colour Mix-up game!

We can create the same Colour 'Mix-up game' in Python. But we will take it one stage further by making the game into a window 'app' that pops-up on your screen using something called TK (which is a module available in Thonny when we write the code). It makes a very nice window for this game to play.

(Start of code) - type in the code in BLACK as shown. Ignore '#' marks are for code COMMENTS only.

```
# Guess the Colours!  Let's Get Coding book project

import tkinter  # This creates the nice pop-up window you see on screen...
import random  # Make all colours a random choice, based on;

# Colours we will be using in sequence; include
colours = ['Red','Blue','Green','Pink','Black','Yellow','Orange','White','Purple','Brown']
score=0 # Start score at zero
timeleft=45 # Countdown timer (45 seconds)

# The function that will start the game and sets Countdown timer (from 45 seconds)
def startGame(event):
•••• if timeleft == 45:
•••• •••• countdown()

•••• nextColour() # Choosing next colour in (random) list of Colours above
# Defining what 'nextcolor' should do (function) next colour
def nextColour():

     # Add global 'score' and check 'timeleft'
•••• global score
•••• global timeleft

     # if and when you run out of time...
•••• if timeleft > 0:

          # In the meantime check text entry...and wait
•••• •••• input_text.focus_set()

          # if and when colour typed is equal to the colour of the text...
•••• •••• if input_text.get().lower() == colours[1].lower():
          # Add one to the global score.
•••• •••• score += 1

          # Clear text for next entry....
•••• •••• input_text.delete(0, tkinter.END)
          # Random shuffle of the list of colours
•••• •••• random.shuffle(colours)
          # Make a random colour value of the text shown
•••• •••• label.config(fg=str(colours[1]), text=str(colours[0]))
          # Make update of the score so far...
•••• •••• scoreLabel.config(text="Score: " + str(score))

# Countdown timer does this function.
def countdown():

# (cont...)
```

•••• What are these dots for?
= FOUR character spaces
Don't use the TAB key!

45

Red | Blue | Green | Pink | Black | White

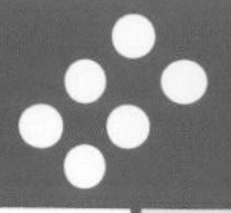

Python: Colour Mix-up game!

Red | Blue | Green | Pink | Black | White

```
# (cont...)

    # Show time left to play...
•••• global timeleft

    # When game is in play
•••• if timeleft > 0:
        # Reduce time by 1 second
•••• •••• timeleft -= 1
        # Change the text line to read time left
•••• •••• timeLabel.config(text="Time you have left: " + str(timeleft))
        # Repeat this function after 1 second as (1000 millisecond = 1 second)
•••• timeLabel.after(1000, countdown)

# Create the TK window (basic TK Set-up)
root = tkinter.Tk()
# Set the title on the window
root.title("Name the 10 Colours!")
# Set the size of the TK window
root.geometry("400x300")

# Make on screen instructions and set size of label in TK
instructions = tkinter.Label(root, text="State the COLOUR and not the word!", font=('Arial', 12))
instructions.pack()

# Add to instructions on new line and set size in TK
scoreLabel = tkinter.Label(root, text=" Press [Enter] to start game and countdown", font=('Arial', 10))
scoreLabel.pack()

# Add a time label on a new line and set size in TK
timeLabel = tkinter.Label(root, text="Time remaining: " + str(timeleft), font=('Arial', 12))
timeLabel.pack()

# Add a display label of the colour words shown (large size) in TK
label = tkinter.Label(root, font=('Arial', 60))
label.pack()

# Make a text entry box for typing in colours (input texts) as answer in TK
input_text = tkinter.Entry(root)

# Start the game when - enter - key is pressed
root.bind('<Return>', startGame)
input_text.pack()

# Input (start and answer session)
input_text.focus_set()

# Start the GUI (Graphical User Interface) for TK
root.mainloop()


# [End of coding] - remember you DON'T have to type any of my comments in Blue!!
```

Note: Python ignores spaces between lines of code and hashes (#). Don't ignore any commas, dashes or underlines '_' characters, brackets or colons (:). Check your code for missing parts, before play!

For our TK project we are using **'Arial'**. But if your system does not have the **'Arial'** display typeface, try another font name on your computer, such as **'Helvetica'**.

•••• What are these dots for?
= FOUR character spaces
Don't use the TAB key!

Note: This code uses a module called TK which is loaded automatically in the background. TK is a really useful Python module, used by many Python projects to call up a (pop-up) Window and buttons that can be programmed and coloured. For simplicity we are using the bare essentials to get you up and running here. For ease of use please use Thonny to run your code. Thonny will recognise TK and and run the program in a 'pop-up' window.

Next: Flying a model Aeroplane in 3D!

20

Coding to FLY an aeroplane!

We shall be trying to do the impossible and try to fly a plane in SCRATCH in 3D.

I hope you have your pilot's license ready as we shall be flying an old fashioned wooden plane held together with bits-of-string and a small pot of green paint and a lot of skill...

This is all possible thanks to SKETCH-UP* which allows us to draw in 3D -if you're able. If not - then I have just the plane for you - ready and waiting...!

I wish this was my idea, but I have to admit another (UK) Primary school teacher* who used it for (3D) Cars and I have adapted it here for our aeroplane. Crash Helmets on!

The Author (likes making 3D models)

* SketchUp is a 3D modelling program used by Architects and 3D model makers.

For Project credits and key information see this book's project RESOURCES page.

Flying a model Aeroplane in 3D!

This is a nice challenge for you to think in 3D. There is a drawing program called SketchUp! which allows you to make a 3D model such as this model aeroplane. Creating a 3D model is beyond the instructions in this book, but I have made one for you, to get started in Scratch and start coding.

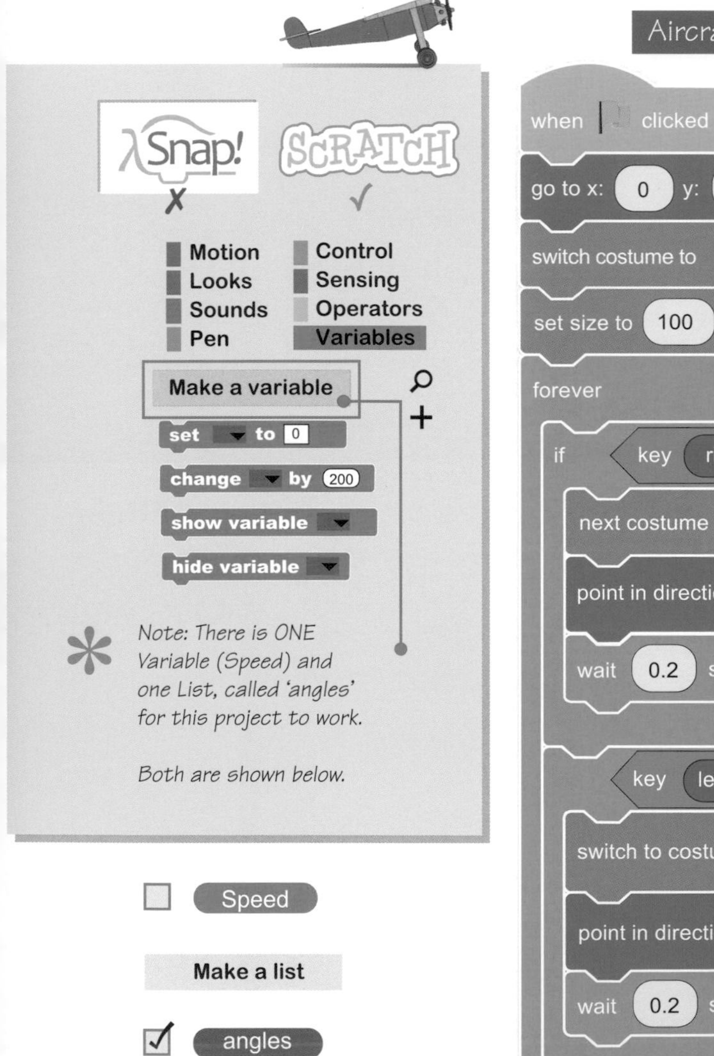

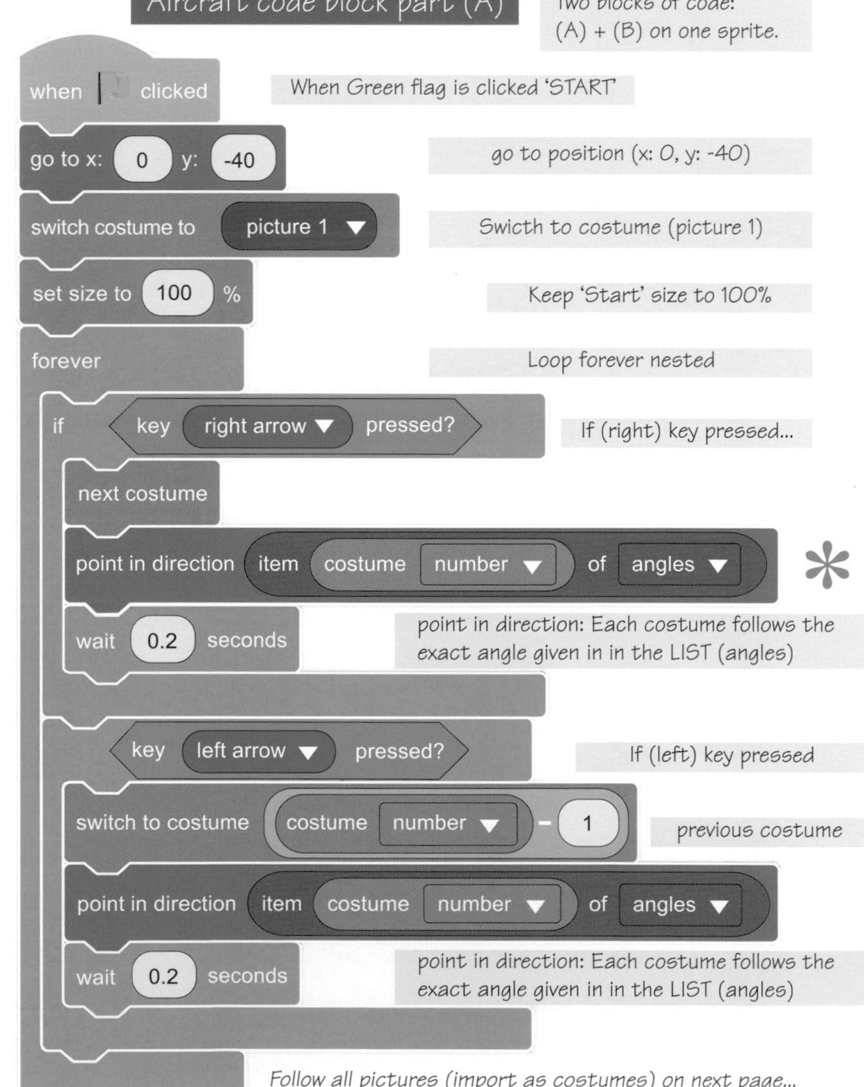

Follow all pictures (import as costumes) on next page...

How it works!

There is only one sprite on this project but it has eight costumes. Each aeroplane costume is a sequence of images. When you click the 'left' or 'right' keys it changes the costume to show the next image which is linked to the 'angle' shown on the (List) in degrees. To create the impression of depth the second block of code (*over page*) makes the aircraft smaller as it travels (*changes in Speed*) into the distance using the 'up' and 'down' keys. Together they give the impression of flying a toy aircraft in a 3D space.

Flying a model Aeroplane in 3D!

This page continues from the previous page... It is extended as there are two blocks of code with EIGHT costumes (to import) for your Aeroplane to fly!

The code block *(shown below)* - block part **(B)** changes the *(speed)* of the airplane and its size. So it gets slower the further away it goes and speeds up when it gets closer. The **'up'** and **'down'** keys are linked to the ***'y position'*** of the airplane. Maths is used to calculate the size and speed.

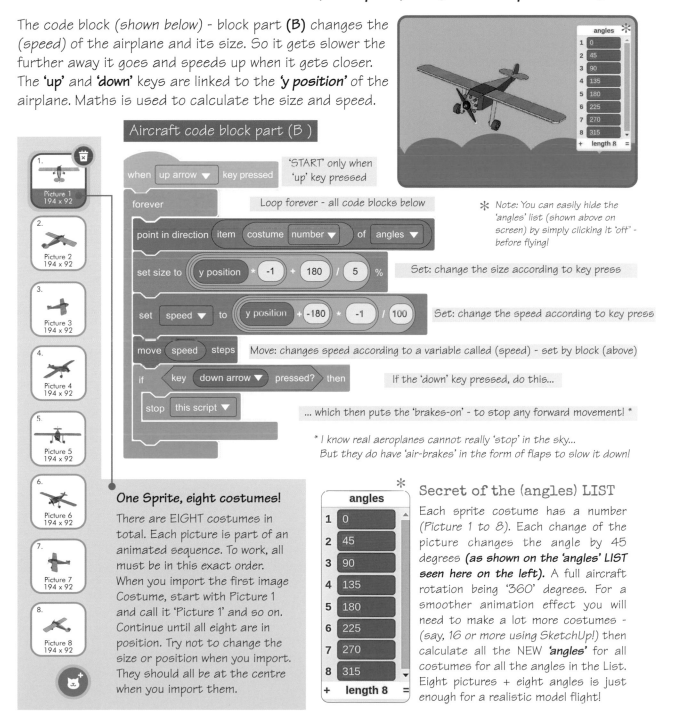

Aircraft code block part (B)

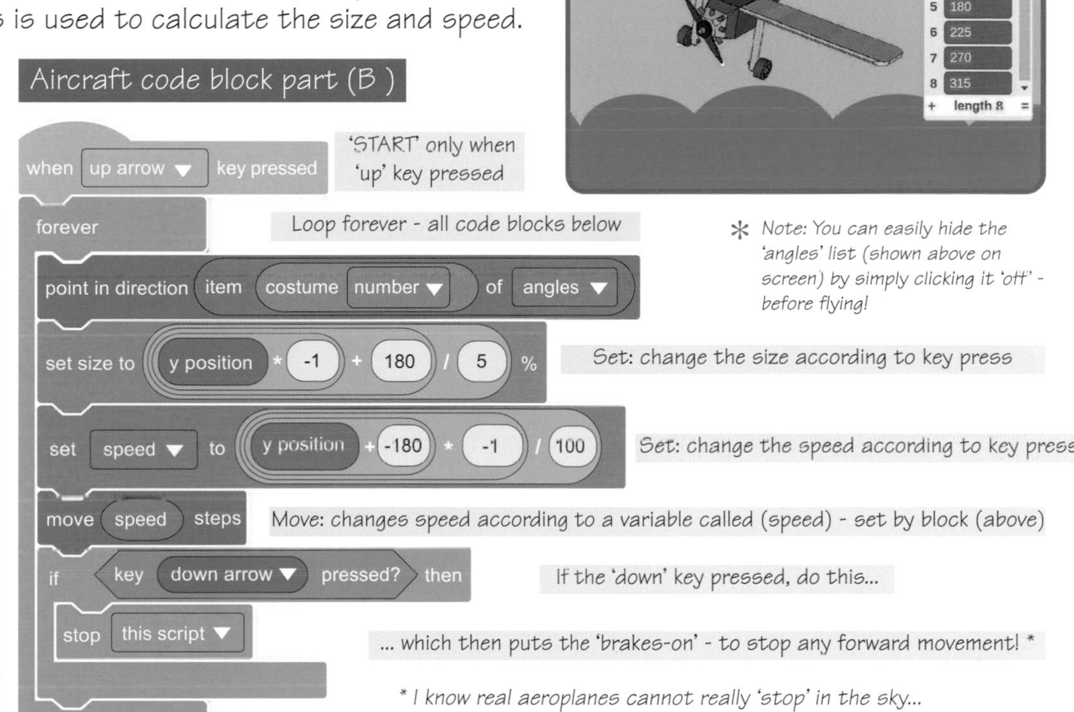

when up arrow key pressed
'START' only when 'up' key pressed
forever
Loop forever - all code blocks below
point in direction item costume number of angles
set size to y position * -1 + 180 / 5 %
Set: change the size according to key press
set speed to y position + -180 * -1 / 100
Set: change the speed according to key press
move speed steps
Move: changes speed according to a variable called (speed) - set by block (above)
if key down arrow pressed? then
If the 'down' key pressed, do this...
stop this script
... which then puts the 'brakes-on' - to stop any forward movement! *

** Note: You can easily hide the 'angles' list (shown above on screen) by simply clicking it 'off' - before flying!*

** I know real aeroplanes cannot really 'stop' in the sky... But they do have 'air-brakes' in the form of flaps to slow it down!*

1. Picture 1 194 x 92
2. Picture 2 194 x 92
3. Picture 3 194 x 92
4. Picture 4 194 x 92
5. Picture 5 194 x 92
6. Picture 6 194 x 92
7. Picture 7 194 x 92
8. Picture 8 194 x 92

One Sprite, eight costumes!

There are EIGHT costumes in total. Each picture is part of an animated sequence. To work, all must be in this exact order. When you import the first image Costume, start with Picture 1 and call it 'Picture 1' and so on. Continue until all eight are in position. Try not to change the size or position when you import. They should all be at the centre when you import them.

	angles
1	0
2	45
3	90
4	135
5	180
6	225
7	270
8	315
+	length 8

Secret of the (angles) LIST

Each sprite costume has a number *(Picture 1 to 8)*. Each change of the picture changes the angle by 45 degrees ***(as shown on the 'angles' LIST seen here on the left).*** A full aircraft rotation being '360' degrees. For a smoother animation effect you will need to make a lot more costumes - *(say, 16 or more using SketchUp!)* then calculate all the NEW ***'angles'*** for all costumes for all the angles in the List. Eight pictures + eight angles is just enough for a realistic model flight!

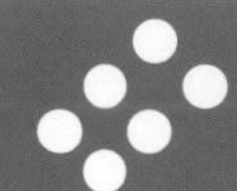

Python: Aeroplane code

This is the simplified version of Aeroplane code found overleaf, not a flight simulator as the code would run to many hundreds of lines of code. But it does give you the basic movements to fly an aeroplane and land it.

(Start of code) - type in the code in BLACK as shown. Ignore '#' marks are for code COMMENTS only.

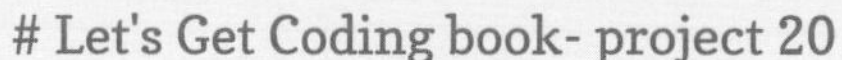

```
# Let's Get Coding book- project 20
# When using THONNY and need to instal the pygame module to play.
# First: 'To install PYGAME module see the book's project RESOURCES on page 136

import pygame
from pygame.locals import *
import time
import math

# Initialise graphics and set up tracking of player (airplane) and (airport) map track.
pygame.init()
track = pygame.image.load("runway.png") # Runway image (in same directory)
player = pygame.image.load("airplane.png") # Aeroplane image (in same directory)
screen = pygame.display.set_mode((800,600)) # Screen is 800 wide by 600 pixels
trackx= 0
tracky= -1000
xpos = 300 # Start x position for our aeroplane
ypos = 300 # Start y position for our aeroplane
keys=[False,False,False,False]
direction = 90 # Direct our aeroplane upwards to start.
forward = 0 # Speed = 0  (unless 'up' key pressed)

running = 1
while running: # set caption title + background colour
•••• pygame.display.set_caption('Fly an aeroplane - (use the arrow keys!)') # The Title
•••• screen.fill((50,143,56)) # This RGB colour (50,143,56 is set to a dark green).

    # If an Arrow key is pressed, do this:
•••• if keys[0]==True:
•••• •••• direction+= 2 # When pressed turn + 2 degrees
•••• if keys[1]==True:
•••• •••• direction-= 2 # When pressed turn - 2 degrees
•••• if keys[2]==True:
•••• •••• forward-= 0.2 # When pressed speed is - 0.2 points
•••• if keys[3]==True and forward <= 0:
•••• •••• forward+= 0.2 # When pressed speed is + 0.2 points
```

Note: We do not need to import a MATHS or TIME module, as it is pre-installed by default in THONNY ready for us to run our code.

This PYGAME project needs to import a module in THONNY. See (Menu) TOOLS, 'click' on MANAGE PACKAGER, to install module. Type 'pygame' in the SEARCH function and it will find it for you, then just click INSTALL. Job done!

•••• What are these dots for?
= FOUR character spaces
Don't use the TAB key!

(cont...) see next page...

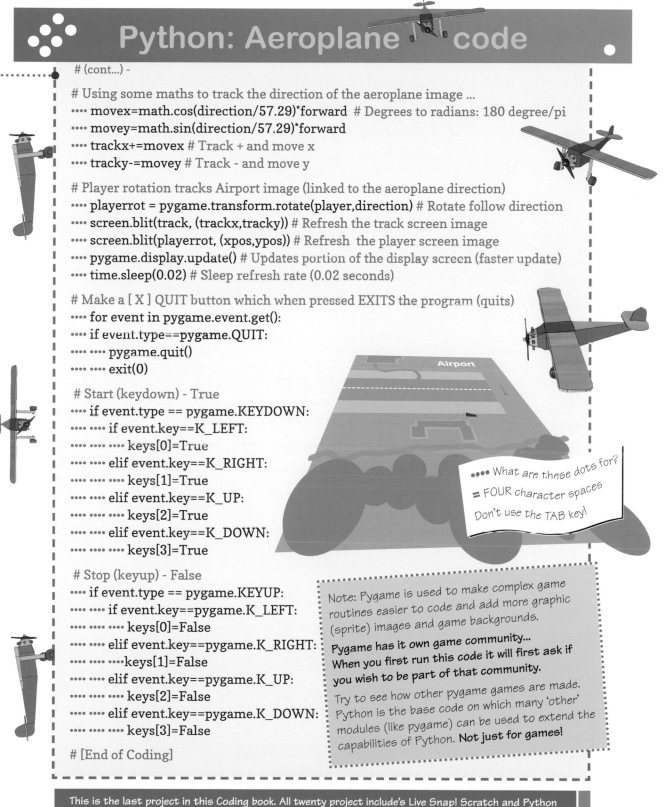

Python: Aeroplane code

```
# (cont...) -

# Using some maths to track the direction of the aeroplane image ...
···· movex=math.cos(direction/57.29)*forward # Degrees to radians: 180 degree/pi
···· movey=math.sin(direction/57.29)*forward
···· trackx+=movex # Track + and move x
···· tracky-=movey # Track - and move y

# Player rotation tracks Airport image (linked to the aeroplane direction)
···· playerrot = pygame.transform.rotate(player,direction) # Rotate follow direction
···· screen.blit(track, (trackx,tracky)) # Refresh the track screen image
···· screen.blit(playerrot, (xpos,ypos)) # Refresh  the player screen image
···· pygame.display.update() # Updates portion of the display screen (faster update)
···· time.sleep(0.02) # Sleep refresh rate (0.02 seconds)

# Make a [ X ] QUIT button which when pressed EXITS the program (quits)
···· for event in pygame.event.get():
···· if event.type==pygame.QUIT:
···· ···· pygame.quit()
···· ···· exit(0)

 # Start (keydown) - True
···· if event.type == pygame.KEYDOWN:
···· ···· if event.key==K_LEFT:
···· ···· ···· keys[0]=True
···· ···· elif event.key==K_RIGHT:
···· ···· ···· keys[1]=True
···· ···· elif event.key==K_UP:
···· ···· ···· keys[2]=True
···· ···· elif event.key==K_DOWN:
···· ···· ···· keys[3]=True

 # Stop (keyup) - False
···· if event.type == pygame.KEYUP:
···· ···· if event.key==pygame.K_LEFT:
···· ···· ···· keys[0]=False
···· ···· elif event.key==pygame.K_RIGHT:
···· ···· ····keys[1]=False
···· ···· elif event.key==pygame.K_UP:
···· ···· ···· keys[2]=False
···· ···· elif event.key==pygame.K_DOWN:
···· ···· ···· keys[3]=False

# [End of Coding]
```

···· What are these dots for?
= FOUR character spaces
Don't use the TAB key!

Note: Pygame is used to make complex game routines easier to code and add more graphic (sprite) images and game backgrounds.

Pygame has it own game community... When you first run this code it will first ask if you wish to be part of that community.

Try to see how other pygame games are made. Python is the base code on which many 'other' modules (like pygame) can be used to extend the capabilities of Python. **Not just for games!**

This is the last project in this Coding book. All twenty project include's Live Snap! Scratch and Python links with coding examples which can found in the project RESOURCES pages starting on page 99...

Options to try:

There are only a few options to play with when using Scratch block coding on this aeroplane project. As this involves importing or drawing in 3D, which you may want to avoid. Start by using the images found in project RESOURCES.

(1) You can change the **background costume** *to this project. Draw your own or import a background. We imported a simple Scratch costume from the costume library.*

(2) The Aircraft images are 3D models based on SketchUp!! (a 3d modelling software). I have taken various views by rotating the model on screen by (about) 45 degrees. I used a screen capture to create each image (eight in total). But it can take skill and time to remove the white background on each image and re-save as 'gif' or 'png' format.

SketchUp! is very good (at 3D models) but beyond the scope of this code book.

But you can still try-out SketchUp! here: https://sketchup.com

All images are provided for this project. Find all the AIRCRAFT images in the book's Project RESOURCES section. Download and import each image as (one sprite) costume sequence. You will also need to import a LIST called 'angles' as shown our previous page 'Secret of the angles LIST'. Alternatively Type in each of the numbers exactly (which are degrees in rotation) as shown in the LIST (see page 95).

> Note: This project will work in Scratch 1.4, Scratch 2 and you may have some difficulty in Scratch 3. This is due to the new way Scratch 3 has hidden some costume function's, one of those is finding the correct Costume number to apply correctly. This was tested on Scratch 1.4 or 2. Improvements both in Scratch 3 and Snap! should make this possible in future.

Python code is a little bit easier to use!

We are using just one of the Aircraft images *(there are eight images in total)*, see the book's project RESOURCES section and download them all. Including a custom drawn background image we are using for our AIRPORT.

This code is fully functioning in 2D but has limitations in 3D, so we are working on using just one image **(aircraft.png)** and using that to fly above our background scene, called AIRPORT. If you choose another aircraft *(one of eight pictures given)*, then you must rename that image to match *(in your own Python code)* and it must also be in the same directory *(folder)* as your existing background image link. Names in all code must match the names of images and must be in a linked directory for linked images to work, *(see my example below):*

Example:

```
track = pygame.image.load("runway.png") # Runway image - (in the same directory )
player = pygame.image.load("airplane.png") # Airplane image - (in the same directory )
```

Other fairly simple Python code changes are to: Change the Background colour *(that which borders the imported background image), see this code line:* **screen.fill((50,143,56))**. Changing the RGB values of **50,143,136**, changes the colour. Experiment! and see what works best for the image imported. Other RGB colour values can be used;

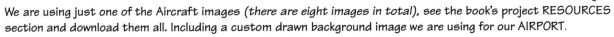

https://rapidtables.com/web/color/RGB_Color.html

As you can see the background colour is that *'behind'* the *(imported)* background image we are using. So I matched the RGB colour to that of my AIRPORT drawing so you would not see the *'edge'* when you fly over the image border.

For additional block and Python coding for this project see project RESOURCES on page 132

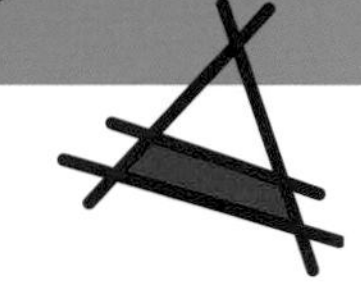

Project RESOURCES:

Using project RESOURCES

Every page of this book has a PROJECT resource page for further information on all twenty projects with a download link.

All book projects are coded in Snap! or SCRATCH (or usually both). Python 3 code examples are matched (not identical) for each project with links to an example project.

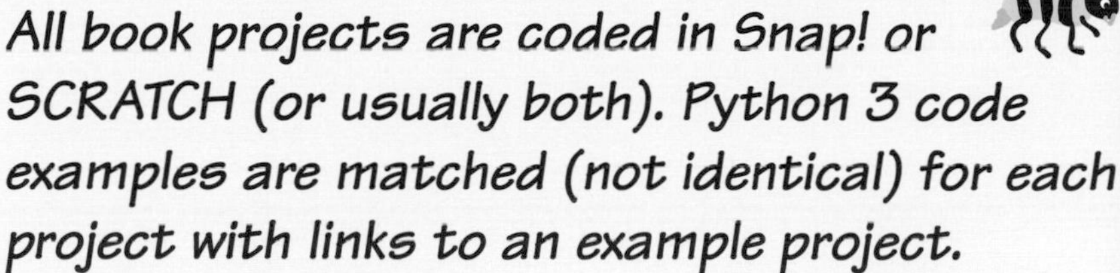

The aim of the book is to match Code with ability (or difficulty) of each project (which is NOT in any particular order but of variety.

The book's starter project in this book is a suggestion (it may not be ideal for the very young in starting out). Each Project is a education challenge based on ability.

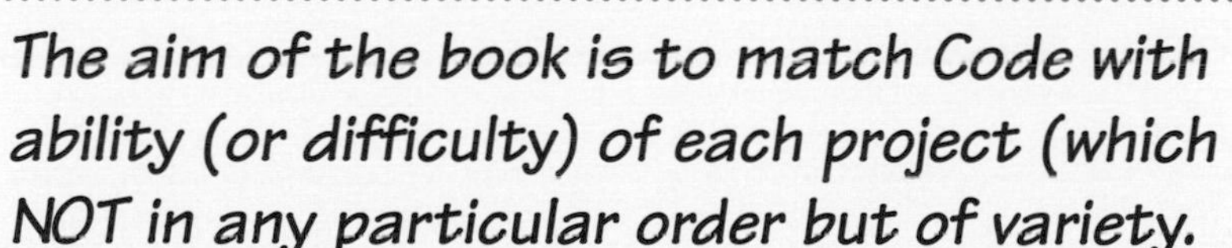

Each project has a secure project or link to an existing (ready made) project or resource.

1. Etch-A-Sketch
2. Pocket money
3. Miles-per-Gallon
4. Dinosaur's age
5. Shopping list
6. Random Star
7. Silly stories
8. Brain Quiz
9. Random Dice
10. Sprout Champ!
11. Morse-Code
12. Bouncing Turtles
13. Knitting patterns
14. Famous Five
15. Mirror reflections
16. Coding Polygons
17. Honey Bees
18. Noughts & Crosses
19. Colour Mix-Up
20. Flying an Aeroplane

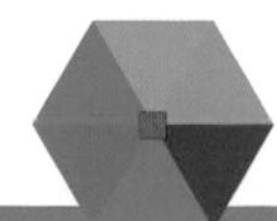

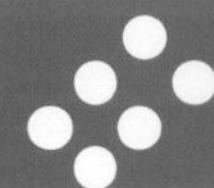

Project resources: (blocks + lists)

Basic blocks in Snap! and Scratch

This Let's Get Coding block uses the standard blocks for SCRATCH 2 and 3 that appear under 'Events' or 'Control' headings. For Snap! and SCRATCH 1.4 , both are found under the 'Control' heading. Both share the standard colour coding whichever you decide to follow.

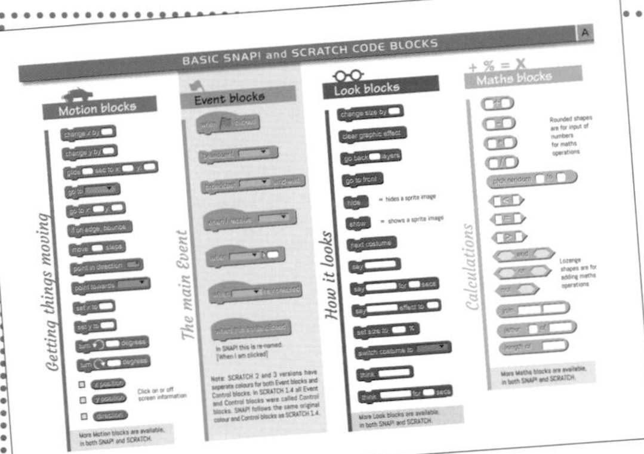

As shown on pages 8 to 9 - are the standard Snap! and Scratch blocks that can be used across both applications.

All blocks follow the same colour and function across Snap! and SCRATCH. But 'Lists' (see below) do differ. This book enables both to be used easily in class or computer club without technical conversion problems. Children will easily recognise all block functions by colour and shape.

<< See pages 8 and 9 for a colour chart of blocks.

Shown: Standard blocks in Event or Control panel in both Snap! and SCRATCH are totally interchangeable. Both share a common (or similar colour block colour), and work much the same way in all our code block projects.

NOTE: There is a difference in how Snap! lists work. Snap! has a totally different LIST creation scheme, which can work in the same way as Scratch, - but it is not obvious how make a LIST easily. The information *(below)* will prepare you to change Scratch 'lists' - into Snap! 'lists' - for any of the projects using 'lists'. The author has decided that Scratch lists are easier than SNAP!, for most of the projects to suit the younger reader that may struggle with Lists. You can try it here!

Making Snap! 'list' blocks work:

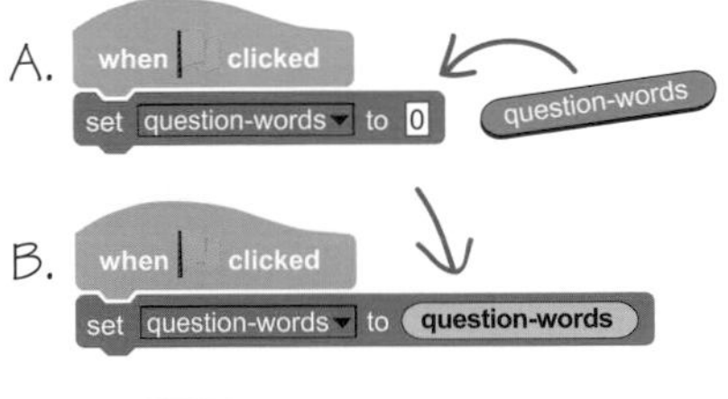

A. To create a Scratch-type list in Snap!, you must first create a variable and then set that (same name) variable to be the list. See: **[question-words].** Start with a variable block.

B. Using the same 'set' VARIABLE block re-assign that name you have just created and insert a new block, after the word 'to' called **[question-words].** As shown.

C. Duplicate B *(right-click on mouse)* add your **'list'** as shown.

Used only for making a Scratch style lists in Snap! - For SCRATCH follow book projects.

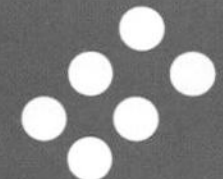

Project resources: (lists)

(2) Making the Snap! 'list' blocks work:

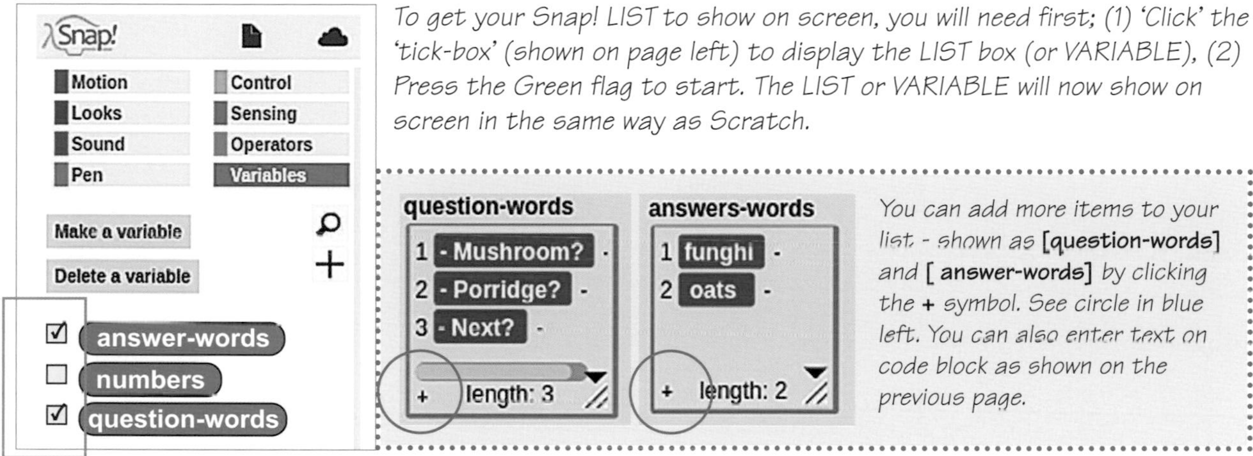

To get your Snap! LIST to show on screen, you will need first; (1) 'Click' the 'tick-box' (shown on page left) to display the LIST box (or VARIABLE), (2) Press the Green flag to start. The LIST or VARIABLE will now show on screen in the same way as Scratch.

You can add more items to your list - shown as **[question-words]** *and* **[answer-words]** *by clicking the* **+** *symbol. See circle in blue left. You can also enter text on code block as shown on the previous page.*

Example: Snap! list block code: Guessing game!

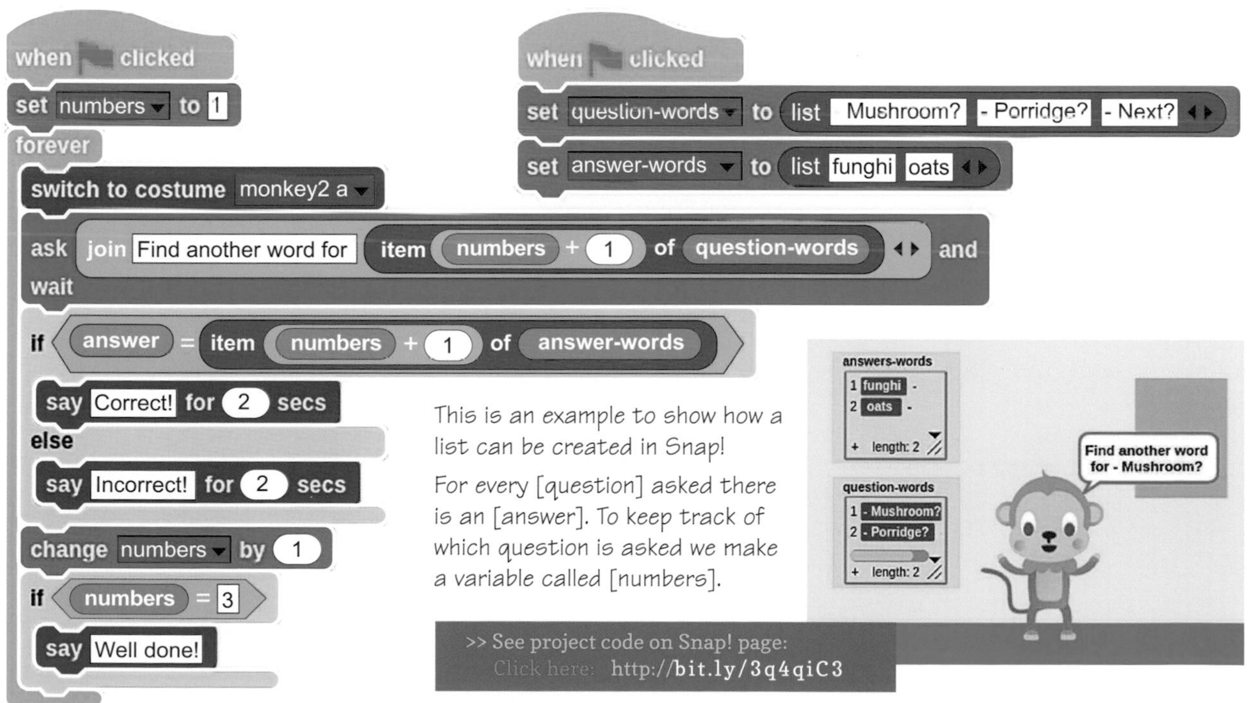

This is an example to show how a list can be created in Snap!

For every [question] asked there is an [answer]. To keep track of which question is asked we make a variable called [numbers].

>> See project code on Snap! page:
Click here: http://bit.ly/3q4qiC3

Scratch 1.4, Scratch 2 and Scratch 3 are all identical for creating a LIST so follow the project pages in this book and you cannot go wrong. In Snap! you may need a little practice first (this page example) to get any similar 'LISTS' working.

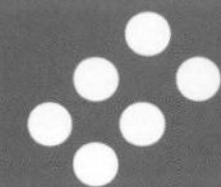

Project RESOURCES: (blocks)

READ ME!

The book's author avoids using technical coding terms for children. Only frequently used base functions are shown below..

Standard Snap! and Scratch code block:

Thread:	***A Thread:*** *allows all the blocks to run (execute the program). In Scratch or SNAP!, this is the green flag [START] button. A Thread is a sequence of code. Example shown:*	when clicked
Statement:	***A Statement:*** *is a command that tells the computer to 'do' something. In Scratch or Snap! any block which reads like a command, (which is called a statement). Example shown on right:*	go to x: y: say
Boolean Expression:	***A Boolean Expression:*** *is something that is either true or false. In Scratch or SNAP!, any block that has an elongated diamond shape is a BOOLEAN EXPRESSION. Example shown:*	mouse down ? = touching ?
Condition:	***A Condition:*** *is something that must be true in order for something to happen is called a CONDITION. In Scratch or SNAP!, any block whose label says IF, WHEN or UNTIL DONE is a condition on your code. Example shown:*	if then
Loop:	***A Loop:*** *can be either a forever, or a repeat, (or repeat until done). Example shown:*	forever
Control:	***A Control:*** *allows a set of blocks to run, change, or start the program. Scratch (2 and 3) has separate EVENTS and CONTROL blocks. Example shown:*	when this sprite clicked broadcast
Variable:	***A Variable:*** *is anything that changes (varies) in the program. When set as a VARIABLE, it can change the program in Scratch and Snap!. Example shown:*	set to 0 change by 200

Note: *Lists are created the same way as a Variable in Snap! Variables are assigned for numbers (and calculations) and Lists for any kind of words. Snap! Lists are constructed - as if they were a Variable. Scratch has a totally seperate 'list' button.*

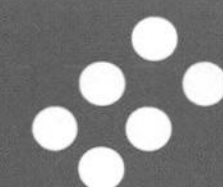

Project RESOURCES: (programs)

A brief introduction to the small (and large) differences in Snap! and Scratch coding platforms, both available free online.

Snap! and Scratch - easy block coding!

This is not a detailed technical book ON BLOCK CODING that includes ANY custom blocks *(now appearing in Snap! and Scratch)* as 'EXTRAS' OR 'ADDITIONAL CUSTOM BLOCKS'. However it's worth noting that such blocks are useful for some other future projects we may make in Snap! and Scratch. The author has made the same code available on all platforms you may use so you can use any computer and you can choose Snap! or Scratch *(or both)* as we progress on projects.

Scratch has 3 working (app*) versions!

Depending on your computer, earlier versions of Scratch (1.4) are ideal for small or old computers and very young children. Scratch 2 is available on the raspberry pi mini computer, whilst all modern computers, can also run Snap! and Scratch 3 on a *Chrome based browser, available for any computer Pi, Mac, Windows, and any Linux version you can think of, including all Google Chromebooks using Android os.*

Main Scratch differences...

(a) SCRATCH 3 is a very different layout to earlier versions and can lead to confusion, even though it offers many enhancements, custom blocks and huge pictorial library with sound effects. It is the front runner. Scr atch 2 and 3 are online but there is also a ***'stand-alone'*** install options for Scratch 2 and 3 available on the raspberry pi.

(b) SCRATCH 1.4 is still popular for very young children with restricted internet access. The original version is still a popular choice on lower spec computers. Snap! is very much based on the original look, feel and layout of the Scratch 1.4.

All versions of Scratch (1.4, version 2 and new version 3) are built-in to any version of the raspberry pi mini-computer (currently at the 'BUSTER' version os). Any book project you have found in this book - can also be used online with Snap! (using any Chrome browser) as easily as you can in Scratch (any version of this application). *app = application

For (basic) Snap! try this video introduction.

https://bit.ly/2R2ByzO

For (basic) Scratch try this video overview:

https://bit.ly/2ImFNV3

READ ME!

Project 'file' formats used in book

(1) Snap! files are all '.xml' files (2) Scratch 1.4 files end in '.sb', Scratch 2 files end with 'sb2" and Scratch 3 files end with 'sb3'. (3) Python files end with '.py'. You can usually open Snap! files in your browser window (or import from Snap! application window). Scratch does not open previous Scratch versions, except that Scratch 3 can now open Scratch 2 files.

.sb3

Note: Scratch 1.4 (.sb) files can only be opened only by Scratch 1.4

Note: picture files that are used used in Snap! are in 'svg' *(Scalable vector format)* for best quality *(import)* or use Scratch for the 'png' format *(Portable Network Graphic)* which is a standard web format used for most *web pages*. Scratch costumes can be importes as 'png' files. All code available from our book project RESOURCES page.

Find: Bit.ly safe weblinks

Weblinks found in this Book are all linked via **Bit.ly** *(to shorten the long 'URL' - **U**nique **R**esource **L**ocation)*. The author uses **Dropbox.com** to store all the book's **'project RESOURCES'**. Coding files + web links are shortened using **Bit.ly** Explore the book's projects with **'LIVE'** links to examples made in **Snap!** and **Scratch 3** online. *(See bottom of this page)**.

Notes*: You do NOT need a password to download any project file. If a link fails to load then check the exact bit.ly link for a typing error. Bit.ly links with the CAPITAL letter 'O' and number 'O' (zero) or the lower case letter "L' (l) for "1" (number) as mixing the letter 'L" and "l" will cause an* ***'404'*** *error, which means' 'file-not-found' that will appear in your browser window.. (See bottom of this page for* ***bit.ly*** *links)*.*

.svg

Explore: project Dropbox links

All examples of Snap! , Scratch and Python code are served via Dropbox. **www.dropbox.com** We use Dropbox ***'file-sharing'*** to share code In Snap! and Scratch with Python 3 formats, for every project found in this book.

.png

** The **Let's Get Coding book** web-site has links to both Snap! and Scratch project files with LIVE coding examples to ALL projects!*

www.LetsGetCodingBook.co.uk/99.html

Project RESOURCES: projects

1

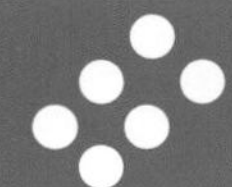

Etch-A-Sketch project

This project Etch-a-Sketch is an ideal starter project. It is very limited in that it can only go in four directions ***(North, South, East, West)***, and then only in a straight line. Just like the original ***'Etch-A-sketch'*** toy game, but ours is made in 4 colours. A huge improvement!

Etch-A-Sketch in Snap! and SCRATCH

If we start with the block coding *(use Snap! or SCRATCH any version)* we can make some fun adjustments. Simply by pressing the **[space-bar]** we can increase the thickness of the line each time (see page code). We can reset it back to zero when we press the Green start button again.

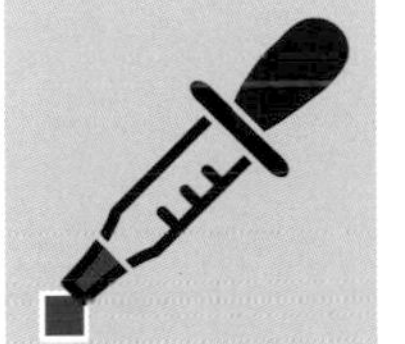

Use the eye-dropper on screen (SNAP!) or choose a colour swatch (Scratch)

How to change Snap! and Scratch

Find colours by using the 'eye-dropper' or pen colour block :

We can add or change colours by using the 'eye-dropper' and click on a new colour easily ***(drag the eye-dropper to a colour on screen)*** grab that colour and it will then appear in the colour well of your 'pen' tool. This may need some practice and a demonstration for children to use.

Project 'Live' weblinks:

This project appears currently on SNAP!:

https://bit.ly/305PqNU

This project also appears currently on Scratch:

https://bit.ly/38aNbxL

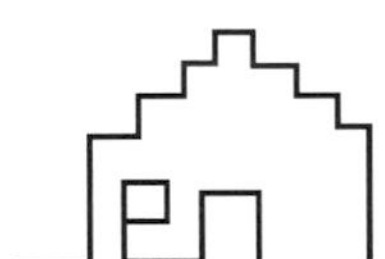

Download the entire coded project:

This project is now available for download: *(SNAP!, Scratch and Python)*..

https://bit.ly/2Hjt6KE

Note: All the book's twenty project files are saved in a 'zip' file format which is a safe way to send files from our Library which are held on a DropBox account. We have tested them on Windows, Mac and Linux which includes the latest Raspberry pi Mini computer using Chrome browser and Thonny.

Project RESOURCES: projects

READ ME!

Python 3

Getting Python code running:

All the projects in this book are tested on THONNY *(which is pre-installed on the raspberry pi mini computer)* as well as Linux, Mac and Windows or THONNY which are all installable on a basic Laptop. But in school it's better to be prepared for a **'Plan B'** in the case of no Python installed...

For Plan B: (use Trinket)

If and when no THONNY installed, use Trinket. Trinket is an on-line IDE* Ideal for some classrooms that have less than the ideal Python 3 installations, there is an easy online alternative called Trinket.* However it is not a direct replacement for THONNY for the projects found in this book require THONNY. ***IDE = Integrated Development Environment** *(a common acronym, there are several others IDE's in various flavours)*. I recommend THONNY as its pre-installed on the raspberry pi mini computer and is the easiest for children to learn compared to many others Python ***(IDE)*** editors. TRINKET will work using a standard Chrome browser found on most modern computers. No installation required. *Trinket is unable to install Python modules, as you would in THONNY.*

www.trinket.io

The *(optional)* Free Trinket tutorials *(below)* are well worth exploring. I have used in schools to reinforce the concept of block coding and then convert to Python to run in a similar way. This helps introduce Python 'Turtle graphics' . It can easily follow-on from the book's 'Etch-A-Sketch' first project. It is a good primer on how Turtle graphics work's in Python. Young coders can simply follow *(safely)* the simple links on each page *(it may take longer than an hour in practice as Video's are sometimes linked along with practice sessions)*. In Trinket 'The Turtle' is called 'Tina' for your Turtle graphics. Unfortunately in Python, there is no actual Pencil costume to import, as easily as a turtle!.

Trinket HOUR-of-CODE

BASIC Python tutorials can be found here: An 'Hour-of-code' is our highly recommended intoduction on what is a good starter code tutorial.

https://bit.ly/3iCODEv8

Note: This does not replace THONNY as many Python modules (such as TK) will not work using such a free online tool. At some point you willl have to install THONNY!

Project RESOURCES: projects

Pocket money, savers and Spenders

In each project *(like this)* **I think it important that children try to 'type' code;** rather than just playing with my examples and then perhaps learn very little. Mistakes are to be expected in code and if a child is not making any mistakes, then perhaps you're either a very good teacher, or rather too good at covering up you're own mistakes. I often make mistakes when I go too fast, I may forget to explain why I put that block of code there and not elsewhere. A good example is in explaining where a VARIABLE should go; ***(Principal/Rate/Time and Interest)*** and how they are used, to calculate *(using VARIABLES to store memory calculations).*

Pocket money - live coding for Snap! (Simple + Compound versions)

https://bit.ly/3iVQk5Y

Pocket money - live coding for SCRATCH (Simple interest only)

https://bit.ly/3jV8Hzo

Pocket money - live coding for SCRATCH (Compound interest)

https://bit.ly/3mF9CyS

Code with (no options) but nuts.

In this short coding example, I have made no options, as it's learning basic Maths skills. I have shown a Squirrel as he is such a great '**saver**' *(of nuts)* for his (or her) winter-time siege. Both the Watermelon and Squirr el are both in the Snap! library and Scratch 'Costumes', easily used to illustrate or just to add interest. Money can be much more interesting when you don't have that much savings. Then just perhaps this money project, creates a little bit of interest *(pardon the pun).*

Download the entire coded project:

This project is now available for download: *(SNAP!, Scratch and Python).*

https://bit.ly/3okeTxt

Note: All the book's twenty project files are saved in a 'zip' file format which is a safe way to send files from our Library which are held on a DropBox account. We have tested them on Windows, Mac and Linux which includes the latest Raspberry pi Mini computer using Chrome browser and Thonny.

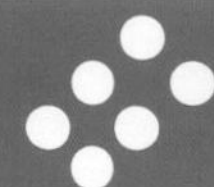

Project RESOURCES: projects

3.

Finding a Cars 'MPG' is a challenge.

This project is in three coded formats; and I have included the VW Beetle as it's not included in Snap! costumes and has to be 'imported' as a graphic. Snap! is able to import graphics in 'svg' format but the drawing options and costumes are sometimes limited. Hence the inclusion of an svg Car file. You may find others. A good SVG editor is a program called **Inkscape** and I have used that to import all drawing graphics into SNAP!.

You will find Inkscape (a graphics editor) at:

`https://inkscape.org`

Although it is NOT aimed at children to use. Many Snap! costumes are 'svg' files as are most *(not all)* of Scratch costume files. SVG is a quality image format *(Scalable Vector Graphics)* that can be used in any Browser applications *(like Snap! or Scratch 3)*.

Scratch has more costumes to choose from than Snap! (We imported our own SVG image).

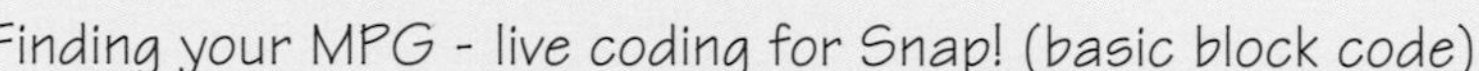

Finding your MPG - live coding for Snap! (basic block code)

https://bit.ly/3jY2YSQ

Finding your MPG - live coding for SCRATCH (basic block code)

https://bit.ly/3oP6anl

Python code extensions:

Create some custom coding for our Python cars. After all, we measure fuel in Litres now *(not Gallons)* and the distance is not in **Miles** either but in **Kilometres**. So using the same basic code as our MPG project we shall adapt that and consider how we can convert that all to an electric car. *(Discuss)* So how do they measure that? We've done that for you below!

Download the entire coded project:

This project is now available for download: *(SNAP!, Scratch and Python)*.

https://bit.ly/3dStCec

Note: All the book's twenty project files are saved in a 'zip' file format which is a safe way to send files from our Library which are held on a DropBox account. We have tested them on Windows, Mac and Linux which includes the latest Raspberry pi Mini computer using Chrome browser and Thonny.

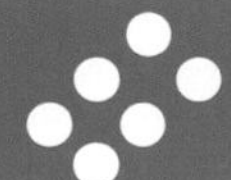

Project RESOURCES: projects

Guess the age of the Dinosaur!

Excluding myself, of course. This is a fun game that is a question and answer session that is easy for children to understand. Even the maths is easy to explain, being either above or below *(a random)* age target. The blocks may look daunting at first, but once underway, the blocks look less menacing and more exciting to demonstrate. You may well have to construct and demonstrate how the blocks expand *(and embed)* to fit the questions and how to link-words-together using the green [join] blocks which is also not that obvious *(for children)* as to why we are using a Maths block to make a sentence work later on *(see code examples)**.

Dinosaurs' like Python code...

Python can be demonstrated to be easier to set up, and easily compared *(with block code)*. Making a story like this is something that could be a another story entirely. This is only my own daft story. Another Zoo *(school)* trip is better or a holiday perhaps? Its only limited by imagination of the young coder. In fact silly is better than serious on this project, but children can still be tripped up by missing out a key block of code. Making the same set of Variables as 'keywords' *(or make a few more)* is a good place to start for making a longer silly story.

Project 'Live' weblinks:

This project appears currently on SNAP!:

https://bit.ly/3p2Nkt4

This project also appears currently on Scratch:

https://bit.ly/3oTTkUD

*Download the entire coded project:

This project is now available for download: *(SNAP!, Scratch and Python)..*

https://bit.ly/3oi0a6e

Note: All the book's twenty project files are saved in a 'zip' file format which is a safe way to send files from our Library which are held on a DropBox account. We have tested them on Windows, Mac and Linux which includes the latest Raspberry pi Mini computer using Chrome browser and Thonny.

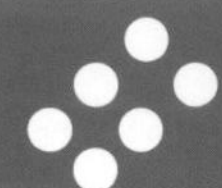

Project RESOURCES: projects

A Shopping list for everyone!

We create an easy to use Shopping list; for Toys and Birthdays. Using the list function *(of course)*. I am using three sprites on the block coding to act like Buttons we can press. **Sprite 1 is [+]** *(as shown)*, followed by **Sprite 2 [O]** and **Sprite [X]**. So pressing a Sprite makes that button interactive by adding, listing and deleting an item in list. The background, I think should be a Toy Shop, although I admit my own project background does looks a lot like a Kitchen shop!

Creating a LIST that works...

The creation of a LIST differs in Snap! to that of Scratch. So that my example ***(shown previously in project RESOURCES page 101)*** is my book example to follow. If not *(and I do agree, it's odd)*, then follow the easier Scratch versions of creating a list and - don't worry too much about it. For this reason this coding book's FIVE list based projects follow the List function based on Scratch - rather than Snap! However both can be made to work equally well with a bit of practice. But in practice it's a bit easier in any version of Scratch for children for lists.

Project 'Live' Scratch weblink:

This project is a Live version appearing on Scratch only:

https://bit.ly/3jUHOjw

*Download the entire coded project:

This project is available for download: *(Scratch1, 3 and Python)*.. *(includes shopping images)*

https://bit.ly/2TO3doT

Note: All the book's twenty project files are saved in a 'zip' file format which is a safe way to send files from our Library which are held on a DropBox account. We have tested them on Windows, Mac and Linux which includes the latest Raspberry pi Mini computer using Chrome browser and Thonny.

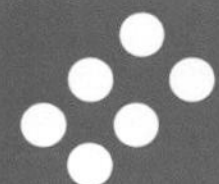

Project RESOURCES: projects

6.

Create amazing random Stars!

A fun activity in a short piece of code. I like drawing programs and this example of code is equally as good in Python as it is when using only the coding blocks in Snap! or Scratch. Most of the calls are RANDOM the important bit of code to point-out is that the Geometry for making such different shapes such as Triangle, Square and Star is made using the same repeat function and angles.

Python code works in same way:

This script uses The Turtle but into Python and changes its shape to a pencil point *(circle)*. I have built in the same routines but in this version of Python *(not using a Python colour module)*, the RANDOM colours function can be enabled with this single line of code....

```
turtle.colour('#%06x' % random.randint(0, 2**24 - 1))
```

This is better explained to older children but an overview of **How-it-works** is here. There are many ways to do this; all colours *(spelt as 'colors' in most programming code)* uses **Red, Green** and **Blue** colours. When we mix **RGB** proportion of any two *(or three colours)* we get a new colour hue. So there are a number of ways of doing this by calculation. This is just one of many other Python solutions. *(None are actually that easy to use!).*

colour('#%06x'	- Vary colour hue by six
% random.randint	- Make a random number
(0, 2**24 - 1)	- RGB colours at random (0,0,0)

How RGB colours work are better explained with an interactive colour map: *One of the better colour maps (or charts) is at* ***Trinket.io/docs/colors***
If we define two* *(both extreme)* ends of the RGB spectrum we get:

(1) RGB colour values start at **(255, 255, 255)** = for pure **White***
(2) RGB random colour (Red) from chart above **(255,0,0)** = for Red
(3) RGB colours values for (Black) is zero **(0,0,0)** = for jet **Black***

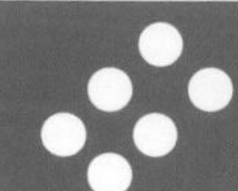

Project RESOURCES: projects

6. »

Python Colours and 'modules'!

So rather than fill this book with technical ***'what works now'*** I do think young coders can consider colour options to use later. The author has avoided the use of TK and Pygame (or other) *'colour'* **modules** on this project. We may use them later in another book project. Python ***'modules'*** extend the range and options of Python. ***Modules*** can be just called up as and when needed. The main idea in this book is to keep it as simple to code as possible and we shall leave ***'modules'*** until later in the book.

We could also try a Colour LIST instead... (see below):

Python list of colours:

```
# Program will stop when we run out of colours in list!
colors=['red', 'orange', 'purple', 'green', 'brown', 'yellow']
# Then replace our single line of code with this:
turtle.pencolor(random.choice(colors))
# Choose random colour from the list (above)
# You can also add as many colours as you wish!
```

Project 'Live' weblinks:

This project appears currently on SNAP!:

https://bit.ly/34XeWro

This project also appears currently on Scratch:

https://bit.ly/31ONDlB

Download the entire coded project:

This project is now available for download: *(SNAP!, Scratch and Python)*..

https://bit.ly/3jUBehS

Note: All the book's twenty project files are saved in a 'zip' file format which is a safe way to send files from our Library which are held on a DropBox account. We have tested them on Windows, Mac and Linux which includes the latest Raspberry pi Mini computer using Chrome browser and Thonny.

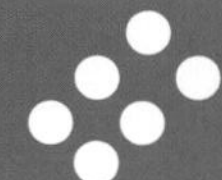

Project RESOURCES: projects

7.

Creating a (very) Silly story!

Something a bit different in making an interactive form - from a list of questions. In this example A Silly Story can be made from a list of items. So in my Zoo story the list of topics is made into **VARIABLES** that I can then use to set as an ***'answer'*** to each question.

In this example I am using Scratch! block code, but it will work much the same way in Snap! when we use the green **[join]** block to respond. In either case it requires bit of imagination to make it work and put a suitable **[join]** one word to another word to make readable as a Zoo story.

Rather than try to plan this for children I would let them just make the story up as they go along. All you need to do is make the first two sentences using two or three key words as a key **VARIABLE**. It is then just a ***'Question and Answer'*** type coding game.

Relating this to a similar Python code is part of the project's aim.

Project 'Live' weblinks:

This project appears currently on SNAP!:

https://bit.ly/34WxKal

This project also appears currently on Scratch:

https://bit.ly/3es6JyC

Download the entire coded project:

This project is now available for download: *(SNAP!, Scratch and Python)..**

https://bit.ly/38wPs6B

Note: All the book's twenty project files are saved in a 'zip' file format which is a safe way to send files from our Library which are held on a DropBox account. We have tested them on Windows, Mac and Linux which includes the latest Raspberry pi Mini computer using Chrome browser and Thonny.

**** Remember:*** *All graphic file format's names end in* ***.png****, or* ***.svg****. Any Python file formats end in* ***.py*** *and Scratch formats end in either* ***.sb3*** *(Scratch 3),* ***.sb2*** *(Scratch 2) or earlier Scratch (1.4) just ends with* ***.sb****, such as* ***'filename.sb'***

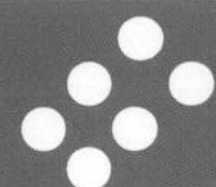

Project RESOURCES: projects

8.

Brain Trainer Quiz!

This is an interactive quiz. Abby is your host and she will ask a series of Maths Questions, all of which you have to get correct. In this program, if you make a single Maths mistake you have to start again. All of these questions are based on a quiz I found in The Times *(UK Newspaper)* and I adapted it to this code. By showing you how to make it, you can make a similar challenge with another set of Maths questions in the same way. Note in this program the calculations are made by the program code *(not just a simple 'yes' or 'no' answer)*, that would be too easy for you!

I am a Sprite called Abby. I appear in the costumes section of both Snap! and Scratch There are four Abby costumes to choose and they should appear in your quiz block code!

It's worth looking at the original press cutting *(below)*, as this is something I try to do everyday over breakfast. You may find something similar in the puzzle section of many other national newspapers.... The puzzle is a ***'bite-sized'*** Maths calculation of a small sequence of numbers. The Python Brain Trainer Calculator can be used in the same way - to calculate the same sequence of numbers as shown here.

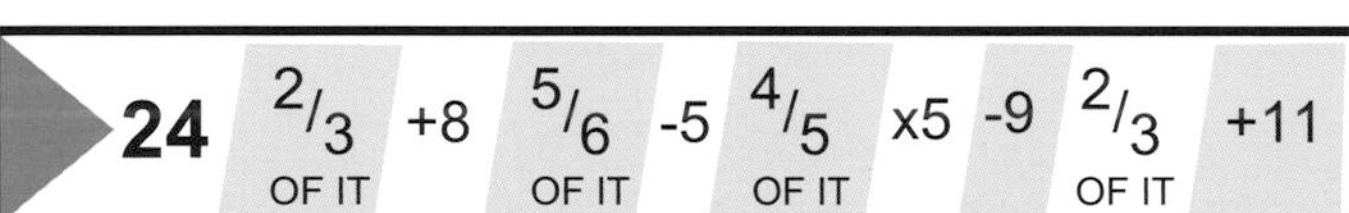
24 | 2/3 OF IT | +8 | 5/6 OF IT | -5 | 4/5 OF IT | x5 | -9 | 2/3 OF IT | +11

From The Times Puzzle pages, a source of similar brain challenges daily.

Project 'Live' weblinks:

This project appears currently on SNAP!:

https://bit.ly/3pKdTTQ

This project also appears currently on Scratch:

https://bit.ly/2IkZ8G4

Download the entire coded project:

This project is now available for download: *(SNAP!, Scratch and Python)*..

https://bit.ly/3neMcAz

Note: All the book's twenty project files are saved in a 'zip' file format which is a safe way to send files from our Library which are held on a DropBox account. We have tested them on Windows, Mac and Linux which includes the latest Raspberry pi Mini computer using Chrome browser and Thonny.

Abby's voice is a series of computer generated sound clips which can be used in both Snap! or Scratch. See project RESOURCES page with coded examples in the weblink on this page.

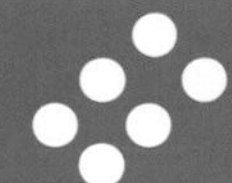

Project RESOURCES: projects

9.

Two Spinning Random dice ...

An easy game that can be extended to be more than one dice. For the more adventurous you may consider a dice to have more than six sides but for our example, a tumbling dice has six sides and we start with two dice. It's easy to have -or add, more dice.

Even more Python Random dice!

Python code can have not only have more sides, but many more dice to infinity. But that can be explored later as it's fairly easy to extend for a quick demonstration based on our code example.

As usual, I have attached graphics for this project for both Snap! and Scratch and was a bit surprised to learn that Scratch does not yet accept graphics in SVG format. For this reason I have also created .png to import as ***costumes*** in Scratch *(any version)*.

Snap! is lot better at importing high quality 'svg' format graphics. Unfortunately Snap! only has only a very basic graphic editing and drawing ability, although it works well enough for this project. Children should draw their own dice, *(if possible)* for this project. It is easy enough to learn using the standard drawing tools in either Snap! or Scratch.

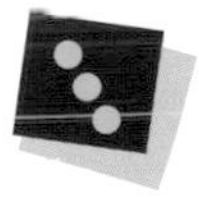

Project 'Live' weblinks:

This project appears currently on SNAP!:

https://bit.ly/3piAIxQ

This project also appears currently on Scratch:

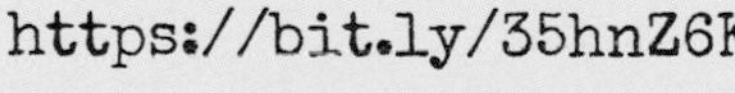

https://bit.ly/35hnZ6K

Download the entire coded project:

This project is now available for download: *(SNAP!, Scratch and Python)*..

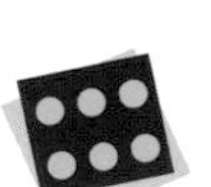

https://bit.ly/32vud0Y

Note: All the book's twenty project files are saved in a 'zip' file format which is a safe way to send files from our Library which are held on a DropBox account. We have tested them on Windows, Mac and Linux which includes the latest Raspberry pi Mini computer using Chrome browser and Thonny.

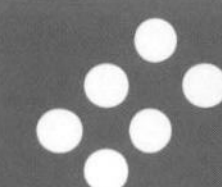

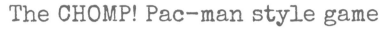

Project RESOURCES: projects

10.

The CHOMP! Pac-man style game

A bit of fun with a chomping sprite. Obviously based on **Pac-man** but made to move in all directions and now eats as much SPROUTS as he can. This introduces the concept of keeping a score as well as how-to-make a simple two-costume animated Sprite. This project is identical in **Snap!** and **Scratch**, but its fair to say that **Snap!** has less then wonderful drawing and edit ability, *(compared to Scratch).*

However the best option is to use an external graphics editor such as INKSCAPE* (www.inkscape.org) to make your Pac-man. This is not very practical in school but ***'at home'*** you may have more time to learn a new skill, *making high quality* ***'clip-art'*** *for your coding is easy!*

The graphics for this project you can download (avoiding having to draw any Pac-man at all), but the most fun is also making your own Pac-man!

Notes: Getting children to eat SPROUTS is ***almost impossible*** so we could easily change that to something else ***not eaten***. The game really is giving points (score) to food being ***'eaten'*** or ***'not eaten'*** for minus points.

Python coding needs 'collisions'

We have to define what the centre of an object is *(for all food collisions)* it has to be defined before we start. It's the same for all Python games. The block of code called **'def collision'** makes up one essential block. Anything that overlaps is a collision. So much easier in Snap! and Scratch!

However there are many more things you can do in Python and one of those 'tricks' is to use a Python module (in Thonny) called TK to make the game work better. TK is a popular module that enables graphics to be easily imported and coded with a simple GUI.*

Our CHOMP! project Python code is designed to be as simple as possible, so I have had to drop some key points, such as the score display and adding some ***(bad)*** food to eat *(such as Jelly)*. But I have created a new CHOMP! 2 version with two pages of Python code that I have now bundled into the Download section. A preview of that code 'CHOMP! 2' is also on the next page, *(see screen-shot photo).*

***GUI = Graphic User Interface*

Project RESOURCES: projects

10.

The CHOMP! final - full version 2

There are two versions of this game to play with.

The first easier to code version is the one printed in the book. The second *(shown below)* is still two pages of code but has more game functionality.

All the Chomp! code versions are on the download links at the bottom of this page.

Project 'Live' weblinks:

This project appears currently on SNAP!:

https://bit.ly/3nlU4k7

This project also appears currently on Scratch:

https://bit.ly/3eUqSOu

Download the entire coded project:

This project is now available for download: *(SNAP!, Scratch and Python).*

https://bit.ly/3nhCSfp

Note: All the book's twenty project files are saved in a 'zip' file format which is a safe way to send files from our Library which are held on a DropBox account. We have tested them on Windows, Mac and Linux which includes the latest Raspberry pi Mini computer using Chrome browser and Thonny.

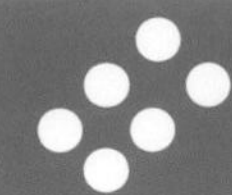

Project RESOURCES: projects

11 »

Morse-Code Sender

The history of the Telegraph is fascinating! and it's the basis of many of our modern communications as well as direction finding using 'beacons' which still guide boats into harbours and aircraft into airports using just **morse-code,** before 'GPS' was made available *(Global Positioning System)* which uses space satellites to compute where you are on land, air and sea). Before all that stuff, we simply just had morse-code. Experienced radio operators could send ***'secret messages'*** by using short sound bursts of dots and dashes and send urgent messages over the radio.

We are using that same technology and try making our own top secret message-making machine using Scratch block code programming.

To make this work is for older children, as we shall be using a combination of Lists and Variables which you have to 'import' into Scratch to work. I have chosen Scratch as it's easier to use for this project. If you want to try and use Snap! then you can try *(and adapt)* my coded example made on page 101. However I would avoid that on this project. The next two pages are for Scratch only.

To start make the **VARIABLES** and **LISTS** as described on page 56.
Make block code exactly as that shown on project page!
Use the same names for **VARIABLES** and **LISTS** to avoid confusion.
You should then have a screen that looks like the one shown below:

This is how the screen looks with LISTS after we have imported the LIST code. We recommend you IMPORT the code rather than type it.

*How to import **'morse-code'** and **'characters'** LIST is shown on the next page.*

»

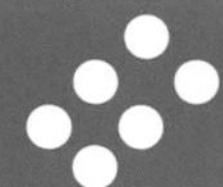

Project RESOURCES: projects

[characters]	[morse-code]
A	.-
B	-...
C	-.-.
D	-..
E	.
F	..-.
G	--.
H	....
I	..
J	.---
K	-.-
L	.-..
M	--
N	-.
O	---
P	.--.
Q	--.-
R	.-.
S	...
T	-
U	..-
V	...-
W	.--
X	-..-
Y	-.--
Z	--..

Creating your first [character] LIST

You can enter line-by-line all 26 letters of the alphabet A to Z in **[characters]** or import them.

Its easier to ***'import'*** the A to Z text into your **[characters]** list if you choose. Each line in your LIST (called **[characters])** will have just one letter per line *(see left)*. The top letter in this list is the letter 'A'. *(There are no lower case letters used in real morse-code, it's all CAPITAL letters).*

For **[characters]** list press the **[+]** button *(to add to the list)* or import *(as shown below in blue circle)* by which you can download the correct file to import. *Download and import the TEXT file called;* ***'A-Z letters.txt'***

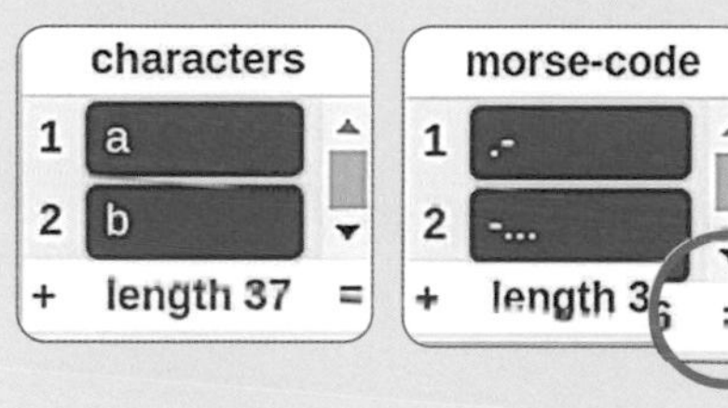

CLICK on bottom right as shown here to ***import*** *the supplied MORSE-CODE (text) into your new morse-code LIST (as shown in blue circled here). Import* ***A-Z letters.txt'*** *file for* ***'characters'*** *LIST and Import the other text file (morse-code.txt) for* ***'morse-code'*** *LIST*

Creating your first [morse-code] LIST

You can enter line-by-line all **'dot-dash-dot'** *(all 26 of them)* into **[morse-code]** or import them...

It's easier to *'import'* the morse text into your **[morse-code]** LIST, rather than try to 'type' it *(and make a silly mistake)*. Each line in your LIST (called **[more-code])** will have a text symbol . The top symbol on this LIST represents the letter **'A'**. Morse is all capital letters.

For **[morse-code]** list press the **[+]** button *(to add to the list)* or import (as shown above in blue circle) by which you can download the correct file to import. *Download and import the TEXT file called;* ***'morse code.txt'***

If you still determined to 'type' your morse-code into a LIST then use a simple key dash letter (as shown on your keyboard) for '-' and a full stop key for the '.' Simply follow the morse A-Z guide shown on the left hand side of this page!

Project RESOURCES: projects

11. »

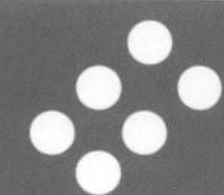

Just a [space] between words

We are using a *'blank'* **[space]** between words. A bit like my own typing or otherwise ***'all-the-words'*** I use would get totally mixed-up and made unclear. So we use the **[space]** key for that. In morse code there is no **[space]** key but a slightly longer pause between words. It works but in our code the symbols are a bit difficult to read *(when output)*. To solve that I have added another symbol such as **') ('** which looks a bit odd until you see it working as it adds a bit more space between words. You could use a double **[space]** key word space as an alternative...!

Test, test, test (debug)!

This is not a quick piece of code to play with, It means error checking to check the sequence *(presuming the LISTS are correctly entered).*

A debug! (bug)

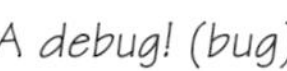

Python code is a doddle by comparison!

This is almost the shortest piece of code in the book. So this is a good example to use and compare. Python is so fast, I have used a timer to slow down the code output. If any errors appear on Python always check your syntax. This is the odd double **underscores** in the **'class'** function which I highlight as a possible problem. (**if __name__ == "__main__":**)

Note: *Checking such computer code workings is often called* ***'debugging'.***

[letter space]

[letter space]

Project 'Live' weblinks:

This project only appears on Scratch:

https://bit.ly/35o5Gg2

Download the entire coded project:

This project is now available for download: *(Scratch and Python)*..

https://bit.ly/3nB33xY

Note: All the book's twenty project files are saved in a 'zip' file format which is a safe way to send files from our Library which are held on a DropBox account. We have tested them on Windows, Mac and Linux which includes the latest Raspberry pi Mini computer using Chrome browser and Thonny.

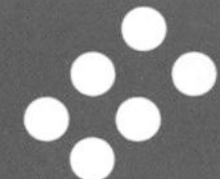

Project RESOURCES: projects

Bouncing Snap! and Scratch Turtles

Bouncing anything can be applied to this block code. I have used bouncing beans in the past which work just as well. So we start with either a drawing or an import of something fun to do. In block code, *(and it's the same in Snap! or Scratch)*, we can easily pick a **[touching-colour]** code block to create a collision for a bounce back. For that to work we need hard outline in our drawing - or a solid colour, I have imported a Turtle sprite for that.

VARIABLES **[speed]** and **[angle]** are used to control the 'bounce' collisions.

Bouncing Python Turtles

Turtles are built-in to Python, so we only have to call them up. They have various shapes we can define *(triangle, square and circle)*, change colours and even size. There is no speed control but we can change the default speed and the gravity control which makes for a more realistic bounce.

Python does not allow us to bounce objects simply based on a colour. We have to define *(using Maths)* the centre of the object to calculate the correct collision response. We also do not have a simple **[if-on-edge-bounce]** so we have to define a screen boundary. But all in all it's fun!

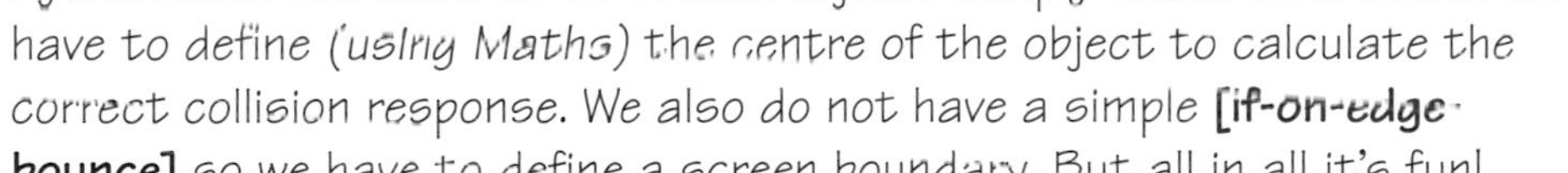

Project 'Live' weblinks:

This project appears currently on SNAP!:

https://bit.ly/38Y12aN

This project also appears currently on Scratch:

https://bit.ly/3pKrNpq

Download the entire coded project:

This project is now available for download: *(SNAP!, Scratch and Python)*..

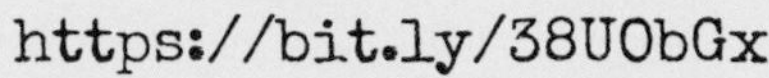

https://bit.ly/38U0bGx

Note: All the book's twenty project files are saved in a 'zip' file format which is a safe way to send files from our Library which are held on a DropBox account. We have tested them on Windows, Mac and Linux which includes the latest Raspberry pi Mini computer using Chrome browser and Thonny.

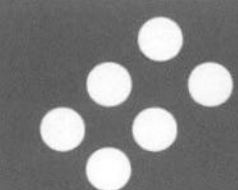

Project RESOURCES: projects

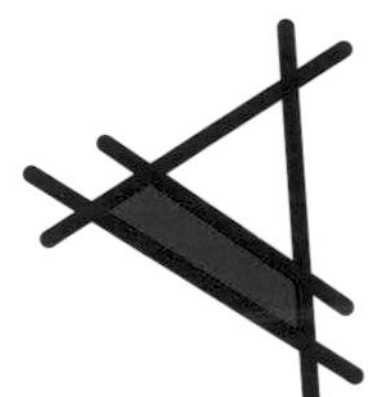

Knitting patterns

Geometric patterns are easily repeated with code, called loops. Snap! and Scratch call these repeats *(set number of times)* or forever ***(non-stop).*** Patterns are everywhere and when I saw this geometric pattern it reminded me of a knitting pattern. This project in block code requires an imaginary circle to work around and the device I have chosen is a simple letter 'A' - made to look like a tent or a simple Triangle, if you prefer.

So draw that using straight lines only. Reset the centre as described on the project *(options)* page and you're ready to code. It's also one of the easiest to block code in the book. Ensure you have clicked the two variables as controls and use the **[space-bar]** to stamp out your pattern.

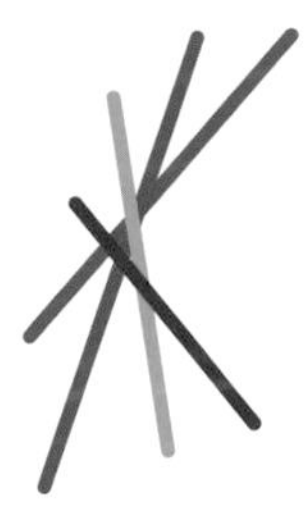

Python coded knits:

Python code works best here. I was so taken with this pattern visually that it had to be made into a theme project for this book. It's heavily maths reliant but as it is a very short Python piece that children could easily type in, we are not worrying about trying to understand the complex sin/cos/pi maths which *(for me)* is as inspiring as any of the other coded projects found in this book. It's just fascinating to see working.

Project 'Live' weblinks:

This project appears currently on SNAP!:

https://bit.ly/3kOM892

This project also appears currently on Scratch:

https://bit.ly/3pOjPeE

Download the entire coded project:

This project is now available for download: *(SNAP!, Scratch and Python)*..

https://bit.ly/39OFESw

Note: All the book's twenty project files are saved in a 'zip' file format which is a safe way to send files from our Library which are held on a DropBox account. We have tested them on Windows, Mac and Linux which includes the latest Raspberry pi Mini computer using Chrome browser and Thonny.

Project RESOURCES: projects

14.

Guess the Famous names!

This project is a guessing game. You can use any names to make a book quiz game. It does help if children have read a popular book such as our feature on the ***'The Famous Five'***. As we are using LISTS the author is using Scratch only *(no Snap! on this)*. So the focus will be on using a LIST and linking that to our ***'guesses'*** and ***'response'*** VARIABLES as input.

Both the Scratch versions and Python code are similar and work much the same way. The main function of RANDOM used in both is to mix up the names *(on the LIST)* to make it difficult to guess each time. Even so it's not that difficult if you keep the names to no more than five or six.

< All of the characters *(Sprite costumes)* are found in Scratch. We need one 'Sprite' to ask the questions. Python is a simple text only quiz code.

Python guesses...

Names in the current **NAME-LIST** are all lower case, *(so any Capital letters in the original LIST name may not be recognised as being correct.)* But IF we change the LIST to include names such as *'Julian' 'Dick'*, or *'Anne'* - it will then accept the capital letter in our LIST *(seen below)*.

```
NAME_LIST = ["Dick", 'George", "Julian", "Timmy", "Annie" , "dick", 'george", "julian", "timmy", "annie"]
```

Project 'Live' weblinks:

This project only appears on Scratch:

https://bit.ly/3meH1Q9

Download the entire coded project:

This project is now available for download: *(Scratch and Python)*..

https://bit.ly/3pQzSsu

Note: All the book's twenty project files are saved in a 'zip' file format which is a safe way to send files from our Library which are held on a DropBox account. We have tested them on Windows, Mac and Linux which includes the latest Raspberry pi Mini computer using Chrome browser and Thonny.

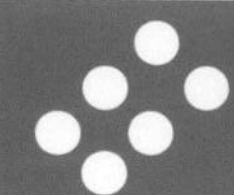

Project RESOURCES: projects

15.

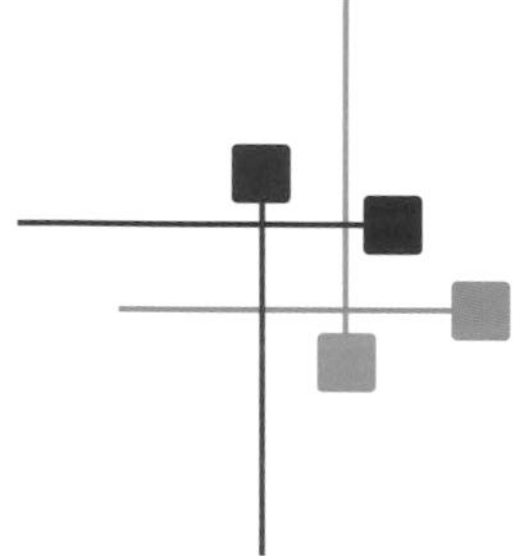

Mirror Mad square reflections

I am using simple square shapes *(you can IMPORT my Turtles later).* This project is both Snap! or Scratch and you only need to draw and code one sprite as described on this project page. The plan is to code one shape before duplicating *(right click on sprite)* which then copies all the code over as well. **Do this three more times.** Name each sprite in turn: ***Red, Green, Blue and Orange.*** Edit each sprite in turn, and change the colour drawing *(edit drawing and pan colour)*, so it matches the name of Red, Green, Blue and Orange (for the name of each the sprites). Follow project **'sprite direction'** on the project page. Note: that each Sprite has a new (odd)direction *(left, right, up and down).* If not check sprite direction again for **'sprite direction'** shown on project page.

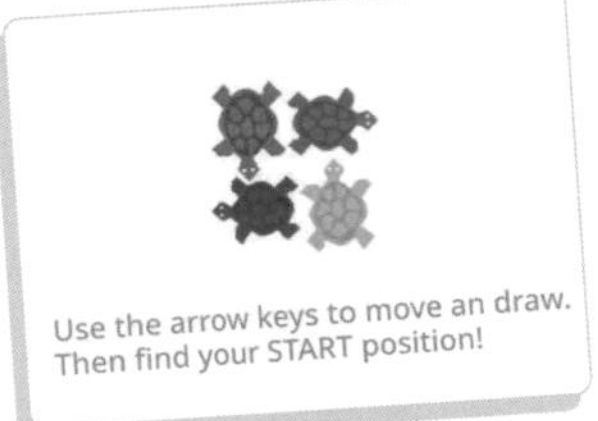

Use the arrow keys to move an draw.
Then find your START position!

You can now IMPORT four coloured Turtles *(in svg graphics format, both Snap! and Scratch tested, created for this project).* Optional import.

Python Turtle reflections

The standard Turtles shapes are included in Python *(other shapes are available should you ask such as: rectangles, circles as well as Turtles).* Creating four Turtles each moving in different directions is the aim of the project. Follow exactly all the Turtle directions given in the code to work.

Project 'Live' weblinks:

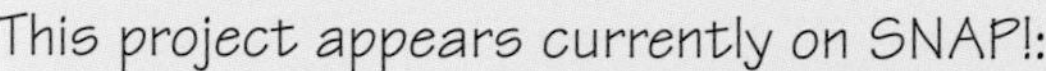

This project appears currently on SNAP!:

https://bit.ly/39ciyIt

This project also appears currently on Scratch:

https://bit.ly/2V2AugB

Download the entire coded project:

This project is now available for download: *(SNAP!, Scratch and Python)*..

https://bit.ly/3pUaVMZ

Note: All the book's twenty project files are saved in a 'zip' file format which is a safe way to send files from our Library which are held on a DropBox account. We have tested them on Windows, Mac and Linux which includes the latest Raspberry pi Mini computer using Chrome browser and Thonny.

Project RESOURCES: projects

16.

Coding Polygon Pinwheels

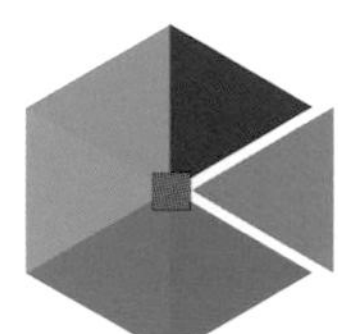

Use a simple grey square as our sprite *(as our pencil or felt-tip)*.
Now use that pen to fill our regular Polygon shape with random colours.

As there is no 'fill' block in any version of Scratch *(to date, although that may change)*, you can find one in Snap! *(see pen section)* and also one exists in Python code. In this book I have excluded all custom code blocks. We won't be using any fill blocks of code in Scratch. Snap! users can try that out later. The main fun is watching our square busy filling in all the gaps in our shape. Nobody should have any problems in dragging all this simple block code into place as even the Python script is relatively short and easy to code.

Python random colours and LISTS

Python does have an *'auto-fill'* function which we can use later and demonstrate working. Plus we can add some colour options in providing a common list of colours as well as the random Colours we have used in our project. I have created two sets of example code in the Download link below. One is for making a LIST of colours *(and how to choose more)* and the other is a simple random colour example. All fun to make.

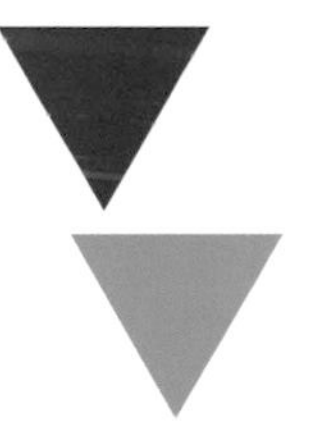

Project 'Live' weblinks:

This project appears currently on SNAP!:

https://bit.ly/377Q7Jd

This project also appears currently on Scratch:

https://bit.ly/3q4uJg0

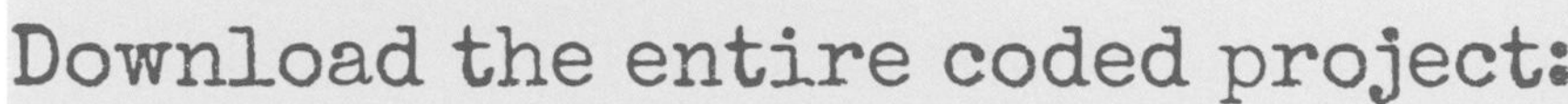

Download the entire coded project:

This project is now available for download: *(SNAP!, Scratch and Python)*..

https://bit.ly/2UZG03k

Note: All the book's twenty project files are saved in a 'zip' file format which is a safe way to send files from our Library which are held on a DropBox account. We have tested them on Windows, Mac and Linux which includes the latest Raspberry pi Mini computer using Chrome browser and Thonny.

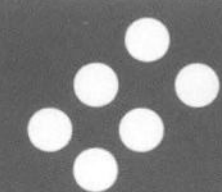

Project RESOURCES: projects

17.

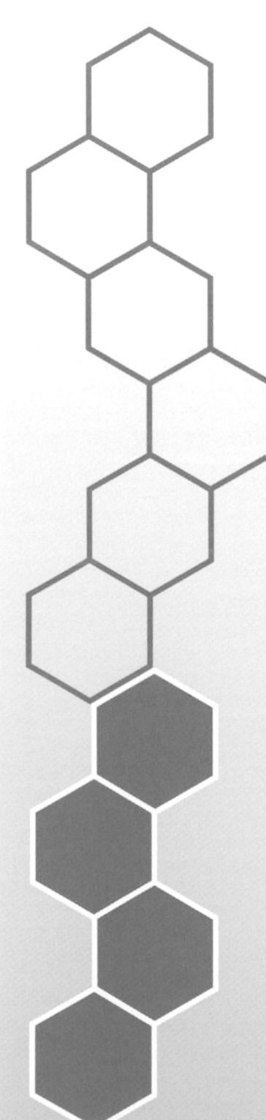

Honey Bees make Patterns

An example of a tessellated pattern made by Bees making Honey. So I would start importing a *(sprite)* Bumble Bee costume *(which you can import - or draw as an option)*. I prefer children to draw a Bumble Bee rather than import. The block code is Snap! and Scratch compatible with no VARIABLES to highlight. The image (Look) re-size block can be adjusted to suit the size of imported image. In our block code there is no colour fill-in of our hexagon shape. I am using one colour to pen outline only. In Snap! you could enable the '(pen colour) 'fill' block for that function. The colours are based on Honey colours that I imagine a Bee would choose. But now understand that Honey does come in many different colours. There's a thought *(for children to play with)*.

Python to Honeycomb

This was the inspiration for this project. One of the reasons I created the book was to explore similarities between coding, platforms and the two main programmes that children can use. Main points are ensuring that the •••• tabbed code indents are *(mostly)* understood to be part of the program sequence with loops and repeats.

Project 'Live' weblinks:

This project appears currently on SNAP!:

https://bit.ly/3q72yxM

This project also appears currently on Scratch:

https://bit.ly/37as7F1

Download the entire coded project:

This project is now available for download: *(SNAP!, Scratch and Python)*..

https://bit.ly/39mcr4v

Note: All the book/s twenty project files are saved in a 'zip' file format which is a safe way to send files from our Library which are held on a DropBox account. We have tested them on Windows, Mac and Linux which includes the latest Raspberry pi Mini computer using Chrome browser and Thonny.

Project RESOURCES: projects

18.

Noughts and Crosses game

Probably the oldest game in the world.

Wins are diagonal, across and down, as shown below.

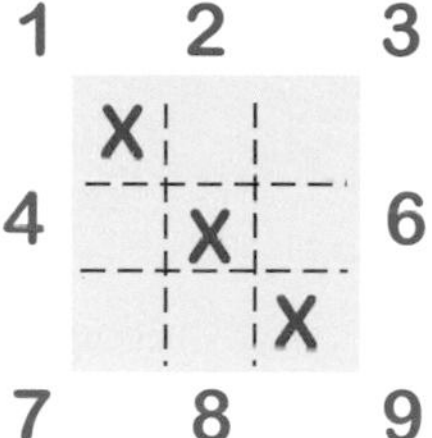

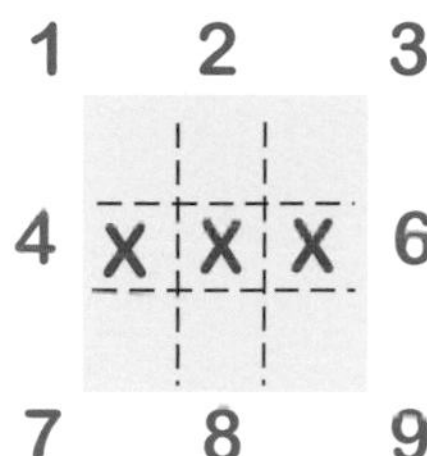

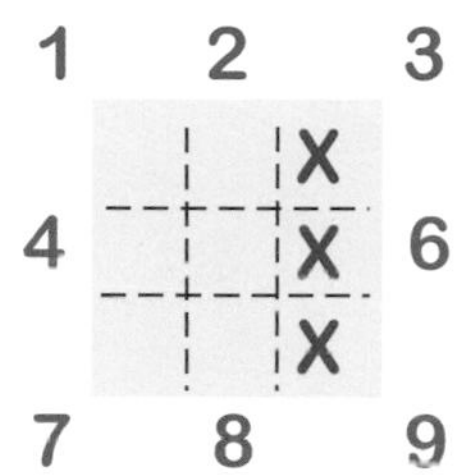

We need to cover all the possible options for both marks: 'X' and 'O'...

Using the code you have already, copy and 'drop-in' the new code additions as marked. Follow the code blocks marked A to C. By hacking our own code we can improve (or make the same code fail) if we fail to follow exact guidelines, it will just stop the game. A missing ., , "I" or ' ' can make all the difference in getting your Python code working. So Debug, and test, (debug and test), then (go eat a biscuit, go for a walk, make tea), debug and test. Computer Programming needs lots of (mostly tedious but essential) tests to make coding work!

```
# (OPTIONS: insert code block A.)
Win = 1
Draw = -1
Running = 0
Stop = 1
Game = Running
Mark = 'X'
# - - - - - - - - - - - - - - - - !!!
```

We are replacing (over-writing) what was there before with this new block of code. Not everything changes, just the code lines we have added. ***(Running, Game and Mark are all identical),*** *so no changes to code there.*

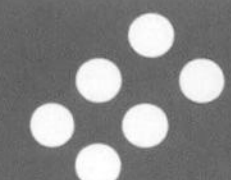

Project RESOURCES: projects

18. 

B.

```
# (OPTIONS: insert code block B.)
•••• •••• def CheckWin():   # Checks if player has won
•••• global Game
   # Horizontal wins (==) means it must EQUAL across three boards
•••• if(board[1] == board[2] and board[2] == board[3] and board[1] != ' '):
•••• •••• Game = Win
•••• elif(board[4] == board[5] and board[5] == board[6] and board[4] != ' '):
•••• •••• Game = Win
•••• elif(board[7] == board[8] and board[8] == board[9] and board[7] != ' '):
•••••••• Game = Win

   # Vertical wins (==) means it must EQUAL across three boards
•••• elif(board[1] == board[4] and board[4] == board[7] and board[1] != ' '):
•••• •••• Game = Win
•••• elif(board[2] == board[5] and board[5] == board[8] and board[2] != ' '):
•••• •••• Game = Win
•••• elif(board[3] == board[6] and board[6] == board[9] and board[3] != ' '):
•••• •••• Game=Win

   # Diagonal wins (==) means it must EQUAL across three boards
•••• elif(board[1] == board[5] and board[5] == board[9] and board[5] != ' '):
•••• •••• Game = Win
•••• elif(board[3] == board[5] and board[5] == board[7] and board[5] != ' '):
•••• •••• Game=Win

   # IF its-a-'DRAW' if (=)  when all board spaces filled, (no wins).
•••• elif(board[1]!=' ' and board[2]!=' ' and board[3]!=' ' and board[4]!=' ' \
and board[5]!=' ' and board[6]!=' ' and board[7]!=' ' and board[8]!=' ' \
and board[9]!=' '):
•••• •••• Game=Draw
•••• else:
•••• •••• Game=Running
# - - - - - - - - - - - - - - - - !!!
```

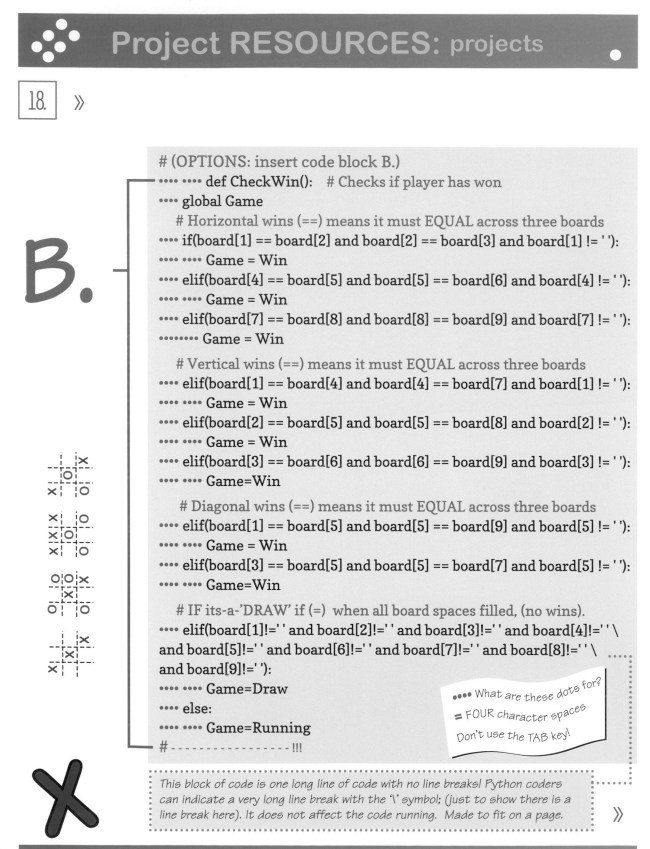

•••• What are these dots for?
= FOUR character spaces
Don't use the TAB key!

This block of code is one long line of code with no line breaks! Python coders can indicate a very long line break with the '\' symbol; (just to show there is a line break here). It does not affect the code running. Made to fit on a page.

»

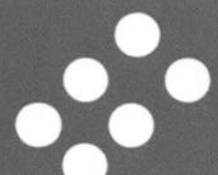

Project RESOURCES: projects

» 18.

C.

```
# (OPTIONS: insert code block C.)
if(Game==Draw):
•••• print("Game is a Draw..")
elif(Game==Win):
•••• •••• player-=1
•••• if(player%2!=0):
•••• •••• print(">> Player [1] Won this game!")
•••• else:
•••• •••• print(">> Player [2] Won this game!")
# - - - - - - - - - - - - - - - - !!!
```

•••• What are these dots for?
= FOUR character spaces
Don't use the TAB key!

As usual with our project RESOURCES download links, we have a links to all the Snap!, Scratch and Python code (all you see here) plus some variations made with and without a 'Winner', and with an option to convert the same code into a colour version using another Python module (using THONNY).

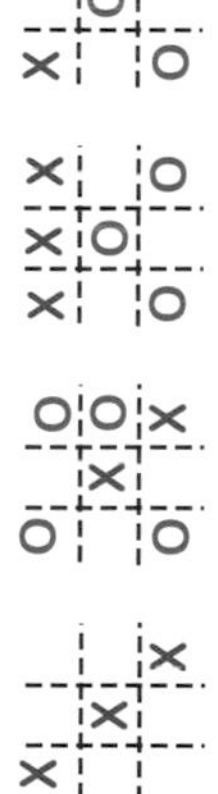

When using a raspberry pi mini-computer; many Python modules' are 'built-in' to the small operating system. Other systems (*Mac, Windows and other Linux computers*) may need a module installation for THONNY to run the code. More details on using and importing a missing Python modules are shown the Python ***'hints & tips'*** section pages 136 to 139.

Project 'Live' weblinks:

This project appears currently on SNAP!:

https://bit.ly/2KLcZX1

This project also appears currently on Scratch:

https://bit.ly/2KNYUbG

Download the entire coded project:

This project is now available for download: *(SNAP!, Scratch and Python)..*

https://bit.ly/2JolYek

Note: All the book's twenty project files are saved in a 'zip' file format which is a safe way to send files from our Library which are held on a DropBox account. We have tested them on Windows, Mac and Linux which includes the latest Raspberry pi Mini computer using Chrome browser and Thonny.

Project RESOURCES: projects

19.

Coding Colourful confusion

For such a simple game, there is a lot going on with this block code. This is a Scratch project only*, *(as it contains a LIST function)*. The most important part is being able to count (and how to count) in the [forever] loop. By asking a simple question we can use an **[IF]** and **[else]** to choose which image to show. There is only one Sprite for this game, but many costumes. This is an important point to make that 'costumes' like 'clothes' can be changed. There is only ONE SPRITE on this game, what changes is the costumes. And we have TEN costumes...!

*All the coding is on the Toucan Sprite. The words that appear are all Costume Sprites (ten in all). They are all words made using Scratch text in the edit window. Choose any **Bold** Typeface on your computer.*

Costume 1

Costume 2

Costume 3

The easiest way to make the costumes is to make one costume first with one large word - the longest word to fit the screen such as 'Orange' in a bold typeface. Centred on screen in Black. It does help to learn how to name the Costumes as you duplicate that costume *(right-click on your mouse)* and change the colour from Black to Red (follow the colour sequence we have shown on page 89 to avoid confusion). Note that all the words shown are in colour *(but are NOT the correct colour shown by the words)*, for example the first Costume is called RED but is in fact BLUE. ***Be guided by the words and not the colour in this game!***

The sequence of costumes is important: ***(Red, Blue, Green, Pink, Black, Yellow, Orange, White, Purple, Brown)*** as each is identified by matching the image (costume) to the word in our Colours LIST *(not 'colours' shown on any costume)*. That's why we need the counter, so the program knows which picture is shown, when the game starts. Making the TEN costumes, to match (an odd colour) and compare to our 'Colour' LIST is the coding challenge. *(See project page 90) - you should have a LIST, as shown on page left.* ***You can probably now guess how this game works!***

Colours
1 Red
2 Blue
3 Green
4 Pink
5 Black
6 Yellow
7 Orange
8 White
9 Purple
10 Brown
+ length 10 =

This is the kind of game children play with when learning Colours! »

** This is a Scratch project. This project could easily be made in Snap! if you are able to follow similar instructions shown on page 100. Scratch is usually easier for a LIST.*

Project RESOURCES: projects

»

19.

Colour Python programming (using TK)

The Python version is an ideal start in using something totally new in this book by use of TK *(or tk inter)*, which is an easy way to create a proper GUI (*Graphical User Interface)* widely adopted in Python for games. Also provides realistic buttons and better score display capability. This is a good example of using TK to improve the overall look of the game code.

All projects in this book have examples to play with and learn from. This is not a computer technical book for fixing problems with code 'syntax' *(which causes most problems - even for experienced coders)* as we cannot rely on a 'word' dictionary. We have to 'spot' our own 'syntax' errors, and that is really hard to do on your own. But in a computer club *(or school)* you can usually find someone to check your code. Debugging your code, *(we all have to do it)* can take a lot longer to 'spot' an error - than it does to write!

Using the Python TK Module:

TK is a very popular module that is essential to this game. In THONNY you will have to ***'import'*** this module if it's not already installed. The raspberry pi mini-computer has ALL *(most)* commonly used Python modules (ready) pre-installed. For everybody else on a Mac, Windows or most 'other' Linux computers this requires an *(easy-to-install)* system update. This can take less than 2 minutes - *(when using THONNY)*. See our Python ***'hints and tips'*** pages section at the back of this book.

Project 'Live' weblinks:

This project only appears on Scratch:

https://bit.ly/3mA7EjC

Download the entire coded project:

This project is now available for download: *(Scratch and Python)*..

https://bit.ly/2VrClM3

Note: All the book's twenty project files are saved in a 'zip' file format which is a safe way to send files from our Library which are held on a DropBox account. We have tested them on Windows, Mac and Linux which includes the latest Raspberry pi Mini computer using Chrome browser and Thonny.

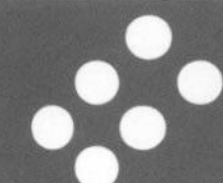

Project RESOURCES: projects

Flying a model Aeroplane

The last of the project's in this book. This is a Scratch only project, *(as it contains a LIST function to flip flight angles)*. It's not impossible in Snap! if you would like to try. This book encourages you to code in Snap!, Scratch and Python and then compare the results. Coding is a game for me, but in a school, I would have to chose just one for an entire term ***(Snap!, Scratch or Python).*** If you're at home, with this book you can try coding all three and see how they all compare on a project basis.

Learning the controls:

If you have worked through the previous projects, you will have learned how to recognise code blocks (often the same code blocks are used in each of the twenty projects, and you will recognise short 'snippits' of Python code along the way. As in any new language practice a 'few-lines' is usually enough to get you started. Coding is a new language for most of us starting out, and your either good at it - or perhaps (like me) a bit slower as I think in terms of how to easily present this, so you can understand it.

In addition: I have no idea on ***'how-to-fly'*** *an aircraft either, but I am willing to try. If you can make such a a model aircraft, you can probably fly one, I tend to think. It's a worthy project to try, although I am not sure what (really) happens when you do actually put the 'brakes-on' when flying an Aircraft. Does an Aircraft actually stop in flight?*

Inspiration in 3D:

Credit where it's due for this is a challenging idea. *I am entirely indebted to Phil Wickins for this inspiring idea in UK schools (and for calculating those tricky distance in Maths).* This is now fully updated for Scratch 3 *(with fully functional lists that extend the idea further using lists).*

For more information see Phil Wickins' education website:

https://bit.ly/31TFSgT

This book is a totally independent production and the link above is for interest only. On the above link you will find the original feature from the raspberry pi magazine that inspired the author to try using Scratch 'Lists' to create the same 3D movement.

»

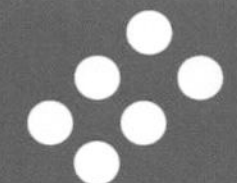

Project RESOURCES: projects

20.

Making 3D Models in SketchUp!

SketchUp!! is beyond the scope of this book, *(although I do teach the SketchUp! basics in Schools).* You can sign-up for free SketchUp! trial for education and it will work in your browser, in the same way that Snap! and Scratch work in your browser window. You can also import your own 3D models *(and create your own models)* that you can in this 3D project*.

sketchup.com

You will need to sign in for an educational account. How to use this 3D modelling program is beyond the scope of this book. You can directly save transparent 3D images in 'png' format. This is what you need to create multiple costumes in SketchUp.

You cannot import any 3D model directly into Snap! or Scratch. This can only be achieved by using animated 'snapshots' of various angles (a minimum of eight) images for all the costumes.

More 3D model test drives?

The options on this code are fairly limited. But you can adopt another 3D model object and import that in the same way I created the aeroplane. For this you will need to know how to make a camera **'Snapshot'** on your computer screen. As all computers have a different idea of what a 'snapshot' is - including my raspberry pi mini computer. You may need someone to show you how to do this. It's also called making a **'Screen-grab'***

***The easiest option is to import an existing 3D model using SketchUp!**

Don't forget to save each view in 'png' format at the viewing angles I have already stated on the project page.

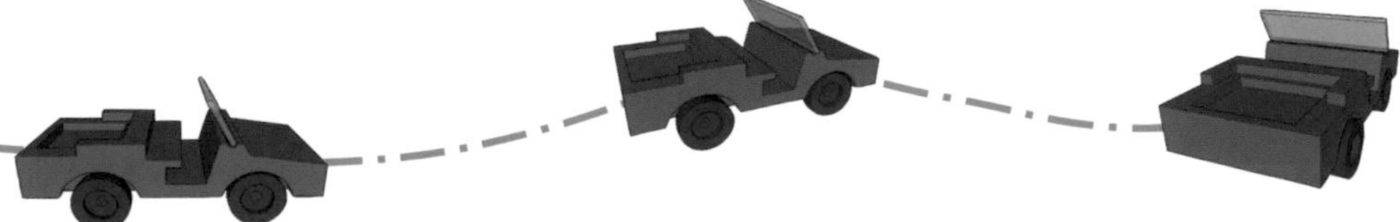

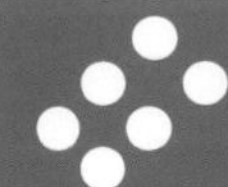

Project RESOURCES: projects

20. »

Import 2D (image) File formats:

See all the file accepted formats on page 104 of this coding book.

You can *(and this is part of the project)* import 8 images of any other aircraft. They need to be similar approximate angles which you calculate *(eight images divided into 360 degrees = angles you will find in my list),* Eight images is the minimum. *Sixteen* will give you a smoother animation!

All costumes you import must be made transparent! You may need to remove the **background** of each image. Take a **'*screenshot*'** from your own computer screen, save as 'png' and then 'cut-out' the picture background for each image. And that is another skill you will have to learn when importing images into Snap!, Scratch or Python.

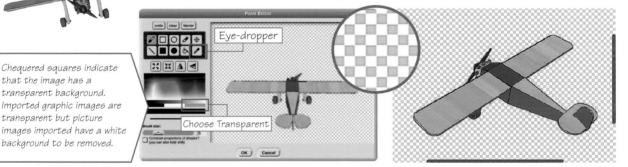

Chequered squares indicate that the image has a transparent background. Imported graphic images are transparent but picture images imported have a white background to be removed.

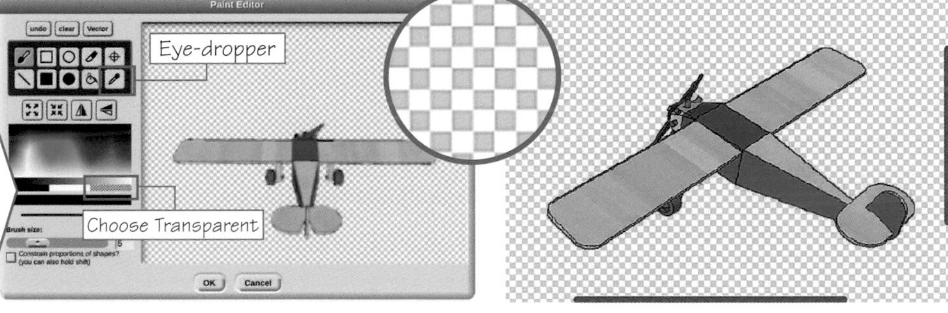

You will know if your images are transparent when you can see the small grey (or light blue) squares in the Sprite picture editing window (as shown above). The transparent background is indicated by this chequered pattern you will see on Snap! or Scratch.

High Flying in Python

We are using the same 3D model and import that into our Python script. We are using a Pygame module that you need pre-installed in THONNY otherwise you will get an error alert. If you're having trouble with installing Python 'modules', I will show you ***how-to-do-that*** in the ***'Python hints and tips'***, section *(see Python Hints and Tips page 136).*

We have two images to import. One is the aeroplane graphic and the other is background image of the airport. Both must be in the same directory, *(or folder if your on a Mac)* as the Python file must be intact with images. You will soon discover that moving any image outside the linked Python file (.py) will cause an error and the program will quit. »

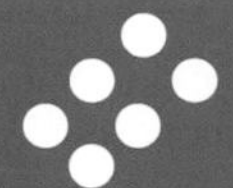

Project RESOURCES: projects

20.

Imported images in Python (A.+B.+C.)

We can use the same images we used in Scratch. A. Use the 'png' format and import another image of your choice. This is a flying game so the image is designed around flight. But saying that, you can choose your own image. The *(imported)* image size and the full name and format type are in my code line you see below ***"airplane.png".*** *(Height: 178 pixels, Width 178 pixels)*

```
player = pygame.image.load("airplane.png" # Open image to see format.
```

B. The other important *(imported)* image is the background that tracks the 'aeroplane' as it flies overhead. For this background image to work, it needs to be of a size *(to scroll)* and set at the same pixel resolution.

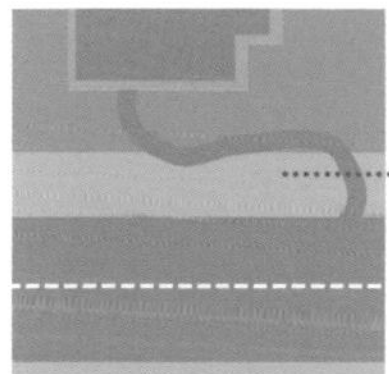

```
rack = pygame.image.load("runway.png") # Note: background image size*.
```

You can make *(and import)* your own **'airport'** import as long as it is of a size that can scroll *(automatically)* with the aeroplane. You may have to make the new Airport *(if you choose to draw one)* using any basic Paint *(or Photo edit)* program and export the final image and size in a 'png' format.

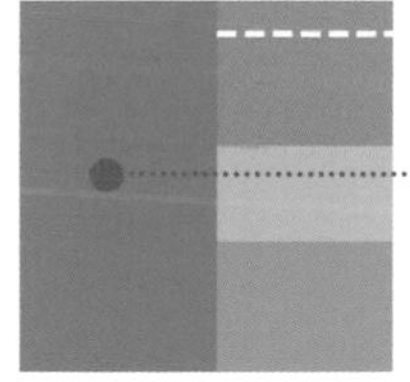

```
screen.fill((50,143,56)) # Change RGB colour- (colour behind 'runway' image)
```

C. Finally ensure your airport image has a border colour *(as shown).*

***Airport image size:**
Width: **1500 pixels**
Height: **1500 pixels**
pixel resolution:
72 pixels/inch

Note: *If creating a new airport ensure the airport image is a large enough size. The image drawing should be at least 500mm Wide by 500mm High. Export should be '.png' format at 72 pixels.*

Project 'Live' weblinks:

This project only appears on Scratch:

https://bit.ly/3ggbyM9

Download the entire coded project:

This project is now available for download: *(Scratch and Python)*..

https://bit.ly/2JQVODk

Note: All the book's twenty project files are saved in a 'zip' file format which is a safe way to send files from our Library which are held on a DropBox account. We have tested them on Windows, Mac and Linux which includes the latest Raspberry pi Mini computer using Chrome browser and Thonny.

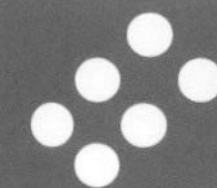

Python hints & tips:

A. Installing a TK module (or a Pygame module)

Find the 'Tools' menu (at top of THONNY screen) as shown.

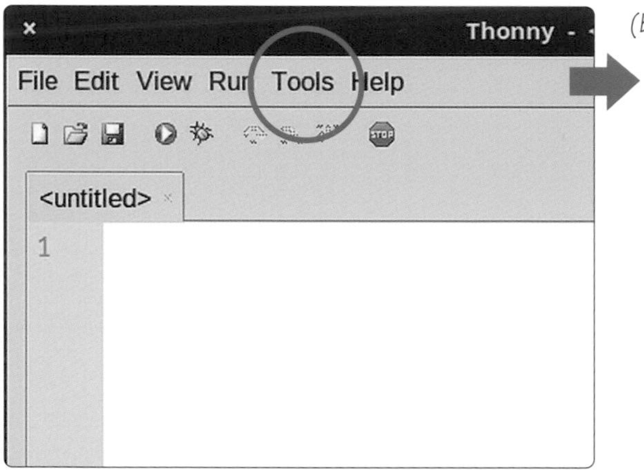

Thonny -
File Edit View Run Tools Help
<untitled>
1

(b) Click on 'Manage packages' under 'Tools' section.

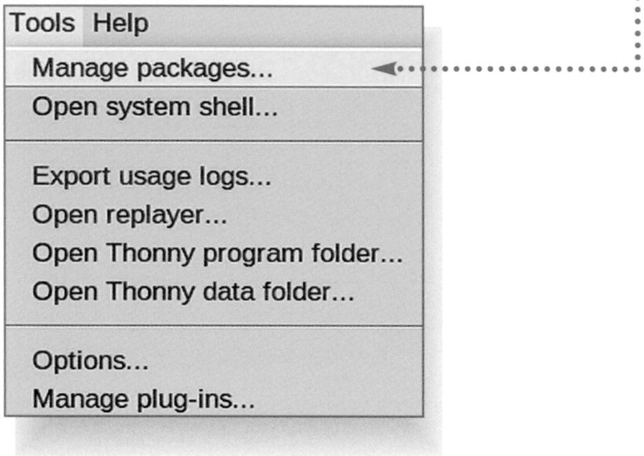

Tools Help
Manage packages...
Open system shell...
Export usage logs...
Open replayer...
Open Thonny program folder...
Open Thonny data folder...
Options...
Manage plug-ins...

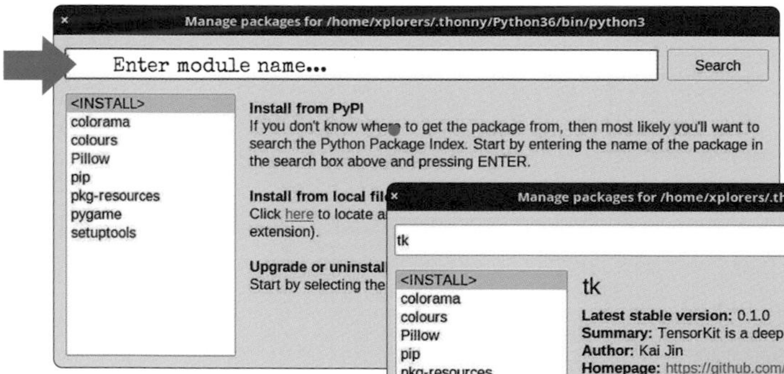

Manage packages for /home/xplorers/.thonny/Python36/bin/python3
Enter module name... Search
<INSTALL>
colorama
colours
Pillow
pip
pkg-resources
pygame
setuptools

Install from PyPI
If you don't know where to get the package from, then most likely you'll want to search the Python Package Index. Start by entering the name of the package in the search box above and pressing ENTER.

Install from local file
Click here to locate and install the package file (usually with .whl, .tar.gz or .zip extension).

Upgrade or uninstall
Start by selecting the package from the left.

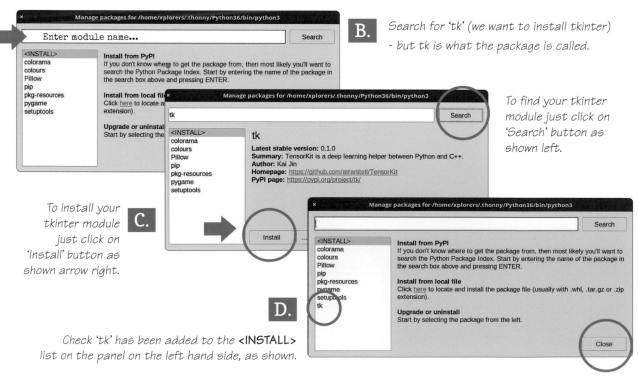

B.

Search for 'tk' (we want to install tkinter) - but tk is what the package is called.

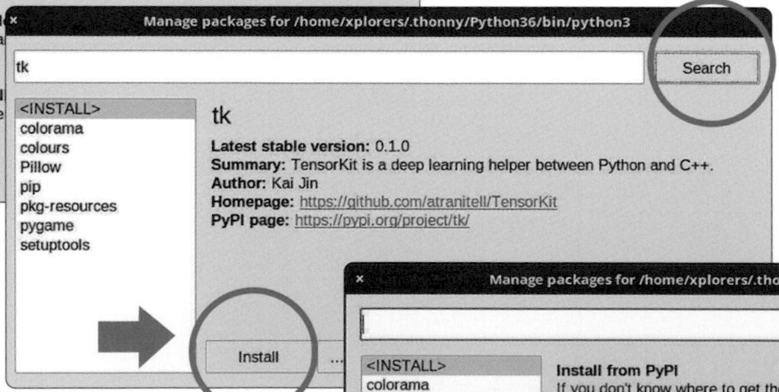

Manage packages for /home/xplorers/.thonny/Python36/bin/python3
tk Search
tk
Latest stable version: 0.1.0
Summary: TensorKit is a deep learning helper between Python and C++.
Author: Kai Jin
Homepage: https://github.com/atranitell/TensorKit
PyPI page: https://pypi.org/project/tk/
Install

To find your tkinter module just click on 'Search' button as shown left.

C.

To install your tkinter module just click on 'Install' button as shown arrow right.

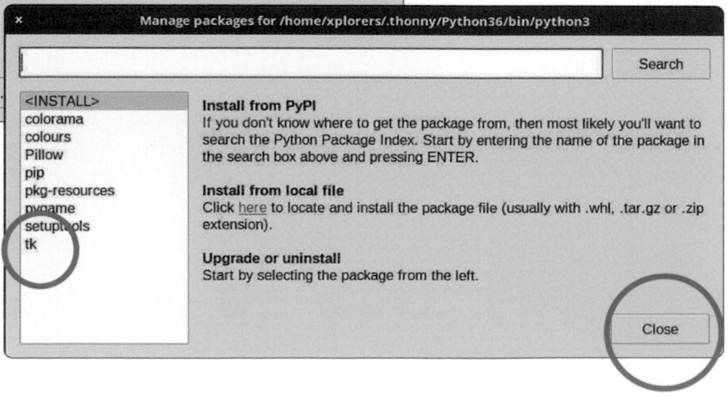

D.

Manage packages for /home/xplorers/.thonny/Python36/bin/python3
<INSTALL>
colorama
colours
Pillow
pip
pkg-resources
pygame
setuptools
tk
Close

Check 'tk' has been added to the **<INSTALL>** *list on the panel on the left hand side, as shown.*

You have now installed your first Python module!

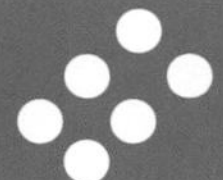

10 Python hints & tips:

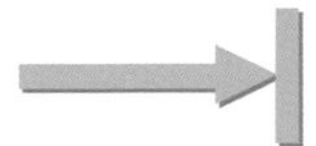

(1) Indents and Bullet points

Throughout the book I have reminded you that the Python indents are not just word spaces. Each indent is marked as •••• *(four character spaces)*. Python should have four character spaces to indicate an indent. Each indent block is a code block *(just like that used in Snap! or Scratch).*

(2) When to avoid the TAB key!

A TAB key may seem like a good time saver *(as it does make spaces)* but the problem with that is the TAB key will not give you exactly **'four character spaces'**. So in this book, I decided that I would make it more obvious on each book project what those indents actually mean. Word or Text programs using TAB does not equal •••• (of four character spaces).

(3) When to use the TAB key!

Using THONNY the TAB key can be made useful, *(when you know how to use it properly)*. When using THONNY *(or other similar code editing programs)*, when you have a block of code to indent, you can simply highlight that same block of text, hit the TAB key - and the entire block will move over four character spaces. Smart eh?

(4) Making a " \ " code line break

When I get to the end of this line it will *'wrap-around'* to the next line *(as in a word processor)*. This is done automatically. Code edit programs *(such as in THONNY or another IDE)* - don't usually do that. A long line of Python code cannot be be broken or it will fail. If you have a very small screen it can be difficult to follow a long line of code. A simple solution is to use a '\' (back-slash) and make a line break. This does not change how the code runs and is a quick and easy way to make it fit on a page. *Example from project page 31, see Shopping list code below*

```
while True:
•••• new_item = input(print("Enter next item on your \
shopping list. Type END when finished: "))
```

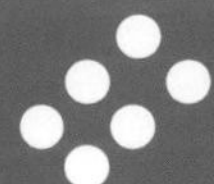

Python hints & tips:

(5) Missing Python modules?

Not all Python code needs a module to run. Some 'operations' are hidden until you import them as in ***'turtle'*** which is built-in to Python. You may need to import ***time, random*** are *'modules' that are usually pre-installed.*

```
import: turtle import*
import: time
import: random
```

On a raspberry pi, most modules are pre-installed and you do not need to install any module for Python to work. To check your installation type in this code your installation *(works on any computer).*

help?

```
help("modules")
```

Save and run as ***'help-mod.py'.*** This will then report a long list of installed Python modules. If you're on a school computer, it may be a short list!

(6) Printable in Python?

The word 'print' in Python code is used only to display a text message on the computer screen, *(which is probably why THONNY does not let you print a page).* Simply open in any word processor and print that out. On a raspberry pi, you can also open your Python code (.py) in a coding editor called **'Geany'*** which is similar to THONNY, and that does have a useful 'print-page' button you can use and it can print the line numbers.

'Geany' is able to print your Python code on any home printer!

**Geany is also available for Windows and Mac computers. www.geany.org*

(7) Using the word 'colour' or 'color' in code?

In this book that I use 'color' and 'colour' as interchangeable but Python code will be fussy how you spell it. Check syntax for 'color' in a code module for something defining a colour, *(as seen in book project 6 - making Random Stars)*

```
•••• turtle.color('#%06x' % random.randint(0, 2**24 - 1))
```

If we used the word 'colour' it will stop working. Python reads American spelling, but when it's not that critical (in a LIST) I will revert back to my own UK specific spelling, *(as seen on project 19 - Colourful confusion).* So beware the odd UK spellings in your code.

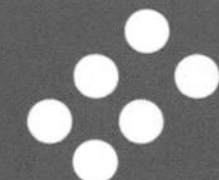

Python hints & tips:

(8) Have you got TK module correctly installed?

Well you can do a quick test, just key in this short Python code, then save and test it. Always include a .py at the end of a filename: **'testmytk.py'**

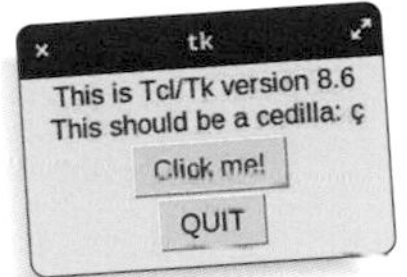


```
import tkinter
tkinter._test()
```

When installed and run- you will then get a mini pop-up, saying 'click-me!'.

(9) Finding (odd) 'Brackets' in your line code...

You may find two *(or three)* odd brackets in one line of Python code. They all do very different things. Don't leave any brackets out, even if they all look a bit odd and you may find multiple **")))"** + brackets on a line end...

(a) Enclosed brackets: ( ) - *brackets within brackets (within brackets) are not that unusual. It may look strange but don't leave any out!*

```
time=int(input("Enter the time (in years): "))
```

(b) Square brackets: [ ] - *Always used for any list of text or numbers. Lists are very useful and always start and end with 'square brackets'.*

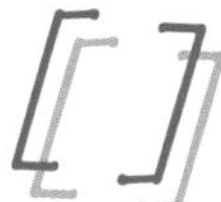

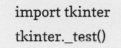

```
colors = ["red", "blue", "orange", "green","brown"]
```

(c) Curly brackets: { } - *Not used for any of the projects found in this book. Arrays are used to input 'dictionary' items into Python code.*

There is no standard Snap! or Scratch blocks that use an ***'Array'.*** ***Arrays*** are often useful, but way beyond the scope of this coding book.

(10) Take a coding *(fun)* break!

Computing is both fun and a logical process. Playing with code means often trying out something new. To make this book I have failed a hundred times on simple projects, I thought were easy *(in Snap! or Scratch)* but then failed in Python, they do not always translate easily. Keeping it all SIMPLE is my very best advice in coding. Read lots of computing books, play lots of games and find out how they all work. Go for a cycle and play!

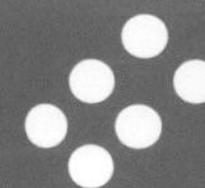

Discover coding:

Find a CoderDojo in your area!

If your child is interested in computer coding then join a world-wide coding club in your area. There are hundreds of free Coding clubs are all over the world called CoderDojo's. You can bring your own *(or any old laptop you may be able to borrow) for a computer.* If you have a raspberry pi *(excellent)* then you will soon find other families coding Snap! and Scratch blocks and learn Python together. You may even find the Author somewhere!

coderdojo.com

The MagPi magazine is also available around the world. Based on the raspberry pi mini computer that gives you a monthly news update on the cheapest mini computer you can buy and see what you can do with a small computer with a few tweaks and add-on's.

magpi.raspberrypi.org

This is the little mini-computer that is fond of educators and children world-wide. Every year a new model emerges at low cost and it's an easy operating system has built-in applications to run SNAP!, Scratch and Python. All you need to run every project in this book plus hundreds of other games and activities to play and code yourself!

raspberrypi.org

Thank you for buying this Let's Get Coding book:

The author takes responsibility for any coding mistakes, although I have carefully checked every project on a range of small computers, *(the most popular operating systems on laptop, desktop - and the raspberry pi mini computer in particular)*. This book has a number of recommended linked programs, that can be easily used. But I cannot explain how-to-use-them-all. All Snap!, Scratch and Python web links are tested as fully working - at time of going to press, but this may change over time - due to 'third-party' links the author has used throughout this book, *(therefore beyond my control)*. As far as I am able all the books projects are tested and working for use by schools, home educators and computer club under adult supervision of a computer tutor or a responsible parent with some prior knowledge of coding.

The CoderDojo clubs, the Magpi magazine and raspberry pi organisation are provided for information only for all parents and educators. The author can only recommend.

All the code is free to share for education at home, school and computer clubs.
See Let's Get Coding book's web site for news and code updates since publication.

LetsGetCodingBook.co.uk

Disclaimer:

The author is not responsible for melting keyboards, flat batteries, computer viruses (all of them), or installations that may (or may not) make your computer stop working for any reason. Hacking computer code is risky, even if it's your own code, you could put the entire world in jeopardy. So for that reason, children reading this book are advised to be careful with any weblinks and to NOT 'click' on any - unless you know for sure where they come from (or where they are going). It is usually the responsibility of the school club tutor, to check that all weblinks are SAFE before proceeding.

SAFETY: read page 104 for all safe LIVE links to project examples!

The internet is a dangerous place for the unwary so be careful.

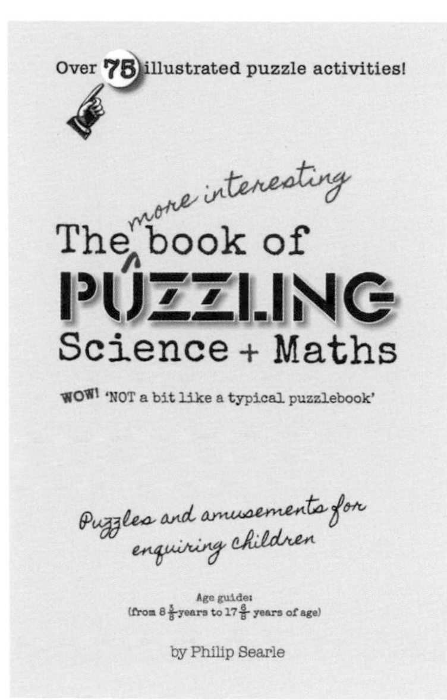

Also by Philip Searle and published by Tarquin

The More Interesting Book of Puzzling Science + Maths

Not a bit like a typical puzzle book!

For an enquiring mind, with an interest in science and mathematics, here is a treasure trove of delights from Philip Searle and son. Puzzles developed by enquiring children and adults for people like them.

Not focusing on either science and mathematics gives the elbow room to look at things that curricula don't cover. Some of the more than 75 puzzles in this wonderful book will be familiar friends, here presented in a lively fresh way for new readers. Many others will be new - there are hours of challenging fun to be had for anybody.

Book ISBN 9781911093510
eBook ISBN 9781911093527